Merry Christmas Dad
from Babe and Mike
1970

The Provocative Pen of
LUCIUS BEEBE, ESQ.

Other Books by Lucius Beebe

Boston and The Boston Legend
The Stork Club Bar Book
High Iron, A Book of Trains
Highliners, A Railroad Album
Trains In Transition
Highball, A Railroad Pageant
Snoot If You Must
Comstock Commotion, The Story of The Territorial Enterprise
Mansions on Rails, The Folklore of The Private Railway Car
Mr. Pullman's Elegant Palace Car
Twentieth Century, The Greatest Train in The World
The Overland Limited
Two Trains to Remember
The Big Spenders

In Collaboration with Charles Clegg

Mixed Train Daily, A Book of Short Line Railroads
Virginia & Truckee
Legends of The Comstock Lode
U. S. West, The Saga of Wells Fargo
Cable Car Carnival
The American West
Hear The Train Blow
Steamcars to The Comstock
The Age of Steam
Narrow Gauge in The Rockies
Dreadful California
San Francisco's Golden Era
Great Railroad Photographs U.S.A.
When Beauty Rode The Rails
Rio Grande, Mainline of The Rockies
The Trains We Rode

The Provocative Pen of

LUCIUS BEEBE, ESQ.

CHRONICLE PUBLISHING COMPANY

SAN FRANCISCO

The essays contained in this book originally
appeared in The San Francisco Chronicle.

Library of Congress Card No. 66–27595

Some Words of Appreciation

This masterwork of Lucius Beebe, made up of selections from his colums which appeared in the *San Francisco Chronicle* during the past six years, is dedicated to the de Young family whose amazing newspaper has been a part of San Francisco for more than a century; and, particularly, to Charles de Young Thieriot, the *Chronicle's* present publisher.

These baroque and splendid literary creations of the baroque and splendid Mr. Beebe are a tribute to the loyalty and graciousness which is so much a part of this West Coast newspaper dynasty. This volume also brings to mind the outright horror experienced on Monday mornings by some members of the de Young family as they turned to Mr. Beebe's fulminations on the *Chronicle* editorial page, and it acknowledges their courage in championing this unpredictable genius of American letters.

Scott Newhall
Executive Editor
San Francisco Chronicle

INTRODUCTION

Time once wired its San Francisco representative: THE WEEKLY NEWSMAGAZINE INTERESTED IN ONLY ONE REPORT ON LUCIUS BEEBE, THE INEVITABLE MILESTONE (signed) THE EDITORS OF TIME.

When the occasion arose on February 4, 1966, to write that inevitable Milestone, *Time* muffed the assignment. It devoted a few patronizing words to Mr. Beebe's "elegance" and reported that he had been a cafe society columnist for the *San Francisco Chronicle*. Which was rather like describing J. P. Morgan as a bank teller. Mr. Beebe, who held *Time* in the same contempt in which it held him, would not have been surprised.

During the nearly six years that Lucius Beebe wrote for the *Chronicle,* his column, "This Wild West," dealt with subjects as disparate as man's cruelty toward his fellow animals and man's idiocy in trying to reach the moon. In its time it covered economics, politics, journalism, religion, history, morals, justice, finance and travel—but never society with a capital S in any form.

Mr. Beebe had begun his 40 years in journalism on a disreputable New England tabloid for which each day he managed to produce a story, real or imagined, of an orgy in the bedrooms of Back Bay Boston or the dormitories of Harvard University. Then as now, high jinks among the upper crust was a circulation builder.

He had attended Yale briefly before his spirited pranks caused his expulsion but he later earned two degrees at Harvard. The Harvard registrar readmitted him to the groves of academe on the understanding that the orgy stories would cease. The Boy Beebe, as he liked to call himself, considered it a fair exchange.

While at Harvard he wrote for the *Crimson* a series of scathing attacks on compulsory chapel at Yale which were widely reprinted. When college authorities caved in under the barrage, that year's graduating class voted Mr. Beebe, in absentia, the man who had done the most for Yale.

Young Mr. Beebe joined the *New York Herald Tribune* at the time of the stock market crash and remained a member of the staff of that then flourishing newspaper for 21 years. During the course of his career in New York journalism, he became a railroad buff and it was during a trip to Nevada to research a book on the Old West that Mr. Beebe and his associate, Charles Clegg, discovered Virginia City.

They were so charmed by this "ghost town which refused to die" on the site of the old Comstock Lode that they decided to make their home in the West. Mr. Beebe, at that time the author of a column on Manhattan high life called "This New York," resigned his job with the *Herald Tribune* and the two descended on Virginia City like a conquering army. The town has never been the same since.

Within a few years Mr. Beebe and his partner had re-established the pioneer weekly, *The Territorial Enterprise,* upon which Mark Twain had once labored. During the six years he published the paper its pages were enlivened with attacks on every known aspect of the human comedy couched in an invective unmatched in the breezy, frontier journalism of the Old West to which it was heir.

In his low-crowned, broad-brimmed black hat, string tie, ruffled shirt, black clawhammer coat, frontier pants and boots, he was the glass of fashion on the Comstock. When, thus attired, the publisher of *The Territorial Enterprise* stepped forth into C Street en route to the Delta Saloon for an eye-opener the tourists who had made the pilgrimage to Virginia City were entranced. Here was a character from The Real West. They went away true believers.

The paper enjoyed the biggest paid circulation of any weekly west of the Missouri and contributed materially to the prosperity of Virginia City, but after six years Messrs. Beebe and Clegg tired of their publishing chores and sold out. They took to splitting their time between Nevada and California even though Mr. Beebe considered the Golden State an overcrowded asylum run by the inmates.

Mr. Beebe joined the *Chronicle* staff in 1960 at the age of 57, in the full flower of his middle years and eager to do battle with the entrenched forces of liberalism and progress. He drove a hard bargain with the management but it turned out to be a better bargain for us than we then dreamed for he proceeded to shower us with articles and book reviews in addition to his column. When we offered to pay him more he refused. It seems we had bought Beebe on the American plan—one fee covered everything.

Most staffers were required to join the American Newspaper Guild but Mr. Beebe never did and the Guild did not press the point. Possibly they would have felt uncomfortable extending the mantle of brotherhood to one who considered the union a branch of the Mafia and who had attacked it in the pages of his own paper with such ferocity that it considered suing for libel. In any case, Mr. Beebe eventually rendered the question moot by incorporating his literary endeavors under the laws of Nevada and becoming the Nevada Alvarado Corporation.

In an age of mealy-mouthed journalism, Mr. Beebe's opinions rang loud and clear, and his capacity for inventive epithet was unsurpassed. Few weeks passed during which he did not cane some scoundrel in his column. And if the blows that were struck seemed at times to lack the usual Beebe vigor, it was only because *Chronicle* editors, with craven concern for the laws of libel, had seized his arm on the downswing.

Whenever, in his column-writing, he delivered himself of what even he considered a choice piece of invective about one of his favorite targets he could not resist returning to the scuffle several paragraphs later and clouting his victim a second time and occasionally even a third. He was rather like a pianist who, having brought off a difficult piece, was so pleased with his performance that he played a reprise or two for his own satisfaction even before the audience had the opportunity to applaud.

When a lawyer took umbrage at the scarcely veiled implication in a Beebe column that he was a shyster and a disgrace to the bar Mr. Beebe was mildly surprised. After all, he had only been expressing an opinion. When the lawyer took advantage of the opportunity offered him to denounce his tormentor in equally insulting (though far less colorful) terms in the pages of the *Chronicle* Mr. Beebe was delighted. So far as he was concerned turnabout was fair play.

Only once during his years as a *Chronicle* columnist did we fail Mr. Beebe and expose him to a suit for libel. He had, by British standards, gone too far in belaboring a London restaurant where the food and service fell below his elevated standards. At that, it took them three years to lay him by the heels and he got off with a modest retraction and a contribution to charity.

Editing Mr. Beebe was not an assignment for those lacking in nerve. He fiercely resisted the editorial pencil and was not above attempting to overawe the pencil wielder. In this respect, he enjoyed an unfair advantage since he stood 6 foot 3 and weighed 220 pounds. He loved long sentences, long paragraphs, and showing off a vocabulary studded with ornate words. His spelling, to use his own term for it, was at times hilarious.

Though a man of honor, Mr. Beebe was occasionally guilty of

sharp practice when it might further his cause in the timeless struggle between editor and writer. A 75-line column somehow grew to 80 lines. The margins on his typewriter moved farther and farther out. For awhile he even took to producing his column on a machine with smaller type.

When inevitably his column was trimmed back, he charged like a wounded buffalo. Many of his complaints were contained in letters that were better than the columns they concerned. After being thrice rebuffed in one effort to launch a libel in the *Chronicle* he left town. The next word came in a one-sentence letter from Virginia City: "I have retired to the Comstock to lick my wounds."

At other times complaints were delivered in person over a hot bird and a cold bottle. Periodic luncheons, in Mr. Beebe's view, were essential to the reestablishment of good relations between himself and his editors. When he was the host, the plot was always the same. Stuff them with good food and paralyze them with strong drink and they will see things my way. They usually did too, until they sobered up.

When the *Chronicle* hosted the luncheons they usually took place on Nob Hill. Mr. Beebe always parked his car on the flat and arrived by cab. He was a four-Martini man at lunch and, having so imbibed, feared to navigate San Francisco's hills on his own. Although he might have the outward mien of an archbishop, he knew when alcohol had unhorsed him. Once he had been taxied down, however, he didn't mind driving home down a crowded freeway known locally as Bloody Bayshore. Apparently it was Nob Hill's altitude that bothered him rather than the traffic.

His penchant for fine food and drink cost him five kidney stone operations, periodic attacks of gout and a liver which, he proudly reported, had at times swollen "to ducal dimensions." He considered these ailments the price of civilized living. When it was suggested that a change of diet might improve his health he retorted that he did not intend to face a miserable old age on bread and water.

By most standards, though certainly not by his own, Mr. Beebe was a rich man. He did not have to work for a living though he worked hard on his many books, articles, reviews and columns. An inheritance from his New England forebears prudently managed by the most conservative Boston bankers provided him with an income capable of sustaining his appetite for Beluga caviar, Bollinger's champagne and Corona cigars. These amenities were further augmented during his life by ownership of several Rolls-Royces, a Thunderbird every other year, a Victorian mansion in Virginia City and frequent trips to London aboard the *Queen Mary*.

With his partner Clegg he owned in his time two private railroad cars. The first, the *Gold Coast,* was succeeded in 1955 by the even more opulent *Virginia City*. They rolled it out on state occasions and for an annual two-week junket to the Monterey Peninsula. The car, according to Beebe, was maintained in part to please his enormous St. Bernard, T-Bone Towser, upon whom he lavished the only affection he was ever seen to display in public.

During his early years in New York he had been classified as a dandy because he possessed a large and elaborate wardrobe, and the mannerisms for which he was noted set the teeth of a number of his contemporaries on edge. Young Mr. Beebe's posture as he back-pedaled rapidly toward the 19th century outraged all to whom progress was a sacred word. With the passage of time, there was somewhat less outrage. For his outlook, his mannerisms and his clothes seemed more becoming in a dignified man of middle age. This latter day approval, however, was lost on Mr. Beebe. He hadn't paid any attention to the disapproval in the first place.

Mr. Beebe possessed a rich sense of humor and an eye for the absurd that was directed not least against himself. He was quite aware that he was considered out of step, that he marched to a different drummer in what was at times a one-man parade. Eccentricity, whether in himself or others, he considered the birthright of a free man. Witness this recollection of ex-newsman Jay Allen's via columnist Herb Caen:

When he arrived in New York in his private car some years back he invited Wolcott Gibbs of the New Yorker to visit him. As Gibbs approached over the railroad tracks, Mr. Beebe, attired in morning coat and striped trousers, appeared on the platform, raised high his glass of champagne, and called out: "Welcome to Walden Pond!"

He loved every living species known to the planet earth with the exception of man. Offered the choice of a world without animals or a world without humans, he would without hesitation have selected the latter. He was particularly offended by politicians, lawyers, pompous journalists, advertising men, children on the loose, folksy bankers, nearly all foreigners and those who might be included in Kipling's "lesser breeds without the law."

He despised most newspapers, airlines, travel abroad (except to

London), organized religion, easy credit and installment buying, the innumerable trashy products that clutter the market place and plastics in any form (he was a sealing wax and lead foil man to the end).

Mr. Beebe detested the newspapers of the sixties as a pusillanimous breed and held them in contempt for lacking not only the courage of their convictions but any convictions at all. He was convinced that the civil rights movement was the bogus creation of Negro confidence men abetted by hysterical and incompetent editors. He was outraged by the Alsops and Pearsons who lived high on the hog through their ability to frighten the public to death with threats of doom via The Bomb, fallout, starvation, lung cancer and pollution of all kinds.

He considered the *Chronicle* a cut—but only a cut—above the other jackals of the press. Perhaps mainly because it had the good taste to publish his column and successfully resisted the efforts of indignant liberals to drive him from its pages. The paper's editorial policy, with which he was in almost total disagreement, caused him to refer to it as the West coast edition of *Pravda*. (At that, we got off lucky. The University of California's seeming inability to quell the student unrest of the mid-sixties earned it the title of Kremlin West.)

During his last visit to Virginia City, he wrote to us in San Francisco: "The *Chronicle* totters up the hill usually a day late which has the effect of invalidating many of its more hideous outrages on the assurance that something infinitely worse has happened since then only we don't know it. I recommend a two-day-old newspaper as a mild hypnotic."

Mr. Beebe was born, lived and died a Republican of such conviction that he would have voted for Cassius Clay had he been the party's nominee. Democrats were moral lepers who looted the U. S. Treasury whenever unleashed by a naive electorate. It was their nature to steal and they were as helpless in the face of temptation as Willie Sutton in a deserted bank.

(He had rather approved of John F. Kennedy, in spite of himself, since Kennedy, like Beebe, was a Harvard man, a Bostonian, wealthy and a gentleman of style. Bobby, however, was beyond the pale and Lyndon Johnson was a Texas sodbuster whose rise to power demonstrated the inherent dangers of democracy.)

The graduated income tax, he believed, was solely a device for despoiling the thrifty for the benefit of the shiftless. All other government programs with the except of the national defense and the post office were vast swindles designed to buy votes and assure their authors a permanent place at the public trough. The Federal government was the implacable enemy of every decent citizen since its twin ambitions were to clout his wallet and curb his freedoms.

Mr. Beebe was a lifelong advocate of hard money and he missed the gold-backed currency and double eagles of his youth. When the silver dollars which were so much a part of Nevada life were scooped up by hoarders, he was not surprised. To him it was a classic example of Gresham's Law in operation; the perfect answer to a government so shifty that it had finally stooped to debasing its own coinage. Ever since the United States had gone off the gold standard (under a Democrat, naturally) its currency had enjoyed the status of a Confederate shinplaster in his eyes. It followed, naturally, that the same political party would eventually be guilty of producing four-bit pieces and quarters which clanked instead of rang.

Some years before his death, Mr. Beebe provided Herb Caen with a self-assessment which embodied some of his feelings about himself and his times. He wrote, in part:

"I admire most of all the Renaissance Man, and, if it can be said without pretentiousness, like to think of myself as one, at least in small measure. Not a Michelangelo, mark you, but perhaps a poor man's Cellini or a road company Cosmo d'Medici. The Renaissance Man did a number of things, many of them well, a few beautifully. He was no damned specialist.

"If anything is worth doing, it is worth doing in style. And on your own terms and nobody's God damned else's. I like people who never give a passing thought to public opinion or the suffrage of society, not who deliberately antagonize it, but simply are unaware that it exists. I'd like my obit to say: 'Everything he did was made to measure. He never got an idea off the rack.'

"I take leave of you with an aphorism of the late Michael Arlen, in his way too a Renaissance Man, although he only did one thing well and that only once: 'I require very little of life. I want only the best of everything, and there's so little of that'."

Gordon Pates

San Francisco
1966

xiii

CONTENTS

CHAPTER ONE

Beebe—Man and Boy

Despite the prodding of his associates, Mr. Beebe never got around to writing what could have been one of the most delightful autobiographies of all time. In many of his columns, however, he touched on various phases of his life. A reading of them, therefore, will give one some of the high spots of the author's 63 years. They extend from the first (and almost the last) time he took to the air at the age of 12 to his celebration of 40 years of newspapering on his 61st birthday, at which time he was pleased to capsulize his philosophy in the immortal phrase: "The disfavor of envious inferiority is a boutonniere that can be worn by a gentleman all day without fading."

Happy Days in Wakefield

In my now almost unimaginably distant early youth in Wake-field, Massachusetts, my constant guide, philosopher and friend was a small, peppery Irishman named Dennis Dailey, a faithful family retainer who worked for my father as he had for my grandfather before him as head farmer or overseer of the Beebe acres which extended from the tranquil shores of Lake Quannapowit to the woodlot in Lynnfield, almost as far from home itself as Roundy's general store.

Dennis had been a drummer boy in the Union Armies and was, as a result of this heady military experience, shrewdly versed in the conduct of the arsenal of primitive weapons of approximate precision, most of them cap and ball, with which any New England boyhood was then surrounded. He was also possessed of a rich and almost limitless vocabulary of expletives which would fire a woodpile at 40 paces.

It was his kindly custom from time to time to hitch up one of the lighter rigs in the carriage house and take me to drink soda confections at the cool marble counter of Bonney & Dutton's drug store in Wakefield town square. During my prolonged skirmishes with lemon phosphates and banana splits he would disappear into the back room with Doc Dutton, from which he invariably emerged in mood radiant, sometimes wiping his constabulary mustaches on a bandana handkerchief and smelling as my father did when he came from the barber shop, sort of.

Once his tarrying with the Doc was so profitable and pleasant that, on gaining the seat of the buggy, he fell right out the other side just as the Rev. Dr. Rice, pastor of the First Congregational Church, was passing by. No matter.

Massachusetts in that dim and distant time had something called local option, which meant that a township could be wet or dry as its constituents pleased. Wakefield was nominally dry

4

and everybody did his serious drinking behind the partition in Doc Dutton's pharmacy. It would have been just as easy and a pleasant drive, too, to achieve neighboring Stoneham or Reading or Gerry's celebrated cider mill at Lynnfield, but this wasn't part of the game and, besides, it took trade away from home.

A Pioneer Passenger

I first flew, if memory doesn't betray me, as a paid passenger in a two-seater Wright biplane with a barnstorming lady aviator named Ruth Law at the Wakefield-Reading Fair of my boyhood at approximately the age of 12.

Aviators then had to pay dolts like myself to ride with them and I collected an unbelievable five dollars for riding out front with Miss Law whose attire was a pair of riding breeches, goggles and a motoring cap turned backward so the visor covered her neck. A pair of propellers made of wood at the back end of the machine were activated by chain gears from a motor conveniently situated where it would flatten the plane's occupants like waffles in the event of a crash landing.

I was enchanted with flying and with Miss Law and would have gone on with her gladly to the Rockingham and even the Rochester Fair if an account of my daring hadn't appeared in the *Wakefield Daily Item* and so apprised my family of my folly. I was then handcuffed to a heavy item of furniture until the Fair was over.

By the time I achieved the ivied halls of Harvard passengers were no longer being paid to fly, but themselves paid a modest fee to ride in open cockpit planes. A drinking acquaintance of mine named Bradley Fisk evolved the theory that flying was a sovereign remedy for hangovers, which everyone had in depth in those days, and we used to go over to Boston airport and take a restorative flight over the Charles river basin after which, revitalized, we would repair to Honest Parker Shannon's groggery hard by the *Boston Herald* in Avery street and start all over again.

An Excess of Zeal

As a fourth generation Boston banker myself, I only escaped permanent enslavement in a cashier's cage when I discovered, and actively practiced the discovery, that a copy spindle was ideally suited to impaling to the counter the hand of a depositor outstretched in an attempt to withdraw funds. While applauding my sentiments to the hilt, the management felt I was carrying institutional loyalty to extremes and I was released to seek employment elsewhere.

An Orgy A Day

Once, in the long ago past, I worked for a newspaper that is now with the ages called the *Boston Telegram,* whose moral tone, because it was in direct afternoon competition with Mr. Hearst's *Boston American,* was so low and its editorial stances so depraved as to freeze, by the very mention of its name, the marrow and congeal the spine of Bostonians who walked the sunny side of Commonwealth Avenue and read the irreproachable *Boston Evening Transcript.*

This is not the occasion to recall the impious scheme of things we evoked through five editions a day on the *Telegram* other than to mention that the word "orgy" was required by a standing editorial regulation to appear somewhere on the front page of every paper every day of publication in something larger than 72 point Cheltenham bold type. We specialized in orgies, especially among Harvard students and the Codfish aristocracy of fashionable Back Bay. The banner headline, "Society Matrons Seized in Fashionable Orgy" was a recurrent commonplace. The fact, revealed when one read below the banks, that the society matrons were named Suzie Slottnick and Jessie Krassmeyer and that the scene of their apprehension was a bagnio on farthest Huntington Avenue made no difference. It was our orgy of the day, the chef's suggestion in the department of elevated depravity.

The Wisdom of Polonius

In May 1922, I first took passage to cross the Atlantic in the Cunard steamship *Aquitania,* then at the apex of its celebrity as a luxury vessel of the type spoken of in the public prints as "an ocean greyhound." As a youth traveling alone, I was assigned, as was the custom of the time at capacity sailings, to share a stateroom with another gentleman whose identity was revealed as that of Claude Graham-White.

At this remove the name may mean little except to students of aviation, but Graham-White was a flying pioneer of impressive dimensions, so valued by the English government as an expert and consultant that he was paid an annual sum, reported to be $25,000, never to set foot in an airplane. He was a handsome, sophisticated and urbane *viveur* in whose debt I shall always stand for many kindly offices of worldliness.

Learning, conversationally, that I was an undergraduate at New Haven and that this was my first trip abroad, my roommate was quietly amused and remarked: "I think you will learn more that will be useful to you in life in six days aboard a Cunard steamship than in a semester at any university in the world."

Claude Graham-White couldn't have been more right. Others may sit at the feet of Yale or Oxford or the Sorbonne as their alma mater, but although I am a graduate elsewhere and have latinate documents to attest to it, I own to being a graduate first and foremost of transatlantic travel and the University of Cunard.

A good deal of gin has flowed under the bridgework since Claude Graham-White instructed me in some of the basic facts of life: gentlemen wear shawl collar dinner jackets, peaked

7

lapels are for musicians (this was 1922); only show-offs drink more than one bottle of champagne at breakfast; the most costly cognac on the wine list isn't always the best; don't ask for Maine lobster on an east-west passage or English channel sole going from west to east; tip the carver at Simpson's no more than threepence.

Don't get in fist fights with Frenchmen, which is insulting, strike them with your walking stick; try not to use the words "bottom" or "bum" in polite English society; they mean something else. When the King of Spain asks you to have a drink in the Ritz Bar, which he will probably do if you're a regular, it's more polite not to order a King's Death, which is what he himself will be drinking, but to call it a Royal Highball.

Nearly 40 years afterward these instructions may, to some, seem vaguely frivolous. In 1922 they were the wisdom of Polonius.

When the Twenties Really Roared

In what would seem to be an effort to update the decor and motif of premises patronized by drinkers who require these amenities from the Gay Nineties theme that has been abroad in the land ever since, just before repeal, the late Christopher Morely inaugurated the Gay Nineties boom with his old-time music hall in Hoboken, there now seems to be a rash of establishments claiming what have come to be known as "The Roaring Twenties" as their patron period. This was a decade, as everyone knows from the variety of literature available in the bibliography and inconography of the period, that was devoted to the flapper, the pocket flask, four-button suits, the Stutz Bearcat roadster, and the cult of F. Scott Fitzgerald.

Hardly a Stutz or Mercer two-seater overturned along the reaches of the College Highway but your correspondent was rescued from the debris and carted off to jail, his coonskin coat

8

smoldering. I was among those present when the inevitable patrol wagon backed up to Webster Hall in the Village to carry off the participants in Cynthia White's annual Pagan Revel and semiannual Communist Debutante Party. I was urged, long before commencement, to forsake the Yard and Campus of Harvard and Yale, respectively, for conduct not strictly academic, and I batted a thousand in the intercollegiate awfulness sweepstakes by being asked by no less august a don than Dean Christian Gauss to leave a Yale-Princeton football prom.

Unlike some name droppers I could name drop, I knew Scott Fitzgerald personally and once helped Katharine Brush pull him from the fountain of the Pulitzer Memorial in the Plaza. I saw and did all these things and many others, but none of them resembled the Roaring Twenties as they seem to be recreated for today's more stylish drinkers.

The decor of the speakeasy of the period, and I had a bundle of cards of admission to stagger today's collector of credit cards, was an austere premise characterized by durable properties and equally durable customers. The bar was apt to be fashioned from poured concrete and the furniture massive, as though designed for some ignoble Westminster Abbey. In the place of the rich crystal of today's fakement, a single naked rehearsal bulb illumined the festive scene. The floor plan of such premises as Winkle's, Dan Moriarity's and Steve & Ed Bozzinetti's was laid out, like the fortifications of Paris, by a military strategist and was calculated for long siege and active resistance to the Federals. When a raid was in progress, the screams of the participants, the shattering of glass, the sound of ball bats on derby hats, and the cries of the maimed and wounded resembled the sunken ditch at Waterloo.

I find it difficult to reconcile the contemporary recreation of the Roaring Twenties with its properties ravished from Venetian palazzos, Moorish mosques, Nob Hill mansions of the Eighties and red velvet swings that are pure Harry K. Thaw-

Stanford White, with the factual reality as I knew it, man and beast, for a decade.

The impresarios of today's Roaring Twenties have something else in mind; the Fall of Babylon in D. W. Griffith's "Intolerance" or revelry by night in Belgium's capital, but not the Twenties whose scars I still bear as thick as marks of Indian warfare at Deerfield, Mass.

The Walker Years in Old New York

I went to work for Stanley Walker on the morning of August 11, 1929, just in time to get myself built into a desk at the *Herald Tribune,* which not only warded off the catastrophes of that dreadful autumn, but all other forms of professional calamity for 21 years.

It was one of Walker's days to be whimsical, and he received me amongst his myriad assistants on the city desk attired in a Sherlock Holmes suit of ratcatcher pattern with deerstalker hat and meerschaum pipe and surveyed me from derby hat to Frank Brothers' brogues (then the occupational attire of city side reporters) through a reading glass of great power and formidable dimensions.

He sent for Beverly Smith, the sunniest tempered and most genial reporter I have ever known, and said: "Beverly, pray introduce the new man to the staff. Don't let him pay for anything." This last had me stopped until we went down the Fortieth Street elevators to Jack Bleeck's Artists' & Writers' Club next door, where I met not only the city staff, but such towering eminenti as Ogden Reid, the owner, Geoffrey Parsons, the great chief editorial writer, W. O. McGeehan in sports, William M. Houghton, Walter Millis and Arthur C. Clark, the patrician Sunday editor.

As this was midmorning, it was explained to me that Percy Hammond, chief drama reviewer, would not show up until dusk. I was not allowed to pay for anything.

Walker had a sly way of getting full value out of a reporter's time and if it was a slack day on the assignment sheet, we were all set to work researching subjects purporting to be background material for special Sunday features.

Many of these deathless word paintings later turned up verbatim in Walker's books along with flattering personal mention of the ghostly workers in the vineyard. I know for a fact that Joe Alsop, Ishbel Ross and Howard White, the society editor, and I each did what later appeared as a full chapter in "Mrs. Astor's Horse."

It was the heyday of the full-dress obituary and the split page of the *Herald Tribune* was devoted every morning to beautifully confected biographical essays of notables who had died the day before, some of them running to 2000 words of immaculately styled prose. These masterpieces were written by people on the staff who were experts or knew the subjects personally and Joe Alsop, Henry Cabot Lodge, Alva Johnston and I polished many a lyric gem for the departed.

One of Walker's obsessions was the possibility that John D. Rockefeller the elder might die on his vast estates at Pocantico Hills where his demise could be kept a secret indefinitely, presumably while adjustments were made in the corporate structure of Standard Oil. A youth with a powerful glass was stationed in a tree overlooking the private Rockefeller golf course and for years reported daily that the old codger yet was animate. It came as a fearful blow to Walker when John D. died at Ormond Beach, Florida, without the *Herald Tribune's* permission, as it were.

The Sunny Side of Grubb Street

The estate of being a man of beautiful letters has come a long way since I read galley proofs on my first book, which was just before General Lee showed up at Appomattox Courthouse. My first editor at Appleton-Century, now Appleton-Century-Crofts and only heaven knows who Mr. Crofts may be, was a banty little gentleman of great charm and personal attainments named Barry Benefield who had just written "Valiant Is the Name for Carrie."

Life was not easy for a serf indentured to Mr. Benefield. He wanted authors to produce. Every morning he would call me at my desk at the *Herald Tribune* to see if I was in operating condition. If the departmental secretary gave him an evasive answer he would, with unerring judgment, call Bleeck's Artists' & Writers' Saloon, then a speakeasy, and command Henry, the senior barman, to cut off my elixir of life forthwith. "Beebe is a scoundrel," he would snarl at the terrified man of bottles. "Don't serve him another thimbleful. Bid him eschew the hooch and get upstairs and start smiting his Remington."

Highest in my regardful recollections of the word foundries, however, is Mrs. William Haskell who followed Benefield at Appleton-Century in the pontifical reign as senior editor of John L. B. Williams. She wore businesslike clothes, black bombazine I think, and a chatelaine watch and her hair was done at the back of her head in a tight pug. She looked like a cartoon version of an early-day suffragette, and when she wanted service her voice rattled all the glasses on the back bar.

Appleton-Century in those days was hard by the McAlpin Hotel in Herald Square and the hellish Mrs. Haskell and I frequently found it convenient to conduct our devotions at the shrine of belles lettres at the bar of that establishment. By merely stepping out the door into Seventh Avenue one could obtain a matchless view of the façade of the old New York Herald building which James Gordon Bennett had ennobled with a pair of bronze bell-ringers from Switzerland who emerged from an ornate portico on the hour to smite the time with bronze hammers on a bronze bell. They were one of the things to see in old New York and I had never seen them in action.

Mrs. Haskell and I would prolong our devotions to the muse

from hour to hour in an effort to obtain a glimpse of this edifying spectacle, but always, and I never knew it to fail, a chance acquaintance would set them up or the bartender would announce that this one was on the house, just as time, treading on the dial's point, approached the hour. The muffled bonging of the Bennett gong would announce that we had missed the Swiss bellringers again and were, of course, obliged to tarry another 60 minutes.

There must have been some sort of symbolism in it. Another day, another dollar. Another book, another round at the Mc-Alpin bar and another date missed with the bell-ringers of eternity.

Father Visits Bleeck's

Once, and only once, I took my father, a Boston banker of formidable dimensions, to Bleeck's. Father had been down to do some business with the firm of Morgan & Company, a bank he always distrusted since he had had an $8 Collins & Fairbanks hat blown off his head when emerging from its portals during the Wall Street bombing of 1917. He viewed the ribald company at the bar with cold distaste.

At one point he asked me if I could identify the two burlesque figures crouching at the corner of the bar in parodies of evening attire and obviously about to be thrown out by the management.

"The tall one, sir," I told him, "is my employer, Mr. Ogden Reid, publisher of the *New York Herald Tribune,* son of Whitelaw Reid, former Ambassador to the Court of St. James's. The other is Mr. Reid's cousin, Ogden Mills, Secretary of the Treasury of the United States. I think in a little while they'll leave and go to the Brook Club."

Father took the Owl home on the New Haven and was never the same afterward.

13

The Last Word

I still think the ultimate commentary on the modern chichi gastronomy was that made many years ago by Whitney Bolton of the *Morning Telegraph* after an elaborate dinner I had given in honor of the publication of Stanley Walker's book "Mrs. Astor's Horse." Whitney had been taken in wine and forced to retire before dinner was over, but next morning his secretary called with a message: "Tell Lucius it's all right; the white wine came up with the fish."

Beebe the Economist

The mantle of Sylvia Porter does not rest with all the voluptuousness of a Poole opera cloak upon the shoulders of the author. His notions of economics have long been a source of bemusement to friends who admire to recall the occasion, years since, when as a form of protest against what he felt to be the exorbitant cost of asparagus on a room service menu, he attempted to steam open a jar from the grocer and had to replaster and paper an entire hotel suite in consequence.

Wake at the Waldorf

One of the occupational hazards of engaging in the production of new theatrical ventures on Broadway when this reporter covered Shubert Alley used to be that implicit in the inevitable parties given for members of the cast, their friends and those interested in the show after the first New York performance. If the show was assured of success, a contingency that could with some degree of certainty be predicated on how it had done at New Haven or Philadelphia during the tryout, these routs were eagerly looked forward to and invitations to them avidly sought

14

both by legitimately interested parties and by touts and hangers-on with scant credentials for professional recognition.

If the show was a bust and the opening night party also the herald of imminent demise, they could be a dreadful business characterized by bogus cheeriness and spurious optimism when everybody knew that next week at the latest the van would come to take the scenery to the warehouse. Memory serves of one such occasion when the highly solvent Jock Whitney who had been financially implicated in the doomed venture had planned a veritable Trimalchio's Feast to be recreated at the Starlight Roof of the then new Waldorf on Park Avenue. Caviar and other rare viands for 500 celebrities was commanded. Enough double magnums of Bollinger, Mumm's and Krug's Private Cuvee were on ice to float a battleship. Flowers from Wadley & Smythe came came to a king's ransom and Meyer Davis in person was on hand to lead the orchestra.

The only trouble was the play itself was a horrendous catastrophe. By the end of the first act Kelcey Allen of *Women's Wear Daily,* a sure bellwether, was running a menacing finger across his wing collar in cutthroat pantomime and Percy Hammond had stalked out in the direction of Sardi's bar after loud assertions that he wasn't coming back. The third act played to a half vacant house and the final curtain rang down with the boom of doom on a handful of embarrassed survivors most of whom could be identified as friends and family of the martyred cast.

The play, oddly enough by Peter Arno, had been called "There Goes The Bride" and the night air of Broadway resounded with obvious witticisms based on the evanescent nature of the whole sorry affair. In such a pass you might imagine nobody would have showed up at the Waldorf to share Mr. Whitney's well-upholstered bounty, but there you are mistaken. The time was in the early Thirties and parties with limitless caviar and quail in aspic were few and far between. You'd have

15

been surprised at the turnout of mendacious ghouls who were optimistic about the chances of the bride's survival while piling their plates with the best unsalted Beluga and foresaw a run to rival "Abie's Irish Rose" as the wine disappeared.

"Pol Roger never before in history buoyed up so many bare-footed liars," was Walter Winchell's commentary.

A Subversive Who Pays Cash

The author recently spent a disturbing hour or two reading Vance Packard's "The Waste Makers" and, in a moment of revulsion, undertook to evolve a mythical character whose potential existence could drive any Madison Avenue sales promotion expert right smack dab out of his head.

To begin with our dream boy has been strongly conditioned all his life to despise trash and is hence allergic to nine-tenths of all the commodities and many of the services which compose the great American consumer market. He was brought up by well-to-do but extremely prudent parents whose every property and attitude was solid, conservative and durable.

The house in which he was born had been built something over a century before by a celebrated New England architect around a core of Dutch brick with a Federal facade and, barring accidents of chance, would be around several centuries longer. The family motor cars like the carriages which had preceded them were solid, enduring Packards and Pierce-Arrows of an age that had never heard of planned obsolescence. They lasted for years and were kept in meticulous repair.

His clothes, like those of his father before him, were tailored of sixteen- and eighteen-ounce hard worsteds and sharkskins by London and New York tailors and had a life expectancy roughly that of their owner. His bootmaker would have cut his own throat if any of his shoes failed to last a decade of constant use. He shaved with straight razors which could easily outlast his own

16

lifetime. The books in his library were those he expected to reread every few years and there were, therefore, no paperbacks or best sellers and very little fiction.

Now in the fullness of his years and with the means to gratify any reasonable whim of possession, our hero is more than ever inclined to take a dim view of high pressure salesmanship. There is neither radio nor television in his home and he will purchase no trade product that he believes to be advertised on these media.

His motor cars are of an English manufacture that owners generally feel to be nicely broken in after 100,000 miles. His cupidity for material possessions is difficult to arouse, although he is a recognized collector in certain restricted fields of historic interest and takes stock only in merchandise and services advertised in newspapers and coated paper periodicals. He hasn't seen a motion picture film in five years.

In his home the plumbing is copper, the hardware fittings are bronze, the kitchen equipment copper, the table service is sterling and the linen is linen. He discharged a servant who served paper napkins with the cocktails and there is almost no plastic in the establishment. Music is provided by a long-playing device of the sort used in public auditoriums and will probably last a lifetime without replacement of more than minor components.

He has no slightest inclination toward camping, hunting, fishing or otherwise violating nature and the landscape and hence is no prospect for house trailers, plastic boats, outboard motors, cookout utensils, tents, hunting attire or trout lures. He takes a dim view of home motion pictures and his only camera is a Speed Graphic of ancient construction. The wine and spirits in his cellars are of the best established brands and if he should see a whiskey in his possession advertised as being "light" or "chill filtered" he would throw it out.

Since he regards drinking as a serious matter, his bar embraces no bartender's aprons with cute mottoes, no cocktail mixers that play "How Dry I Am" when activated and there are no frivolous or patented hors d'oeuvres from Japan or Hawaii. His guests are served a plate of anchovies or sardines with English water biscuit. He has never been in a supermarket and sneers diligently at most of the achievements of the packaging industry.

He carries no single credit card, pays cash on the barrel whenever possible and, where charge accounts are essential to convenience, pays bills the day they come in. By the third of each month he owes no money to anyone.

Our boy, in a word, is proof against the blandishments that have built a precarious national economy on the purchasing of merchandised trash. No sales pitch can unload on him properties which, after a calculated minimum lifetime, will wear out, evaporate, disintegrate, decompose, collapse or require replacement if he can help it. Such matters as light bulbs which burn out after a minimal usefulness are beyond his capacity to eliminate, but he makes their existence a virtue on the basis that they constitute a warning against fallible merchandise in other categories.

This discouraging character evoked for purposes of dismay to hucksters generally is not, as it turns out, so fictional as an economist of the planned obsolescence school might like to imagine. It is, in fact, I, the writer of this horror story and probably a subversive of important dimensions.

Probably it's a good thing there aren't many like him. The American economy is insecure enough already.

A Curmudgeon's Stewardship

It so happens, fortuitously, that this column will appear on the sixty-first birthday of its vagrant and often, no doubt, fallible conductor, and at the same time marks approximately four decades of editorial activity on four different newspapers, a period largely enlivened by reciprocal insult, bad feeling and the exchange of metaphorical dead cats and decayed vegetable matter.

This is neither the space nor, contrary to the hopes of many readers, the occasion for an *apologia pro vita sua* but it may well be the occasion for a brief account of editorial stewardship which has endured and maintained continuity since the first outraged subscriber to the *Boston Telegram* in 1922 called on the managing editor at 99 Portland Street and demanded the dismissal of the Boy Beebe and that instanter as an affront to God and public morality. I think I had submitted an irreverent report of a temperance meeting in Tremont Temple.

The powerful boot of the m.e., a tough and temperamental fellow named Leo Taffe (whose temper was uncertain until after the fifth drink of the morning which he had not yet had), was applied in the appropriate place. The editorial rooms of the long since defunct *Telegram* were on the fifth floor achieved by a steel and cement stairwell down which a descending body ricocheted in gratifying manner. On the sidewalk outside, the prostrate and barely recognizable advocate of temperance was collared by Murph the cop as an undesirable early morning drunk and thrown in the tank.

"The thinnest skinned sons of bitches in the world," Mr. Taffe remarked, replacing the bottle of rye that occupied the file drawer in his desk marked "City Hall Contacts, Confidential," "are reformers and liberals. All they want of a newspaper is everything their own way and the suppression of all opposition. The anointed can't take it."

Over the years it has been my almost unexceptional experience that Mr. Taffe was so right. The identifying hallmark of the true, deep-dyed liberal, the dedicated sorehead and witless do-gooder is intolerance of any opinions but his own and the clamorous demand that the voice of heresy be unequivocally stilled. The discovery has been a source of inspiration throughout a professional lifetime predicated on the realization that combat is part of the human condition and that combat against the dedicated forces of spurious benevolence in the world is the most satisfying of human occupations.

The risk of being detested by mannerless inferiority is not just the calculated risk of the practicing journalist of any discernible integrity; it is his vindication.

The commentator motivated by any sense of responsibility to his readers, his employer or to himself cannot be simply an unctuous playback for the golden opinions the human race has come to form of itself through the simple but defective device of believing its own publicity. To do so is a profound disservice to a completely inconsequential placental mammal who, through his innate capacity for murdering other animals, has contrived to dominate a molecule of galactic dust floating on the outer perimeter of a sea of time. The human race has always paid the highest going price to its priests to tell it it was immortal and its press agents and secular comforters to tell it it was consequential. Both are, however, mendacious and often hilariously disproved by the headlines in an adjacent column.

"A newspaperman mistakes his calling," said Raymond Moley, strictly an old pro himself, "when he enters a popularity contest."

The measure of a true professional on this basis is not his friends but the enemies he has acquired and should cherish as his justification for existing at all.

Of a winter's evening, before a blazing fire of letters to my employer demanding my dismissal and suppression instanter as an enemy of the people, I warm myself with the recollection of creeps, humanitarians and other shysters whose disapproval I have incurred.

As I have suggested before in these columns, the disfavor of envious inferiority is a boutonniere that can be worn by a gentlemen all day without fading.

No Paris After Death

I claim no kinship to the ineffable Henry James, but there are those to whom the dismal cliche about good Americans going, when they die, to Maxim's in Paris is demonstrably fallacious.

Americans of taste and perception, when they die and if they have any choice of routing, go to Simpson's in the Strand or Brown's Hotel, or punting on the Thames, which they call Isis Water when it passes by the most radiant abode of humanism since Athens, or they go to work in the stacks at the Victoria & Albert Museum or to feed the swans on Avon.

Whatever may be their predilection, they don't go to the screaming, sooty abode of chaos that for a thousand years has spuriously referred to itself as "The City of Light," which is filled with foreigners, many of them Frenchmen.

CHAPTER TWO

Manners, Morals and Mores

Mr. Beebe found most aspects of modern times hilarious and believed that, by any standard you cared to apply, the nation had been moving down hill since the turn of the century. He found nearly every action of man farcical and could not help, nay enjoyed, making invidious comparisons between the meretricious aspects of the present which affronted him and those aspects of the past which, in his memory, were of solid gold.

Help Stamp Out the 20th Century

Every now and then in the course of censure, correction or, at infrequent intervals, approval and encouragement to which one lays himself open by an expression of opinion in the public prints, this department is attacked, most often in painful holograph or single space typescript, for failure to adapt itself to the Twentieth Century.

The idea that anybody who resists the Twentieth Century is somehow subversive and a nogood is wide-spread and deep-rooted, but it may be suspected that it finds its most ardent partisans among those who themselves would admire to live in another time but haven't successfully contrived the mechanism for doing it.

The same people who denounce somebody they disapprove of for embracing an Edwardian or Victorian cast of thought and intellectual posture seem, to my casual observation, to have no such prejudice against more remote areas of history and speak with respectful admiration of the Age of Pericles or the Augustan Age or the Age of Johnson, Swift, Pope or Dryden. The hanker for retrogression is respectable if its objective is at sufficient remove, so that these spacious periods in history are enviable and engage general approval while the Age of McKinley, the best time in all foreseeable probability Americans will ever know, does not.

The reason would seem to be that the Elizabethan Age is unattainable by a wide margin of time; the Age of McKinley holds the mirror to only yesterday's satisfactions, to good times only recently lost that existed within the recollection of a still living generation. The Athens of Pericles is gone beyond all possibility of recreation, while the years of Edward the Good are only half a century over the horizon and, besides, the plumbing in 1905 was fully as effective as it is today and the local phone service almost as good. It is the narrow margin of deprivation that makes it so disturbing.

To have been born in 1600 strains the imagination, and anyway there were all those rats spreading the bubonic plague. Anybody could have been born in 1860 and a great many people had parents who were ready and willing to tell at first hand of how good things were only yesterday. To miss the boat by a day or a week isn't so painful; to miss it by moments is maddening.

Since it must be apparent to the veriest dolt that the Twentieth Century, at least since August, 1914, has been an unmitigated catastrophe, it would seem the part of prudence to live in some other period as much as may be practicable without violating the sanitary code or building regulations. I am agreeable to subscribing to the theory that progress is a good thing only it's been allowed to go on too long, and the time to have taken a firm stand was between 1905 and 1910 in the era of hard gold currency and the two bit drink at the Waldorf.

It has the advantage of a position that can be abandoned for strategic reasons if there seems a possibility of women's suffrage or a graduated income tax. One can always fall back on Tudor times and the age of Henry VIII, a period of voluptuary satisfactions if only one could avoid the poxes, both great and small.

Dreadful Art of the Postage Stamp

The wires from Washington, in addition to their daily budget of bad news for everybody, including the taxpayers who voted into office the most corrupt and larcenous Administration since the unfortunate General Grant, bear incidental tidings of a new House Office Building that is going to cost you and me $125,-000,000 for the most expensive shack-up in the world where the privileged pickpockets we elect to public office can plan

27

further infamies against their constituents in luxury without parallel since Imperial Rome.

It is the prayerful hope of the Administration that these and other incidental intelligences of outright thefts of billions from the public revenues by the Texas gang may be buried from the attention of newspaper readers by the happily opportune threat of a fine war which would divert public attention from anything so trivial.

If these blessings can be showered down on the Party of Absolute Corruption in terms of an ever soaring public debt that will ensure a perpetual rise in confiscatory taxes for generations to come, why is it that patrons of the Post Office cannot, except on very rare or holiday occasions, be allowed a five cent postage stamp that can be contemplated in the cold light of day without emesis?

They come off the presses in melancholy succession, each special issue more primitive and hideous in its meaningless vacuity than the last. The latest is one of the triumphant botches of all time, honoring, of all things, "physical fitness and the "centennial of Sokols" an entity I had always imagined to be the name of a Broadway newspaper paragrapher.

Last week it was the anniversary of the Battle of New Orleans, a not very creditable American victory in a war that was over before the battle itself was fought. The stamp matched the occasion and was so fearsome a confection of incompetence that the sight of it would have routed Pakenham's regiments if the squirrel rifles of Old Kentucky hadn't. A recent issue commemorating Audubon was so dreaful a farrago of improvisation that, had he been exposed to it, that distinguished naturalist would have drowned its designer in his own pigments.

Of all the ever multiplying services of the Federal government, the Post Office in its over-all operation by and large contrives to give the most abundant satisfaction to its customers. It's a pity that the postage stamps which are its symbolic heraldry to the world should be no better than those of High Colonic or Western Hernia.

The Cigar as Status Symbol

The recent and also brief-lived campaign waged by the Federal government against the cigarette industry which, happily, increased the consumption of the miserable things beyond all previous figures, also focused attention on the long-neglected cigar to an extent where American women were found to be smoking Upmann Specials for all the world like Frau Sacher and the Austrian grand duchesses of other times.

The recent spurt of cigar smoking by American women lacked any sense of conviction or validity, perhaps because their use was promoted and publicized in a variety of nasty tubes and holders in emasculated shapes with filters that robbed the smoke of its authenticity. The woman who smokes a conventional corona or panatella has never been anything but attractive as long as the cigar retained some of its original dimension, although it must be admitted that the last two or three inches of anybody's cigar lack esthetic overtones.

Miss Amy Lowell, probably the best known of American lady cigar smokers, expertly handled a full corona size, all-Havana smoke, and her arrival in the club car of the New Haven Railroad's *Knickerbocker* or *Merchants Limited,* precincts otherwise unequivocally masculine, was accepted without raising an eyebrow. Seated between Massachusetts Governor Channing Cox and the revered Robert Lincoln O'Brien, editor of the *Boston Herald,* and reading a volume of Keats while the smoke rolled around her in clouds, Miss Lowell was one of the inspiring sights of her time and place.

More than anything else, of course, a cigar is an index of a certain degree of affluence. No status attaches to cigarette smoking even if the brand is the legendary Sub Rosa sold by Sullivan

& Powell of Burlington Arcade and widely celebrated a generation ago as the brand used by Raffles, the gentlemanly burglar of fiction.

But cigars are possessed of a lordliness and opulence suggestive of J. P. Morgan, Jim Hill and other magnificoes of the Chauncey M. Depew era. The best of them quite literally reek of money, the more modest brands suggest aspirations to quality and the upward mobility cherished in our social order.

Decline of the Derby

As the last practicing derby hat wearer in the United States, at least so far as reasonably acute observation has, in recent years, been able to establish, this department is moved to look with sorrow and pity on a generation of men who haven't experienced the solaces and convenience of the most practical, durable and comfortable, if not the most beautiful, man's hat ever devised.

I am at a loss to ascribe its decline since it seems only yesterday that no man of any calling from bank president to ward heeler but regarded the hard *chapeau mellon* not so much as a symbol of status, since its universality precluded exclusiveness, but as a convenience in almost every circumstance of city and country life.

Like suits from Poole in London or, only a few years ago, Wetzel in the United States, they are indestructible. Except for the normal swelling of the head that is an attribute of longevity, I am morally certain that a derby I wore at Yale in 1922 would be as serviceable today and certainly as modish as when I was in the habit of wearing it to the Plaza Grill in the years of Connie Bennett and the great tea dance.

The hard hat I now wear, to the politely concealed amusement of San Franciscans, who are the politest people in the land, has seen at least a dozen summers since I purchased it in

London and the reserve or rainy day derbies in the hall closet are probably older.

It should be remarked parenthetically that my hat occasions no remark in my residence at Virginia City on the Comstock Lode in Nevada, but for a different reason. It is felt there to be a vestigial trace of the old frontier and a great deal more Western than the over-exploited Stetson which is indigenous to the Southwest and not the Far West and would have been as risible in Virginia City in the '80s as it was in Delmonico's.

The Silk Hat in American Life

The silk hat is still the handsomest yet devised for masculine headgear and the morning coat or cutaway the most graceful and becoming of garments, compared to which the evening tailcoat of universal acceptance is awkward and graceless. American Presidents have worn both and worn them becomingly from early in the 19th Century down to President Eisenhower who, for some unaccountable reason, balked at the attire approved by his distinguished predecessors. It won't be a salute of breath-taking splendor if President Eisenhower is remembered for nothing more than being the first President to turn up at his own inaugural in a soft hat.

Over the years the silk top hat has been a symbol of varying and often contradictory connotations. When William Lloyd Garrison was attacked on the streets of Boston for his abolitionist sympathies, it was by "a mob in silk hats" and the suggestion was one of rabble dimensions. A high silk hat with a black mourning weed was at one time the symbol of blue-nosed clerical sanctimoniousness and as such was adopted by Rollin Kirby in his now famous "Thou Shalt Not" prohibition cartoons.

Conversely, John L. Sullivan used his tiles, made by the cele-

31

brated Boston hat firm of Collins & Fairbanks, for wine buckets and filled them with iced bottles of champagne. At the turn of the century, the top hat and caped opera cloak were oriflammes of the Stage Door Johnny and the night life of Bustanoby's and Rector's. Largely, the silk hat was the accepted headgear of convention and worn by successful businessmen and, as such, became in the lexicon of class hatred a symbol of rapacity.

Early in the game a London hatter named Gibbus attempted to improve on the silk felted hat with a collapsible opera hat made of watered silk on springs. It didn't need constant brushing with a hat lure and took less space in crowded places of assembly and it made a delicious plopping sound when snapped open.

New York first nighters of the Thirties still recall the Broadway opening at which an afternoon newspaper critic, who was widely known for his addiction to the bottle, was taken in wine during the performance and staggered up the aisle using his opera hat as a receptacle for emesis. A witty old lady in a front seat remarked audibly that "she did wish those critics would wait till they got to their office to write their reviews."

Notes on the Sad State of the Beard

Time was, within the memory of living man, when a beard lent a man a certain distinction and was an object of general approval and esteem in the community. It was eminently masculine and carried with it professional implications or associations with an older and generally more commendable social order.

By and large, although few men cared for them after the advent of the Gillette razor, beards were a thing of fair repute in the community and only evoked mild cries of "beaver" from amiable humorists.

Today the estate of the beard has sunk to almost unplumbed depths. It has become the identifying badge of the self-pro-

32

claimed wierdy, the ineffectual intellectual, the oriflamme of creeps, and a mangy badge of discontent and contamination. Young men with a grievance against something feel that growing a peculiar growth on the face proclaims them to be rebels in a just cause, but generally speaking, the growing of whiskers is viewed with suspicion or explicit contempt. The beard is the badge of the out, the witless, and the frustrated, who can imagine no more valid expression of revolt than defiance of the code of personal sanitation. A brief survey of the types on the street you see wearing beards reveals a sublimation of everything you don't want to be seen with.

Obviously there are exceptions to any such generalities, most of them among musicians of established reputation, but on a wide front the growth of hair on the masculine face in extravagant dimensions is socially and economically suspect. Either the wearer of whiskers is a college boy growing them briefly for Frontier Days or he's a bottom drawer psycho.

Because all such social mores are established by identification with specific personalities, it is easy to point to the preposterous Fidel Castro as a prime cause of the disrepute in which beards find themselves. Toothbrush mustaches achieved a status of ill omen with Hitler, and Castro has put the curse on the stringy chin whiskers that were once the glory of Yankee sea captains and Confederate generals.

The beatnik-Castro association with whiskers was undoubtedly what prompted a trustee of a local educational institution, on discovering an instructor with full muff or beaver, to make inquiry into the propriety of his being on the staff. As was pointed out on several hands, whiskers in the learned professionals have a long and honored background of precedent, but today for reasons of association, a beard is as suspect among right-minded people as a copy of *Pravda* would be.

The folklore of beards is a mutable one and it is within reason that they should stage a comeback one of these days, but it will take some notably handsome whiskers in exalted places and worn by men of irreproachable social status to accomplish it. Castro and his mangy followers have done beards almost irreparable damage in our time.

The one ingratiating beard currently available in these parts is, perhaps symbolically, a sort of prop. It belongs to Bad Water Bill Fryk, who, together with his faithful burro, Gravel Gertie, poses for tourists in Virginia City's C Street in summer and turns up in other seasons at all the Death Valley authors' conferences and meetings in the Sierra saloons of E. Clampus Vitus. Bad Water's facade is one of patched Levi's, the battered canteen and turned up sombrero of the Frederick Remington type prospector, together with the howdy pardner vernacular of the Old Frontier. Under the layer of alkali dust, carefully applied to the beard each morning, Bad Water is a cultivated fellow who uses the subjunctive and says "whilst" like at Oxford. Rumor has it Bad Water is a Harvard man.

Are Barbers Becoming Extinct?

There seems to be something ominous and distinctly hostile to the American scheme of things that has always embraced barber shops as part of our national culture in the imminent arrival of the $2.50 haircut in San Francisco, a jump of two bits over the already preposterous $2.25 charged most places and one which, it is safe to guess, will put more barbers on relief than members of this ancient and now vanishing calling may like to think about.

Barbers, for all their alleged philosophical turn of mind, conversational versatility, political sagacity and other qualities of intellect and the senses, are completely unable to see handwriting on the wall that is clearly legible to most other discerning people.

"Nobody wants to cut their own hair or have the butler do it for them" will be the obvious reply of the barbers' union, but along the turn of the century just as a Boston character named Gillette was beginning to become known, the barbers were convulsed with mirth at the idea of anybody shaving themselves. Their references to bandages and arnica and cut throats delighted auditors and the mangled victim of self-shaving with a "safety razor" was a standard of music hall humor and the pages of *Life* and *Judge*.

I know, I know: monetary values change and we have inflation and everybody is richer, but the fact stands that there were a lot more barbers and barber shops in proportion to population when you could get the works, a shave, haircut, manicure, shine and singe, the last of which is now obsolete but once enjoyed a wide vogue, for $1.50 than in today's market when the full menu will cost close to $10 exclusive of tips.

I know because as a youth I used to get the full gospel treatment once a week downstairs in the Touraine Hotel in Boston for less than two dollars including the hat boy, shine boy and young lady with a Gibson girl hairdo who buffed my nails, and emerge frizzled, singed, gleaming and smelling of Ed Pinaud fit to turn heads as far away as Brimstone Corner. The whole thing was a success when I got home and my father, lowering the bedsheet pages of the *Boston Evening Transcript* to glare at me over his bifocals, would mutter an unflattering remark about Saturday night in a parlor house.

The decline of being barbered over the decades since that remote and golden time has been in largest measure attributable squarely to the high cost of something that used to be within convenient price range of everybody.

I like to think, too, that barber shop business has been abated not only by the economics of the trade but by its esthetics in the form of the so-called sanitary barber shop which has overtones of an operating room instead of a gentleman's club. The old model Koch's Patent barber chairs with mahogany furniture and red plush cushions and brass footrests and the hot towels that came from an enormous nickel-plated globular vault in the middle of the room had an appeal to the senses that is lacking in the surgical antisepsis that displaced them. A haircut that is only superficially removed from an appendectomy somehow lacks charm.

Still and all I'd hate to see the barber shop follow the honest swinging door men's saloon that once was the true glory of America into the discard and the museums, to be an object of curiosity like the blacksmith shop and the wonderful marble-topped soda fountains of yesterday. That melancholy day gets closer with every price raise for a haircut, and by the time it hits $3 the calling of being a barber will be as obsolete as the snuff grinder and frilled shirt laundress.

'White Christmas' Is a Dog's Breakfast

According to the printed reports of Tennessee Williams' new play on Broadway, its principal performer is a fellow fresh out of the hatch who spends his time trying to get "White Christmas" on the car radio and who, on his wedding night, had such an attack of the shakes that his wife slept in a chair in preference to the nuptial couch.

The author explicitly associates mental unbalance with the playing of "White Christmas" and that is all right with me.

For of all the dreary dirges and meretricious ballads known to the seasonal repertory of cliches, this half-time shuffle toward the graveyards of melancholy seems to me the most depressing, ghoulish and depraved. It's the sort of tune that, on a slightly overcast day, might well make a sensitive man go shopping for rope.

It has about it all the emetic sweetness of Liberace with the light of mother love in the eye that isn't watching the cash till, the professionalized tin-pan cloyingness of cheap perfume on an elderly prostitute.

Just what deludes shopkeepers and resort proprietors into the demonstrably demented notion that "White Christmas" is going to mesmerize the customers into unzipping the billfold in gestures of unimaginable largesse and transform tightwads into big spenders simply escapes me.

When I hear "White Christmas" I go home. Sometimes I'm actively ill, which isn't encouraging to the happy barroom trade. The tune and its revolting words have about them all the charm of those suicidal threnodies that were once chanted in the back rooms of Berlin night clubs in the early Nazi era. A stench of serecloths drenched in a perfume called Parfait Amour. A graveyard whine.

Don't get me wrong. I'm not running down the glad Yule spirit and getting in on a Scrooge act, an attitude that has for me all the sophistication of the village atheist pose.

But spare my palsied eardrums the whining bathos and sanctimonious bleat of "White Christmas." As music I find it only a little more hilarious than the dead march from "Saul," and as sentiment it's a dog's breakfast. And if ever that gloomiest of all concepts is fulfilled and Santa Claus is discovered to have committed suicide, you can make book that, like Tennessee Williams' bridegroom in the play, he became deranged from listening to the repulsive strains of "White Christmas" on the radio.

Be a Patriot! Light Up!

In the years of my youth, a period approximating, as it now seems, the Custer massacre, cigarettes were not a highly regarded article of commerce. Their use generally was restricted to the lower orders of society, pimps, race track touts, Congressmen and the like, and certainly none were ever smoked in my father's house by any member of the family, although now and then guests asked if they might be excused to go into the garden and smoke a cigar after dinner.

Smoking in the presence of ladies was unthinkable and there was still a statute on the local Boston law books against smoking pipes on the public street, pipes being associated with the Irish and not to be tolerated in the presence of gentlefolk.

There were, to be sure, exceptions to the rule. My friend Edwin Arlington Robinson, was notoriously a smoker of Sweet Caporals, but he was a recognized and widely acclaimed poet and was accorded the tolerance usually extended to genius. A bleak and craggy Down Easter, he had been a mighty skirmisher with the bottle in earlier times and cigarettes were regarded as a sort of tapering off. Most other men of letters of the time smoked pipes, and cigars were, of course, the universal hallmark of manhood and symbol of prestige according to their quality and cost.

Nor was this prejudice against cigarettes a parochial one confined to Puritan New England. As evidence of bad morale among the ship's company in the sinking of the *Titanic,* witnesses attested that in the lifeboats many stewards and other members of the crew lit cigarettes in the presence of ladies, not to mention the Grim Reaper and the greatest catastrophe of modern times. It was, incidentally, the most serious evidence of misconduct ever made against the company's servants on that ill-starred vessel.

Tobacco in those days wasn't especially big business, certainly nothing to attract the hostility of a predatory Federal Government bent on taxing out of existence every possible source of revenue except the billion dollar union racket, some of whose components are wealthier by far than the industries they seek to impoverish by extortion.

Now the wowsers, do-gooders and reforming trash generally,

including "medical authorities" from mail order schools of osteopathy with nothing better to occupy their childish minds, are grinding out a sustained barrage of anti-cigarette propaganda. The Surgeon General of the U. S., presumably a handy fellow in the realm of gunshot wounds, has appointed the usual committee to investigate the potentialities for lung cancer, and publicity-mad politicians of the more debased order are rallying to denounce the sinful cigarette as a smoke screen for the evasion of more potentially dangerous issues.

To date the principal source of this septic fright talk about lung cancer has been England, where socialized medicine has reduced the once haughty practitioners of Harley Street to a confraternity of seedy pensioners dependent on the favors of a Ministry of Health that is a shining example of bureaucratic incompetence, corruption and political expediency.

The massed forces of bigotry, superstition and infected politics are ganging up on tobacco in general and cigarettes in particular with an ultimate view to their total prohibition. And don't think for a minute this cretin babbling about lung cancer isn't going to cost you and me money. Tobacco taxes last year yielded $3.2 billions in State and Federal revenue, and any least dime's abatement in this sum is going to be compensated by some other confiscatory rooking of the taxpayer to support the nest of boodling elected mendicants in Washington, D. C.

The time for all men of independence and integrity to start smoking is right now.

I doubt if I have smoked ten cigarettes in the last ten years but I am going to re-establish a habit I neither admire nor take pleasure in as a patriotic duty.

The cold war that is waged every minute of the day and night between the voters and taxpayers of the United States and the Government at Washington is getting hot with a meddlesome, impertinent and paternalistic hierarchy of shiftless time-servers trying to move in once more on the personal liberties of those of us who maintain them with their front feet in the public hog trough.

For 13 long years I fought the good fight along with 160,-000,000 other American patriots allied against the infamies of prohibition. I've got scars on my liver to show for it.

I'm not too old to enlist again in the unceasing battle that all Americans have to fight all the time against the enemy that is Washington, your enemy, my enemy and everybody's enemy, the Federal Government of the United States in all its bureaucratic infamy. May I offer you a light?

A Taste for Heroes With Hair on Them

Unless all the signs prove false, the people of the United States are in for the inspirational brainwashing in favor of clean living that accompanies any national triumph in any field of competitive endeavor, this time in the name of our astronauts.

What must vastly amuse the cynical observer of Americana is the flood of hallelujahs that these achievements must inevitably raise in favor of baby, mother, the Flag, clean living, temperance and the inviolability of marriage and the American home.

It has happened before, this whitewashing and decontaminating of national heroes until their saintliness, purity and Galahad dimensions generally turn the collective stomach of intelligence. They tried it on Colonel Lindbergh, if memory serves, who was a fairly natural fellow until the image makers deprived him of any normal masculinity and character, but the colonel proved an idol with feet of clay. When the thrice damned prohibitionists advertised him as a fellow who recoiled from strong drink, Colonel Lindbergh, to his everlasting credit, suddenly called in the reporters and photographers to record him gloriously downing Daiquiris by the bucket.

It wasn't always so with the heroes of American folk legend. Until comparatively recently, when the Methodists started remaking the image of desirability, the men who attracted worshipful attention to themselves in the national scheme of things were almost inevitably men of bounce with redeeming traces of low character about them.

Examine briefly the outstanding public favorites of a better time in the land and you discover an imposing, indeed a radiant, array of lechers, drunks, saloon brawlers, blasphemers against all godliness and low fellows generally.

Take a specially choice American hero of positively epic dimensions that have endured long after his passing from the scene, Buffalo Bill Cody. From manhood until the day of his death, Pahaska smelled of strong waters. Much of the time he was soused to the sombrero, and had to be helped onto his horse. His employers had him enjoined by court order to stay sober and take only six drinks a day, a shyster legal trick which the colonel resolved by taking his drinks in a fire pail. Much of the time he spent chasing the squaws.

As handsome and virile as he was boozy, his taste was catholic and legend has him making his escape from the boudoir of an English peeress in the classic manner: "It is my husband! Go, quickly and by the window!" When he once reproved Gene Fowler for an editorial liberty in Denver with the words, "Young sir, my hairs are hoary!" Fowler replied: "Aye, sire, and not with eld."

Or take another national hero of a bygone and more illustrious day, John L. Sullivan, the Roxbury Strong Boy who could lick any s.o.b. in the place and did it two or three times a night for fun. Sullivan's personal morality was of an order to curl the hair of virtue, and he was worshipped by 100,000,000 people as all that was enviable.

Americans used to like their folk heroes with hair on them. If they have lost their taste for free-wheeling individualists with some savor and gusto about them, all is indeed lost and the national jig is up.

The Expense Account Society

The expense account society that has been brought into existence by the past attitude of the Treasury toward this aspect of the national business structure is not only one that costs the Federal Government a good deal of money but is a much resented affront to a great many people who are themselves unable to swell it in expensive resorts and restaurants and travel abroad tax free and out of various corporate pockets on the slim excuse that they are doing company business.

There are precious few Americans of private means who can or will patronize restaurants where the luncheon tab for the chef's suggestion can come to $45 for two, but such plush premises as the Four Seasons in New York are jammed to the reservation desks with expense account patrons paying $200 for dinner for five.

Probably corporate expense accounts are the greatest single inflationary agency in the entire national economy, in addition to which well-upholstered jerks pre-empting the best of everything in restaurants, theaters, night clubs and airplanes are a damned poor advertisement for big business. They make more enemies among a class of people naturally sympathetic to corporate vastness than all the radical agitators and socialists put together.

An abatement of the expense account society could win the Government wild plaudits from a great many taxpayers who, by indirection, are tired of picking up the tab every time some crumb bum with an executive title, who couldn't treat a friend to a Coke on his own money, decides he wants a week in New York with a suite at the St. Regis and ringside table at El Morocco every evening.

It's a rare business deal that can't be consummated with a 5-cent postage stamp.

42

Into the Footlights of Oblivion

The indiscriminate sale and wholesale distribution of lethal pesticides as long as they only killed off the Nation's wild life and now and then a household pet aroused no indignation anywhere, except on the part of a minority of conservationists like Miss Rachel Carson, who were immediately branded as crackpots and alarmists by the poison industry. The Borgias of the chemical vats suggested that Miss Carson was a discredited "cultist of the balance of nature."

Well, the balance of nature, cult or no cult, is now getting a good deal more attention since it has become a recognized asset to the undertaking business. Indignation and terror commenced to boil when it was found that the same chemical concentration of lethal elements that has killed off the robins in California could and, indeed, was killing off humans as well.

A classic cliche of old fashioned melodrama used to be the big murder moment when the would-be killer got the poisoned chalices mixed and himself fell, clutching his throat and screaming for absolution, into the footlights. The spectacle of a ponderable segment of the population clutching at its throat and reaching for a stomach pump I confess to find a refreshing and instructive revision of this old theme.

The chain of death that commences with the irresponsible spraying of the landscape with dieldrin, aldrin, tedion and heptachlor, chlorinated hydro-carbons which would have found instant acceptance in the kitchens of the Medici, has remarkably few weak links. Beginning, perhaps, with a field mouse and progressing then to a game animal who eats the mouse, it moves almost irrevocably on its way to kill the ultimate consumer who will be the man who shot the bear and sent his friends a nice rack of bear chops for Christmas. The stuff lingers around a long time in the human system, augmenting sometimes over a period of years and has a pronounced potentiality for being passed on from one generation of humans to its own issue in the next.

The robins have gone from the general awareness in California and I must confess myself enchanted at the possibility that some of the people who poisoned them, a tolerably large number, I hope, are today walking around with stuff in their liver and kidneys which will one day soon send them, too, clutching at their throats and screaming for absolution as they fall into the footlights of oblivion.

A Nation of Dietary Sheep

Gene Fowler, something of a cynic where the medical profession was involved, coined the aphorism "Doctors and undertakers always wink in passing." Most reasonable people who have a profound respect for the medical profession in its aspects of propriety would improve on this to agree that diet-sponsoring quacks using popular communications to exploit their obsession don't merely wink in passing the undertaker, they pause and embrace him.

A vast proportion of diet partisans and quasi-medical practitioners advocating seaweed and sunflower seeds for longevity comparable to that of Old Parr are, of course, frauds pure and simple with a crooked commercial pitch or interested angle. Witness the recent example of a New York publishing firm which was in cahoots with a disbarred veterinary to sell its diet fad books as a tie-in with a patent nostrum so fraudulent that the entire setup was eventually exposed by Federal agencies. It makes no difference to a nation of suckers who will embrace any medical fraudulence so long as its practice involves renunciation of the good things of life, including common sense.

The elder John D. Rockefeller was the quintessential end

product of American dietary gullibility and contrived at fantastic cost of money and personal deprivation to extend his life well beyond the allotted Biblical span. He surrounded himself with platoons of doctors and male nurses until his residences were indistinguishable from an emergency ward, existing on a diet of goat's milk and graham crackers in infinitesimal quantities while technicians stood by day and night with oxygen tanks and adrenalin.

His mind and reason for existence had long since gone, but there flickered dimly within the mummy casing the will to continue certifiably animate longer than most. He managed it, too, but few people envied him.

Now let's face it, if anyone wants to live as long as John D. Rockefeller, suitable precautions taken over a lifetime may accomplish this debatable end. From cradle to grave, or more realistically, from incubator to incinerator, he would be well advised to remain in bed, never venturing out of the house, and subsisting on an alcohol-free, salt-free, meatless diet of skimmed milk and the variations on butcher's paper available in all diet shops, with no sex experience (you know what a strain *that* is on the heart) and of course no walking up stairs. That's almost as bad.

A dedicated physician in constant attendance with oxygen tanks handy and a male nurse to wheel him to the bathroom in a rolling chair will be a great help. He will see no visitors on account of germs and have no pets or flowers on account of possible fatal allergies and he won't read the newspapers, because you know what politics does to blood pressure.

With an antiseptic senility thus assured, he may be certain of an eventual and gratifying obituary, next to which in the adjacent column will be the equally admiring obit of a low character who achieved his precise age smoking black cigars in chain from breakfast to bed, consuming a quart of proof spirits every

45

day of his life, eschewing all green vegetables and subsisting largely on underdone red meat and with a record of a hundred mistresses and as many spectacular motor accidents.

Remember the case of Auntie Belle Livingston whose way of life and conduct were so depraved that everyone said she'd come to a bad end from alcohol. She did, too. She was 83 at the time.

How to Live Low on the Hog

One aspect of the alleged American civilization that must arouse mixed emotions in observers from more settled societies is the passionate dedication for masochistic self-immolation in the holy name of staying or getting thin.

In a land of fantastic plenty where more and better food than was ever known before in the history of the world is available to everybody, a large element of American society is busy hiring self-styled medical authorities to put them on diets and is patronizing patent dietetic arrangements warranted to have their rib cages showing through their skin within a fortnight.

Some of the dietary devices may well be sponsored by responsible firms and entrepreneurs of recognized integrity. Others are in the electric belt category. Many of them give sanctimonious smirks in the direction of the medical profession with self-righteous exhortations to "consult your physician." The doctors are happy, if consulted, to concur, since the first clause in the contemporary Hippocratic oath requires all doctors to tell all patients no matter what their ailments, if any, to stop drinking and smoking and to eat as little as possible to sustain life. The doctor who doesn't go through this routine with each and every patient will, if detected, be read out of the medical society.

The life insurance firms, too, are glad to get in on the act, petitioning their clients to avoid any practices or habits that may give a suggestion of pleasure and to "consult your family physician," thereby contributing to everybody's misery and discomfort.

The whole routine is a sort of self-supporting or perpetual motion act, with the vendors of patent slenderizers promoting the medical profession, the medical profession promoting the insurance swamis, and the morticians cheering everybody on in the name of selling narrow gauge caskets at the same price they charge for coffins for people of reasonable dimensions.

A clue to the character of the whole preposterous cult of being undernourished is that none of the soothsayers and get-thin prophets purely and simply suggests that folk stop eating so much. They must stop eating and buy for money a product calculated to take the place of chow. There is a commercial pitch to every diet advocate. Nobody gets in on the act who hasn't got something to sell.

As a result, millions of Americans now fat and happy will undertake at fantastic expense to become thin and miserable, while enriching beyond the dreams of avarice the owners of proprietary brands of pulverized chalk impregnated with synthetic chocolate flavor.

One could go on far, far into the night reciting grim anecdotes about what happened to folk who wanted to be thinner than God intended. But the saddest tale, I think, concerns an amiable old Frenchman known to some of us a few years back as the Prince Curnowsky, King of the Epicures. He wasn't a Prince, but that didn't matter. He was a big eater like "Diamond Jim" Brady but an extremely sophisticated one whose approval could be the making of a Paris restaurant almost overnight.

Well, the Prince got a little heavy around the waist and had to have his dinner jackets let out. Finally, however, he fell into the hands of a Paris diet advocate who cut him down from three squares a day to a single meal, and a miserable one at that, of only five or six courses and no more than two wines, which,

47

to a man of his habits, was starvation. And one night the old gentleman, now thin, thoroughly unhappy and in perfect health as a result of malnutrition, went to open a window when a fit of faintness overcame him and he fell into the courtyard and was killed.

If ever a man died of starvation, it was the Prince Curnowsky, ex-King of the Epicures.

The Expatriate Drinker

That sterling repository of our national yesterdays, American Heritage, has just released an issue devoted in its literate and pictorial entirety to the 1920s, in all probability the last era in the record that is available to being viewed as a well defined and clearly identifiable entity.

I find no mention of one of the great manifestations of the time which should be at least a footnote to any history of prohibition and its attendant infamies.

I speak, of course, of the expatriate drinker.

As clearly defined and as articulate in his grievance against the Yankee homeland as any literary or esthetic rebel who found spiritual consolation and fulfillment on the Left Bank, the alcoholic exile was a part-time refugee from the American wasteland who has not received his historic due in the annals of the period.

His spiritual home was the Ritz Bar on the Cambon side of that auspicious Paris hostelry. His money was, to be sure, unassailably in dollars and he might either be a commuter aboard the then weekly sailings of the *Olympic, Berengaria* or *Paris* or he might establish semi-permanent residence in France. Often enough he was explicitly patriotic in every aspect of national temperament excepting for what came in bottles. There he was red revolutionary, tracing his ancestry to the participants in the Boston Tea Party and the great Whiskey Rebellion in

Pennsylvania. He was often homesick, eagerly questioning the latest arrivals from the Atlantic sea lanes and shuddering at the gruesome details of life and death in the speakeasies of the homeland.

Among the platinum-plated expatriates of the Ritz Bar there grew up a body of legend and folklore while their ritualistic drinking was surrounded with protocol. It was a men's bar exclusively at noontime and women, among them Connie Bennett and Marion Davies, were, much against their inclination, herded by the management into a smoke-filled female groggery across the corridor variously known as the Dog Kennel and the Black Hole of Calcutta.

The thirsty but mannered regulars assembled outside the entrance to the Ritz Bar as noontime approached awaiting, as it were, the noonday gun to start the day's serious drinking. To be seen inside the place before noon identified you as a certifiable alcoholic and no-gooder. To be late was unfashionable, with the result that when Count Johnny Perdicaris looked at his wrist watch and shouted "Now" a small man could be maimed in the ensuing crush.

Strict protocol was observed in seating the devotees of the men's bar itself. Banquettes on the left as one entered were reserved for young gentlemen from Yale, Harvard, Princeton and the members of the American Embassy staff presided over by Myron Herrick. Those to the right were occupied exclusively by South Americans, stiffly starched, pomaded and tightly buttoned, a long row of heavy-rimmed single eyeglasses, mostly with poodles.

Many of the Ritz Bar regulars like Donald Rogers, a former member of the consular service, had been trapped there for years. Rogers was notorious for engaging passage on each successive boat and then not making it until the clerks at Cunard and White Star no longer made actual reservations for him.

Red letter days at the Ritz Bar were those when Alfonso, regnant King of Spain, and his friend Berry Wall, king of the dudes, came in for a drink known in His Majesty's absence as a King's Death but called a Royal Highball when he was present. It comprised a quart of ice cold champagne in a large glass with a generous slug of vintage cognac and a handful of fresh strawberries for panache. His Majesty allowed this was a refreshing beverage with which to begin the day and wiped his mustaches on a king-sized handkerchief from Charvet's just across the way with a crown in the corner. Your correspondent admired these and one day the King gave him one which is still in the bank vault in Reno.

It may do as an index of the time. Our heroes were still kings and there were kings around to be heroes.

The Infamy of Jury Awards

Perhaps the most unmitigatedly asinine aspect of the American legal structure, and to rate such a superlative you have to be far gone in idiocy, is that which permits juries to award damages with no control over the outrageous sums demanded and often granted for the most trifling of causes.

Professional litigants, trading on the maudlin sentimentality of juries in which women are permitted to sit and represented by cry artist shysters on a contingency basis, make a handsome living blackmailing corporate and individual defendants for sums simply dreamed out of thin air which are often awarded without hesitation by juries unable to count that high and who have to spell out the figures with their lips when they read them.

Recently a laborer was awarded half a million dollars by a jury of sniveling illiterates for the loss of his legs in an accident that was a standard occupational hazard of his calling.

Almost as outrageous a sum was a short time back awarded by a jury to a housewife who claimed she had been disfigured and her "beauty" ruined by defective cosmetics. It may be doubted if even the personal pulchritude of Semiramis or Helen of Troy was worth $334,000.

That the cosmetic industry is the world's most monstrous over-all swindle and might well be eliminated from the cosmic scheme of things along with the packaging industry and the legal profession isn't in question. No woman's beauty, unless she is a professional prostitute, has any cash value worth mentioning.

Next to damages for alleged and in 99 cases out of 100 totally imaginary physical harm, the libel racket is the most shocking of all indictments of a system which permits juries to determine the amount of cash damages. Most libel is altogether imaginary. In perhaps one case in a thousand it is conceivable that a professional man's standing and reputation can be harmed by contrived defamation.

To state for the record that a surgeon of fair repute is secretly in the pay of the local undertaker could conceivably do hurt to his gainful practice. For a politician or public officeholder to claim libel against his good name, which is completely non-extant, is simply hilarious.

When a Chicago newspaper at the turn of the century alleged that Theodore Roosevelt was a rumbum and an alcoholic, an enlightened court awarded him damages of less than a dollar. Most reasonable men would account such personal characterization as purely honorific.

If potential damage awards for libel were limited by statute to a reasonable sum, say four bits, the Nation's courts would be less littered with this sort of trash.

To entrust a jury empaneled from the shiftless unemployed whom the sheriff's officers are able to dragoon into service with the awarding of money damages is simply a travesty on the justice the courts so noisily maintain is their stock in trade.

If actual damage can be proved and is available to redress in cash, the sum should be entrusted to a responsible magistrate

51

presumably trained in the law and not available, as are the witless housewives and small tradesmen of juries, to the breastbeating of legal hamfatters retained on a contingency fee basis. There is, of course, risk even here, but it implies some chance of justice by placing it in the hands of only one man who may be a scoundrel instead of 12 who are certain to be.

Sad Decline of a Masculine Refuge

If anything were needed to point up the rapidly degenerating facade of American society and the ascendancy of a septic domesticity, it is the report that pool halls, long a resort of masculinity in its more explicit aspect, are being promoted as family recreation centers and that more than 500 colleges, universities and boys' and women's clubs include pool as part of the curriculum in their physical education courses.

The face-lifting and consequent regenerating of pool halls has been credited to the allied and apparently interchangeable popularity of bowling and is claimed to have been of recent date, but this department is in a position to point out that the renaissance of billiards can be traced to the year 1937 when Brunswick undertook to market a new and approximately portable billiard table.

To forward the fortunes of a formerly shady and therefore universally agreeable sport and elevate it to respectability and oblivion, free samples of the product were sent to a number of New Yorkers whose example, it was felt, if they were photographed tearing the cloth with an inexpert cue, might incite countless and solvent thousands to imitate their publicized example. Franklin P. Adams received one of these devices and so did, if memory serves, Miss Tallulah Bankhead, Marc Connelly, Peter Arno, James Thurber, Harold Ross and your reporter. Few of the recipients of these ponderous favors were

52

maddened with delight. Mostly they were delivered while we were away from home and in no position to prevent their unloading, with bloodshed if necessary, and the gloomy beneficiaries met forthwith at the bar at Jack & Charlie's to take steps.

Miss Bankhead, who lived at the Elysee, reported that the management had allowed that a billiard room could be connected with her suite for an additional $2000 a year, which was more than she cared about. Grover Whalen, who happened to be handy at the bar at the moment and spoke quiet unofficially for the harbor commissioners, said we would all be liable to jail if we threw them in the North River. If the *Queen Mary* went aground on a hidden reef of billiard tables off Pier 60 we could be indicted for barratry.

It was Harold Ross who came up with what proved to be a truly radiant solution to our problem. For a small fee an expressman called and took away no fewer than twenty billiard tables from as many ungrateful recipients of Brunswick bounty and delivered them, over a weekend while he was at Lake Bomosseen, to Wit's End, Alexander Woollcott's digs over by the East River.

The closest approach to actual respectability achieved by any billiard table in your reporter's recollection was that in the bar of The Players at 16 Gramercy Park where it was in constant requisition among the actors who were the club's principal membership and made up a large part of the deficit. Otis Skinner admired also to sleep under it, a circumstance which gave rise to one of the deathless legends of The Players.

One morning about three o'clock a new member of the club, Scudder Middleton, then editing John Hanrahan's *Stage* magazine, while loitering at the bar just before closing, chanced to spy a neatly dinner-jacketed figure in a position of recumbent repose under the club's main source of revenue.

Hastily recruiting the night porter who was wielding a listless broom and Charlie the barkeep, he exorted them to assist him. "It's Otis Skinner," he exclaimed in frightened tones. "The president of the club. This is terrible. Perhaps he's had a stroke. Help me move him."

The aged porter, a character who wore his hat sideways on his head, was unperturbed and went on with his dusting.

"That's all right Mr. Middleton, don't you fret," he soothed, "I know it's Mr. Skinner and that he's president of the club, too. I allus sweeps around him."

The Real Hat of the Old West

A strong case can be built by any perceptive historian for the derby and not the Stetson as the authentic hat of the Old West. The Stetson was almost unknown outside the Texas ranges until it was popularized around the turn of the century by Remington, but a short time spent in any photographic file of the Old West from Chicago to San Francisco in the '70s, '80s and '90s including those regions where firearms were conspicuous and the stagecoach had not yet been supplanted by the steam cars will show the hard crowned derby in florid and almost universal abundance.

The best known photograph of Bat Masterson shows him in a pearl-gray bowler. Wyatt Earp, the paradigm of the brass-knuckles peace officer, was a notable derby fancier. The members of the Hole in the Wall gang in a group photograph taken in Kansas City to a man are attired in the hat we celebrate, although this was on the occasion of a city excursion and may have been an affectation of urban attire rather than native habit.

Black Bart, the poetically inclined stagecoach robber of the Mother Lode highways, was depicted in the standard Wells Fargo wanted poster advertising a reward for his capture in a rakishly low crowned, curly-brimmed dicer. Any group of travelers over the vast Nevada, Montana, Colorado and Oregon distances posed

54

on a Concord stage top headed for Leadville, Silverton, Pizen Switch, the Dalles, Austin, Eureka or Hangtown will show a handful wearing the accepted hat of the region.

In an age before the general availability of soft cloth visor caps, the derby hat was the conventional attire of the working locomotive engineer. It didn't blow off in the slip stream outside his cab window and was a primordial sort of crash helmet, the lineal ancestor of the tin hat of today's working stiff.

It was also the favored headgear of timber cutters in the Northwest, and Stewart Holbrook, the jongleur of "Holy Old Mackinaw," when he first arrived in the Oregon timber regions in 1915, wore a Boston derby and was surprised to find himself properly attired for Tillamook and Snohomish.

Havoc Among the Hearse Jockeys

Although the power of propaganda in book form has long been discounted by cynics who are fond of remarking that the authority of the printing press to resolve public opinion disappeared with "Uncle Tom's Cabin" or, at the latest, with Upton Sinclair's "The Jungle," the hard fact remains that Jessica Mitford's "The American Way of Death" is congealing the marrow of the mendacious ghouls of the undertaking business and raising plain unadulterated havoc with the big time casket and cerement industry.

In California especially, where the partnership between high pressure undertakers and the notoriously available Legislature at Sacramento has made it the least reasonable State in which to die and where no known limit exists to the lengths of persuasion and mendacity to which shroud vendors will go to promote expensive funerals in execrable taste, Miss Mitford has occasioned banshee screams of indignation among the more ostentatious hearse jockeys.

The simple funeral advocates are being denounced as "irreligious," "materialistic" and even "communistic." Not to be buried with the benefits of stylish footwear, a $15,000 bronze coffin and air-conditioned limousines to the graveyard is "un-American" and the suggestion is being covertly circulated that the funeral societies are actually being organized by the Kremlin.

A fine wake, declares the California Funeral Directors Association, the ranking tong of advocates of stately and expensive sarabands of death, is as much a status symbol as a good address and going first class on Charon's barge as much an ostentation of success as its equivalent on the *Queen Mary*. Not to die beyond one's means is against "American tradition."

Repeal of California's arbitrary and absurd burial statutes will only, of course, be accomplished over the dead (and presumably expensively embalmed) bodies of the funeral directors' lobby at Sacramento, for years now the most notorious group operating in the already septic precincts of a corrupt legislative hog trough of almost limitless dimensions. A single graveyard management, that of Forest Lawn in Los Angeles which is widely admired in body snatching circles for its aggressive merchandising methods and stimulation of impulse buying in the shrouds department, does a gross business of more than three million a year in an industry where the profit markup may run as high as 90 per cent, and it's a leadpipe cinch Forest Lawn isn't going to pass a dividend without protest.

What was Wrong With 1905?

Now and then some dolt rises up in meeting in the columns of the enquiring reporter or letters to the editor with the horrid pronouncement that, if elected, Senator Goldwater "will set the country back 50 years." Were it indeed possible by some superlatively benevolent tinkering of the time machine to turn back the clock and replace the scattered pages of the calendar, it would be to restore an infinitely better world than anybody now alive is likely ever to see again.

Envision, if you will, a world where the most hideous manifestations of contemporary barbarism were mercifully unknown, one which was innocent of even intimations of jet travel, radio commentators, television comedians, mendacious opinion polls, the graduated income tax, women in trousers, nuclear fission, sports shirts, television dinners, peace marchers, sit-ins, plastics, condominium apartments, parking meters, Hollywood diets, beatniks, tailfins, the 30-cent dollar, Bobby Kennedy, the Rev. Billy Graham, zippers on men's pants, Hilton hotels and once a day mail delivery.

I am aware that a hanker for the irrevocably vanished past, the *temps jadis* of the poet, has existed in all ages and that a dim view has been taken of it by the deluded gulls in the community who subscribe to the illusion of progress. Somewhere in "The Illiad" Homer complains bitterly of contemporary degenerate times and looks backward to a more heroic age when warriors were bashing in the heads of the opposition with rocks no man of today can even lift. To look backward in admiration and affection is supposed by partisans of the truly dreadful here and now to be an index of insufficiency, an inability to cope with the changing condition of life which has confronted every generation of recorded time.

It seems to me that Senator Goldwater could do a lot worse than promise to turn back the clock to the first decade of the century which now appears to most people to have been a radiant time of ineffable serenity, prosperity and abundance. At least it lacked the disasters, say, of women's suffrage, the universal motor car, credit cards, international airports, repudiation of the national currency, tranquilizers, freedom riders, digit dialing and the one-ounce Martini.

Statistics: Lies With Affidavits

At heart a cynic and basically distrustful of mathematics on the ground that its fabric may well comprise total and absolute error, I am the sort of churl who drives advertising copy writers, to drink and brings dark despair to people who advance powerful arguments backed by imposing arrays of figures.

If I see a gasoline advertised to possess six secret ingredients calculated to lend it the potency of 90 proof bourbon or a brand of baker's bread with eight specially healthful components, I am the sort of curmudgeon who says "Name them!"

Surveys that claim attention to the melancholy circumstance that alcoholism impairs the national economy to the extent of $5,000,000,000, I rudely greet with "How do you know?"

Statistics have always seemed to me the mathematics of mendacity, lies with affidavits, the elaborate machinery of falsehood and deliberate deception. Show me a man who quotes figures to prove a point and offers in evidence statistics to advance an argument, and I'll show you somebody who, for whatever reasons may motivate him, is out to sell you a spurious bill of goods and trade on your gullibility. Hell isn't entirely paved with good intentions; much of its parquet is covered with phony statistics.

No better evidence can come to hand than the spiraling mathematics of hysteria that have been the pattern of the current fallout-doomsday-survival assault on American credibility. I know damned well that when an expert says flatly that 56 per cent of a given community will perish instantly in an all-out atomic attack, or that fallout will produce fatal casualties of 769 out of every 1000, or that a piano crate sheathed in tar paper and stocked with two weeks worth of enchiladas and ginger pop will provide a survival ratio for its inmates of one out of two, that the man who invokes this sort of thing is a fool, a knave or an exhibitionist, or a combination of all three, and the newspaper that reports his statistics of Armageddon down to tenths of one per cent is not giving its readers the break of reasonable appraisal of the news to which they are entitled.

The editor who quotes, without intelligent questioning of its validity, any statistic placed in evidence by any Government

58

agency, advertising firm, politician, aspirant for office, medical "expert," efficiency "expert," sociologist, temperance advocate, race agitator, social reformer, or other generally recognized merchant of mendacity in wholesale and retail quantities is betraying his trust to his constituents. All quoted statistics of any sort should be preceded by the word "alleged" like an inexperienced reporter trying to avoid libel. Figures trying to prove something should be identified as perilous as poisonous medicines are identified by skulls and crossbones. All figures are at best guesswork; most are purely and simply mendacious and calculatedly false.

The Cult of Preposterous Women

Miss Vanessa Brown, an intelligent play-actress—if the terms are not inherently contradictory—spoke words of uncommon wisdom the other day when she remarked that women are made out on the stage and screen to be horse's behinds for the simple reason that most playscripts are written by men and hence in malice against womankind.

"There are very few good parts that recognize the importance of women," deposed Miss Brown. "It's an injustice to our sex."

Men may admire women. They may respect them. They may even love women; it's a sentiment one hears well spoken of. But they don't appreciate seeing them in positions of importance and the fact is attested in our democracy that despite the opening wedge of woman suffrage, very few women have been elected to public office of consequence. The availability of the ballot was widely heralded as the agency which would banish corruption in politics at every level of our national administrative life and usher in a new era of responsible Government untarnished by masculine availability to power and pelf.

The promised millenium failed to materialize and in the few instances where female politicians acceded to office, such as in Texas, their use of authority brought little credit to their sex.

59

Not only do men not want women to achieve a status of importance; there is very little evidence that women do either.

But the boys most effectively interested in portraying women in the role of horse's rumps are not the script writers who cast them as dreary housewives in soap operas or virginal gun molls in thrillers. The characters who really make females into clowns and freaks of the first magnitude and get handsomely paid for it are the most exalted arbiters of female fashions in the ateliers of haute couture in Paris. They are the wicked little men who dream up the hairdos of fashion.

Never before in the course of the war between men and women as envisioned by James Thurber have such effective agencies been devised for making the female person preposterous as the chamberpot hats, the used look, the unwanted look, the idiot look, the street accident look, the nightmare look, the halfwit look and the gassed look, with which their heads and hair are invested in the name of high fashion and the momentary mode.

For the past several years the ultimate in style has been a tinkle pot atop an explosion in a mattress factory combined with smears of eyeshadow that make the wearer resemble nothing so much as the late Alla Nazimova after a particularly nasty motor smash. Women of reported general intelligence in other fields have worn these faces in public to the accompaniment of inextinguishable laughter on the part of all sane persons of either sex.

It's the sort of thing that encourages the belief that women don't particularly want to be taken seriously and would prefer to be mistaken for Harpo Marx.

Today's Gold Brick

Installment buying is this generation's equivalent in the boob sweepstakes of such now cobwebbed devices as the panel game, the gold brick, shares in city hall and the Spanish prisoner hoax, all of them beloved of the con men of the curly-brimmed derby and ratcatcher suit age of American innocence.

That purchase of merchandise on tick amounts annually in the national economy to billions of dollars is the explicit justification of Get Rich Quick Wallingford and irrefutable evidence of the truth of the axiom that there's a sucker born every minute.

The gullibility that sees its own advantage in purchasing on time everything from the washing machine, the idiot tube in the parlor, the Thunderbird and last year's vacation in Hawaii to gasoline at the filling station and home sites in Country Club Acres has changed Monkey Ward and Sears from merchandising institutions to banking services. With interest rates on installment buying running several times the legal rate on money borrowed from accredited sources, sellers would be fools not to get in on the greatest thieving act of the age.

God as a Commodity

The particularly witless group of clergymen who, a short time back, undertook to dissuade President Johnson from, as they said, "using God as a national resource" have chosen for themselves a fairly hard row to hoe.

Not only are they denying God's most satisfactory of all aspects so far as most people are concerned, His availability to universal invocation as witness to the rectitude of their conduct, speech and feelings, but also they are taking on the entire weight of history which is firmly and massively against any such foolishness.

It is almost impossible to refer to any aspect of the historic record, either since the Lord God Jehovah was invented by Jewish theologians and passed along as the principal corporate asset of the Christian church approximately 2000 years ago or in earlier times and equally barbarous places where other gods

61

were worshipped with equal or greater fervor, and not find heads of state on chatty terms with the Almighty. President Johnson is only the latest of the long parade of generals, statesmen, rulers and movers and shakers generally who have invoked God's partnership to cut the throats of competition which was just as noisy in its claims to divine approval.

Almost alone of the historic forces in the record, the modern Communist states reject the practice of involving God in their semantics and there is a general feeling that in so doing they may well be missing a bet.

God began being invited to champion private causes long before He turns up in the literature of early Christianity. The entire Old Testament is a record of His explicit partnership with a long succession of prophets and potentates whose motives, at this remove at any rate, seem to lack special sanctification.

An even greater workout was in store for the agencies of heaven in the middle ages of the Christian record when God had become fairly common currency, conversationally speaking, and the church was everywhere. The ministers who object to President Johnson would have had a bad time of it at the court of any medieval baron whose predatory assaults upon his neighbors were conducted with sanctimonious appeals to God to witness the rightness of the aggressor's cause.

Coming down to modern times in our own national record almost everybody of consequence, Washington, Lincoln, General Grant, President Kennedy, Admiral Farragut, President Wilson, all freely enlisted the approval and active support of heaven in their several projects and nobody seems to have objected that God was being turned into a national resource like stockpiled aluminum or surplus wheat.

Sadly one must conclude that the gaggle of reversed collars who took President Johnson to task are either unaware of history or else groping for newspaper space, a commodity grievously in short supply for the cloth in these secular times. As a source of newspaper attention it is inspired since it entails no serious controversy and will occasion no reprisals. Neither will it add to the stature of a calling already approaching obsolescence.

The Refusal to Face Reality

One more nasty nice-nellyism that is appearing with increased frequency in the national lexicon and distresses, I am sure, the more mature and perceptive element of newspaper readers is the clammy euphemism "emotionally disturbed."

In the special case of newspaper libel it is possible that to describe a person as "emotionally disturbed" isn't actionable and that to specifically charge him with clinical insanity may be. I've heard it argued both ways. For journalistic purposes it may be a necessary evasion like saying a character "was feeling no pain" to indicate delicately and legally that he was honking drunk and had been thrown out of every saloon in the precinct.

"Emotionally disturbed" is nothing more than a lifted pinkie synonym for mad, crazy, nuts, bughouse, insane or off one's chump.

This shifty verbal evasiveness and refusal to face factual reality has for many years now been a characteristic of the language both English and American and is nothing new to the student of our national mores. For some reason that completely escapes rational explanation, undertakers don't like to be called undertakers, but insist on invoking the obscene word "mortician" which actually incorporates the root word of death which they are trying to disown.

In England they used to be known as "The Worshipful Company of Upholders," which had a great deal of style. I suggest it to the California undertakers whose ruthless arrogance and legislative dictatorship are going to get them a fearful comeuppance one of these days. A good billboard campaign with the slogan "When Death Calls, Summon a Member of the Worshipful Company of Upholders" could work wonders for a detested monopoly.

Less hilariously but still essentially childish are the real estate hucksters who insist on being known as "realtors" and factory sites that are advertised as "industrial parks." We incline to laugh condescendingly at such Victorian elaboration of the language as "tonsorial artist" for barber and "mixologist" for bartender, but are daily confronted with straight-faced references to "mobile homesites" which means a parking lot for trailer camp trash.

The evocation of sleazy euphemisms in the language, most of them having to do with decay, disease, mortality and other depressing realities of life and death, isn't only tacky but somehow indicative of a decline in the national character, an over-civilized approach to unpleasant realities that, basically, there is no evading. The emetic newspaper usage of "passed away" for died is as good an example as any at hand.

I once worked for a paper, the *New York Herald Tribune,* where, despite heroic efforts on the part of its great city editor Stanley Walker for a realistic approach to news reporting, the management had a great aversion to the Grim Reaper and we had no bodies, corpses or remains anywhere and they were officially interdicted by the paper's style book. You had to look sharply to know if the character you were reading about was among the quick or had cooled.

We had a splendid obituary page in those days with full dress jobs of sending off the deceased of social and financial standing and the chances were that if you read about somebody within this hallowed editorial ground he was no longer lunching at the Bankers' Club.

Source and fountainhead of this inhibition was our owner, Mrs. Whitelaw Reid, who was getting along in years and, although bright as a button, was reluctant to have mortality discussed in her paper. We also had a style rule which ordained that people were not on board or aboard yachts or vessels or trains, but in board them. Lord knows where this one came from.

When, therefore, Mrs. Reid died in Paris the news accounts of her final homeward progress across the Atlantic said cheerfully: "Mrs. Whitelaw Reid is in board the *Mauretania.*" There was no hint anywhere that she wasn't dining at the captain's table.

Footnotes to the War on Poverty

Gold table service as the normal complement to Rolls-Royce motor cars in the garage and only male domestics in the front of the house emerged on the scene of American affluence in the mid-Nineteenth Century when full gold table service appeared in the New York entertainments of Mrs. William Backhouse Astor and the elder August Belmont, who was the American representative of the Rothschilds and was expected to live accordingly. He did, too, and one evening paid $60,000 for a pair of canvasback ducks for supper. This was the amount he had lost at baccarat in the gaming rooms of John Morrissey so that when, at the free buffet provided for the patrons of that august establishment, he wolfed a brace of under-done ducks, he was able to itemize their cost at $30,000 each. Just to show he could enter into the spirit of the thing on terms of approximate equality with the Rothschilds, Morrissey took Belmont's $60,-000 and with it made the down payment on a pair of $75,000 diamond and sapphire mounted opera glasses from Lemaire of Paris for Mrs. Morrissey with which she was able to stare haughtily at Mrs. Belmont at the Academy of Music.

It was an age that knew what money was for.

Antedating these auspicious doings, the wife of the Mayor of San Francisco, Mrs. William K. Garrison, as early as 1854 had been in the habit of entertaining with a solid gold tea and breakfast service made by Shreve from 500 ounces of prime gold at a cost of $10,000 which might well represent five times the sum in today's shinplaster currency.

By the end of the century the hostesses who didn't serve up to 100 guests off gold flat service wasn't in the elegance sweepstakes even as an also-ran. A nice heavily washed gold service (Mrs. Garrison's is the only solid metal service in the record, with one exception) stood a tycoon $1000 a place setting.

The only other solid gold service in the record was that of the greatest magnifico of the age, William C. Whitney who retained an underbutler whose sole duty was the care and maintenance of this fabled asset which had stood the owner a reputed $300,000 from Tiffany.

A contender in the elegance sweepstakes was Electra Waggoner of Texas who objected to her guests discharging firearms at table. Not that she minded their taking pot shots at the Titians and Rembrandts which lined the walls and were already gunshot beyond repair, but she hated to have the hot cartridges ejected to burn holes in her $50,000 dining room carpet. To solve the difficulty she had handily located at each place setting a tastefully woven solid gold basket at a cost of $1500 each.

In concluding this brief resume it may be worth reporting the exchange between Mrs. Jack Gardner of Fenway Court, Boston, and Chicago's legendary Mrs. Potter Palmer. On a tour of the Potter Palmer castle on the Chicago lakefront Mrs. Gardner was shown around by Honore Palmer acting for his mother. They viewed the throne from which Mrs. Palmer received at receptions, the picture gallery awash with Van Dycks and Vermeers and eventually came to the butler's pantry with its fabulous resources of crystal and china and its gold table service complete with place settings for fifty.

"And what do you do when you have company in for dinner?" asked Mrs. Gardner.

A Slur on American Manhood

About the only one of Dr. Genevieve Kupfer's findings on alcoholism which will raise any eyebrows, blood pressure or Martini glasses is the unequivocal definition by the lady doc of a heavy drinker as anyone who drinks three times a week and takes three or more belts of Old Reprehensible at a time. The inextinguishable mirth this lady-like appraisal would have aroused in the circles of my youth, a period when the American people, 160 million strong, stayed drunk as sailors for thirteen long years in the Second American Revolution called prohibition, would have been deafening.

I know, I know, the heroic exploits of other times grow in the telling and assume a dimension that tends to magnify the original fact. Sordid love scuffles in dreary roadhouses assume the perfumed overtones of the Lunts in "Reunion in Vienna."

Shore dinners at Connecticut beach resorts, with a gallon of warm gin under the table and a bathroom handy for the universal emesis that accompanied its consumption gleam through the mists of antiquity like Trimalchio's Feast. Or at least like supper with Henry VIII and Cardinal Wolsey having at whole roasted steers and tossing pheasant carcasses under the table while regiments of pages did a double scurry with sack and Rhenish to appease the royal thirst.

Still and all, Dr. Kupfer's three drinks at a time were widely consumed between breakfast and luncheon by undergraduates of my acquaintance at Cambridge and New Haven, and the universal highball was so deplored by the university authorities that the reading rooms at Baker Memorial Library at Harvard were equipped with abruptly sloping book-rests to discourage whisky as an accompaniment to economics.

Bradley Fisk and Bydie Kilgour, who lived in lordly affluence in Apthorp House, filled a three gallon water cooler with fresh gin every morning and kept open house so that friends on the way to Music 1 (The History of Roman Band Instruments) or noble Professor Kittredge's course in Shakespeare might arrive in a state elevated to that of the theme of their instruction.

The Beacon Street hostess or patroness of a debutante ball at the Somerset who estimated the capacity of her guests at three belts of the ardent or less than a bottle each of the product of the Champagne never entertained a second time.

But not even the magnifying glass of time can conceivably paint the lily of alcoholic heroism that found its finest hours in the Fakirs' Ball annually staged by Cynthia White or the Harvard-Yale boat races in June which could easily have been rowed in the spilled drinks which swirled ankle-deep on the ballroom floor at the Griswold Hotel in New London.

When, inevitably, at three in the morning, the police backed the wagon up to Webster Hall to remove Miss White's revelry, in toto, to jail, extra patrol wagons had to be borrowed from as far away as the Bronx. At New London, with the passage of years, the yacht basin in front of the Griswold became marked on navigational charts as of unsound anchorage because it was floored with a parquet of empty bottles.

These were the glory years of rebellious patriotism and American manhood when the three drinks of Dr. Kupfer's modest assessment were consumed by a large and devoted segment of the population as the merest eye-opener or phlegm-cutter in preparation for a hard day's work at the barricades, which were of solid polished mahogany. The happy insurrectionists were generaled by as splendid a staff as ever directed a war effort, all named Tony, Mike, Eddie and Lou and whose insignia of rank was a white apron and bar rag. The definition of hard drinking in those heroic times only included the patriot who, every day of his life, was carried from the field of battle, inanimate on a shutter before noon.

CHAPTER THREE
The National Scene

As a lifelong Republican, Mr. Beebe fought constantly against the attempts of the Federal government to squeeze all the juices out of life. He viewed with contempt the great fallout panic of the early sixties and was outraged by the population explosion, both in the United States and throughout the world, which seemed to threaten eventual standing room only even in his beloved West.

An Agnostic in the White House?

Everyone protests loudly that religion must not enter the presidential campaign; isn't it equally proper that all traces of religious belief as an influence in the conduct of the Nation's affairs be eliminated from the Presidency and the Federal Government after the election as well? The sanctimonious obeisance to religious philosophy as a part of public policy may, if followed much longer, flush us right down the drain of history.

So long as wars were conducted with black powder between states allegedly motivated by Christian considerations—everybody called on God to witness the righteousness of his border dispute in those days—a certain element of religion in affairs of state was at least tolerable. The missile age has pretty well outmoded the Christian ethic and the sooner the ritualistic observance of religious matters in government is eliminated the better will be our chances of survival in the face of an enemy uninhibited in his conduct by any but the most practical morality.

The Russian state forms its policies on a basis notoriously devoid of spiritual guidance from any Christian God, and the Russians seem to be doing all right. So far, in the war with the rest of the world, they have coppered most of the bets, and if the Western world continues to be incapacitated by a metaphysical confusion as to who attacks whom first, its chances of survival are dim indeed.

It's bad enough to have an aging pantaloon in presidential office who permits, and even encourages, religious belief to be involved in State utterances, but Mr. Eisenhower is a soldier first and politician second. He undoubtedly figures that no positive harm is involved in placating the churchly, and that military success has seldom been actively impeded by an oblique salutation in the direction of religion. Besides, Mr. Eisenhower is an old man and spiritual insurance is easy to sell him.

The point is that we are confronted with an enemy who thinks in terms of expediency and gives the back of his hand to heavenly intervention in human affairs, and who continues to succeed wildly on these terms. There is no longer room in the conduct of the affairs of the United States and the West generally for the luxury of spiritual reflection and a passive religion. The underdog submission of Christianity is at a demonstrable disadvantage when arrayed against the top-dog dynamic of aggressive Communism.

So why not give enlightened disbelief a whirl in Washington? Remove not only the sectarian aspects of religion but the whole elaborate mishmash of Christian revelation from the national lexicon. Our affairs, let's face it, aren't doing too well "under God" and it may be that we can work to better advantage under new management.

The Matter Nobody Wants to Mention

One doesn't, I think, have to be a student of economics or educated in the mystique of banking and money to get a profound sense of uneasiness about the state of American prosperity and its implications of fraudulence and insecurity. The signs are on every hand and too obvious not to be disturbing. Some are superficial, some are deep rooted and extremely menacing, but all of them add up to a suppressed suspicion, perhaps atavistic in the light of 1929, 1907 and 1893, that we may be headed for hell in the proverbial handcar.

The suspicion is getting around that the United States as a Nation is broke. High as a kite. Stony. Where the woodbine twineth.

The sudden disappearance of hard money in every form is a minor symptom of it. The Treasury Department can issue reassuring bulletins about the drain on coinage imposed by vending machinery and the like, but it won't wash. The sobering truth is that a ponderable part of the population has very little faith in the Federal Government's sorry certificates which are not even backed by silver any more. They've seen their purchasing power diminish in a decade from a sixty-cent dollar, which everyone was assured was necessary to pay for the 1941 war, to a four-bit dollar and now to a thirty-cent dollar with no end in sight.

They figure that a shoebox full of silver dollars and halves stashed away may help out for a few days or hours when the shinplasters become totally worthless.

The basic defect behind the whole fraudulent façade of American economics is, of course, that there is no sound medium of currency against which to equate other values. When Roosevelt II repudiated the national currency and the country went off the gold standard it also repudiated the only known permanent, immutable and universally recognized medium of exchange and standard of values that human contriving has yet come up with. The theory that a Nation's wealth and backlog of potential are in its resources and consumer economy is dandy, but if there is no standard of values by which to measure them they simply don't exist. It's a metaphysical concept much like the noise made by the falling tree in a forest if there's nobody there to hear it. Where there is no standard for its measurement, wealth becomes merely an abstraction unless, of course, you translate it into Jack Daniel's and canned goods which isn't practical on a universal scale.

The Civic Horror Story of Our Time

I would like to make it mandatory that every San Francisco resident, taxpayer, commuter and property owner spend a week of every year confined within the boundaries of Manhattan Island. I would like to see every real estate dealer, engineer and banker involved in the financing of real estate and construction sentenced to spend a full month on Manhattan Island and this

74

goes for every member of the municipal government in the most remote manner concerned with the city's future.

If these sentences were faithfully imposed and if the persons concerned survived the filth, squalor, oppression, nervous frustration and strangling atmosphere of New York city, the future of San Francisco as a place to live and do business would be assured.

Today New York is a charnel house in arrested motion, a necropolis of the living dead. Life for its inhabitants is a continuing battle against obstructions, inconveniences, frustrations and hazards, all of them devised in the name of progress and in fact motivated by avarice, which make the picture of life in any American city of a century or so ago, for all its filth, disease, crime and crowding, one of lyric satisfactions. Every known agency for human comfort, safety, pleasure and professional justification is concentrated there, but to avail oneself of them is as difficult and often impossible as it would be for a dweller on the Montana prairies with the nearest neighbor a hundred miles distant.

A community where movement is impossible and where breathing is largely strangulation isn't a city, it's a corpse. New York has already become a place where the simple getting from here to there and the transport of merchandise through the streets is a virtual impossibility. It is perhaps the only one of the world's great cities where, in a mechanized and industrial century, the best way of getting anywhere is by walking and the distances are prohibitive. Its taxi meter rates are among the lowest in the United States but, ironically, taxi riding is one of its more expensive occupations because of the abominations of its traffic.

Its disease is a simple one: too many people, too many office buildings, too much business. Where more space, more traffic routes, more parks and more air was needed, the community sat passively by while monstrosities of new office buildings, some of them adding 25,000 workers to a single city block, were built, not singly but by the score. To add to the congestion which confronts out of town commuters at the vital bottlenecks of their daily arrival and departure, it has torn down the Pennsylvania Station and has built an additional entire city on top of Grand Central.

Where once sheer inconvenience and frustration made life a chore, civic elephantiasis has now made it impossible.

New York, doomed and in its final illness, can and should be a horrible example to California businessmen and politicians like the superfluous Governor Brown whose precise measure of statesmanship is that he glories in having the largest population.

Taking satisfaction in mere magnitude of population is like pointing with pride to terminal cancer. The end result will be the same for a city or a person.

The Poor People's Millionaire

Richard Nixon made a prolonged, and to some of us at least an incredibly primitive, pitch for the underdog vote, and the electorate gave him the brusheroo, but fast. They wanted nothing of his father's hamburgers and mother's home-made pies. Instead the voters scurried down the street to patronize the plutocratic Mr. Kennedy who makes no attempt to conceal the fact that he knows how to open a double bottle of champagne and never made any apology at all for being a rich man's son.

There have been well born and well-to-do men in the White House before now: Chester Arthur and the two Roosevelts come to mind. But never before has a bundle in the dimensions of several hundred million dollars been delivered at the White House service door, and this in the name of the common man, the shirtless, the sockless, the shiftless and worthless, the confirmed constituents of the Democratic party.

Although the tradition of austere and simple beginnings, preferably in a log cabin on the Kentucky or Illinois frontier, looms large in the American legend and the image of plain antecedents is still evoked, *vide* Mr. Nixon, by aspirants for office, it long ago became an institution more honored in the breach than the observance. In the Nineteenth Century and well into the Twentieth, the United States Senate was famous as the most exclusive rich men's club in the world.

But Mr. Kennedy, who may conservatively be described as a rich millionaire, is something altogether new in the role of President of the United States. He is, by no further remove than that separating him from an elderly parent, the peer of Fords, Rockefellers and some of the more obnoxious Texans. He is immeasurably more solvent than the Vanderbilts, Fricks, Belmonts, Whitneys, Stotesburys and Morgans who only a few years back passed as people who didn't have to consult the right hand column of the menu.

The emergence, unabashed and without apology, into the political arena of a several times over multimillionaire, by whatever narrow margin, must give some long thoughts to old line politicians still thinking in terms of rail splitters, Sockless Jerry Simpson and the professional poor man's friends who could once have been counted on to put the boots to any silk stocking candidate the opposition might nominate.

Among these, too, must be the Republican leaders who steered clear of Nelson Rockefeller as an opponent to Mr. Kennedy on the grounds that he was a man of towering wealth and that Mr. Kennedy's millions would make him a pushover for the poor-mouth pitch of the Vice President. It might well have been that Mr. Rockefeller's millions would have been the only weapon in the Republican political armory capable of overwhelming the Kennedy assets. It's a safe bet that it will be a long time before any political convention of either party in future discards a potential candidate for high office simply on the grounds that he knows how to use the subjunctive and doesn't look uneasy in dinner clothes.

The Great 'Export Democracy' Bust

The persistent notion that great numbers of people in other parts of the world pant to live by the same social and political standards as do citizens of the United States or, if they don't want to, ought to, is a national delusion that dies hard.

The source of our national grief, and one that grows in intensity as the melancholy record unfolds, is that despite our tireless plugging of the commodity for now nigh unto two centuries, there are very few buyers for the peculiar institution of political democracy. Here and there a few reluctant folk are conned into making a down payment on what they patently regard as a dubious bill of goods to begin with, but few of them come through after the down payment and almost none consummate the full purchase.

American partisans of democracy could, if they would, learn a lesson from the fate of American religious missionaries who made a dreadful nuisance of themselves in Asia and Africa in the Nineteenth Century when they undertook to spread the Christian gospel accompanied by the moral prejudices of Circleville, Ohio, to large numbers of contented people already far gone in the practical satisfactions of pagan sin. The plumper and younger missionaries ended as the chef's blue plate suggestion, which served them right.

American exports of a more tangible nature in the last few decades have proven enormously more acceptable than the Christian ethic or a republican political philosophy. Heaven knows, most of them have been an affront to civilization: high rise hotels, cola drinks, television and radio sets and their accompanying mental climate, sports attire, le jazz hot, ball point styluses and can-of-worms traffic intersections. Most of them are abominations and their advent as explicit a manifestation of the advent of barbarism as the advance scouts of Attila the Hun.

But, unlike our holier endeavors and more sanctimonious articles of faith for export, they don't arouse hostility and execration on a universal scale. It may yet be that Conrad Hilton is a better salesman for the American way than Woodrow Wilson. It's a sobering thought.

Calamity Howlers and the U.S. Image

If there's any assertion that leaves me cold in the current contest on the part of politicians, newspaper editorialists and self-appointed critics of or experts on the world scene to out-scream each other it's the statement baldly made with no supporting evidence that the United States in pursuing this or that policy of conduct "has set relations back thirty years." Or that the American "image has suffered" or that "American prestige is on the wane." There is no page in the morning editions that doesn't carry, for what shock effect this most idiot of all editorial devisings may be worth, the intelligence from some far part of the globe that "American influence has suffered a severe setback."

There is a starry-eyed school of ineffectuals and idealists who have an idea that the conduct of international affairs is a sort of popularity contest and who are grieved when an American diplomatist gets poked in the nose in the streets of a South American slumbucket seaport or the Marines are hissed in Tokyo. We've had national experience of being popular. We were deliriously beloved almost everywhere immediately after the conclusion of the 1914 war and again in the closing years of Roosevelt II. On both occasions the United States was taken to the cleaners, its collective pockets picked by the hard-boiled realists we counted our friends and our hat thrown into the street after us.

Now, the better educated element of Yankees are beginning to know it's a sign of maturity and importance to be hated. We've tried the popularity dodge and been rooked, swindled and looted by contemptuous nations and people not worth a spit in the eye. Ill will, distrust, hatred and envy are the natural consequences of wealth and power and the fundamental basis of all international relations and always have been. There is neither altruism nor very much honor between nations and the best that can be hoped for is a reciprocal appreciation, such as that which for the moment seems to exist between the United States and Russia, of everybody's potential for causing damage to everybody else.

Your Uncle Sam walks too tall nowadays to be available to the spitballs of envy.

'Conquest of Space' Is for the Birds

The plea in extenuation of bankrupting the American people is that the "conquest of space," as it is grandly called, represents the highest aspirations of mankind, and that the emplacement of an American flag on a fairly remote planet will constitute a transcendent and ineffable triumph of American genius, even if somebody else has already done it first.

Permit me, in the most genteel manner, to dissent and remark that the whole idiot business represents the terminal stages of paretic insanity and that the thrice-damned politicians who advocate its financing out of the common pocket should be placed under observation and restraint. Impeachment proceedings were once inaugurated against a President of the United States on provocation that seems microscopic in comparison and political thieves and burglars have spent collectively centuries in the jailhouse for looting the public funds of a microscopic fraction of the sum suggested.

The gigantic folly of getting to the moon is going to cost the American taxpayer, already a participant in a catastrophic national bankruptcy, something like an estimated hundred billion dollars and, knowing his Washington as a citadel of total bureaucratic mendacity, he can double or treble this economic calamity with little fear of disapproval.

This fantastic outrage is encouraged by Democratic politicians who regard money as something too frivolous to consider and by a gaggle of high-ranking military officials on the payroll of the rocket industry who give newspaper readers the grue with the chilling intelligence that whoever gets to the moon first will control the world. This is at best a military hypothesis, which is to say water from a contaminated spring, because except in times of actual conflict, the American people have learned to have a very low opinion of the military mind, an intelligence that is prone to panic, especially after a well-upholstered luncheon at the Carlton Hotel with an I.B.M. executive or representative of Boeing.

We are doomed from whomever you hear it: overwhelmed by Russian submarines if you give ear to an admiral, finished by Russian land superiority if you are belting squareface with a general and kaput at the hands of Russian spacemen if you give credence to the fly boys or have your lapels clutched by a vice president of United Aircraft.

But if the precise source of our national extinction varies with each military Cassandra, they all have this in common: they have a calculating and ruthlessly greedy fist in your pocket.

The hypothesis has been evolved in recent years that entire nations can become exposed to actual clinical insanity, a theory most frequently advanced to explain the conduct of Nazi Germany. If, however, you are looking around for symptoms of certifiable mental aberration you need go no farther than the universal American syndrome of space panic and idiot one-upmanship with Russia.

No republic military authority has invoked evidence that achievement of a foothold on the moon will lead to instant and irresistible dominance of terrestrial affairs. The notion is advanced on the sole say-so of a few profiteering peddlers of cosmic mendacity.

Getting a man on the moon hasn't the factual significance of a baseball statistic or the intrinsic value of the price of a Coke. Let the Russians have it and leave you and me our hundred billion dollars. We can spend it as well as the Pentagon and, what's more, it's ours to begin with.

The Moon Solution

Mostly, of course, astronauts and their dreary wives are regarded as copyright property of *Life* magazine and the private preserve of Henry Luce whose special genius for picking winners and whose dedication to the national interest is implicit in his early backing of Fidel Castro's revolution in Cuba. Castro for a time was a Luce exclusive and the champ in the *Life* stables, where he received such radiant publicity that he was eventually able to make Cuba an outpost of the Communist Russian empire.

More recently, as the glamor wore off Castro, he has been replaced in editorial favor in court circles of *Life-Time* with the asinine astronauts who are fully as tiresome as Castro was to *Life* readers but as of now don't seem as potentially dangerous.

Unhappily, the moon folly can't remain a copyrighted property of *Life* and an exclusive with *Time,* in which case it would be possible to ignore it by shifting one's readership to *Look* and *Newsweek.* The stuff will spill over and even your daily newspaper will be fouled up with its tasteless tedium.

The obvious solution of a whole flock of problems would be to allow Russia to be first and uncontested to the moon. It would save the American taxpayer untold sums of money and it would provide absolute assurance that the Russian people would be submerged, perhaps for all time, in the orgiastic flood tide of self-adulation that their government would unleash.

Meeting Eternity in a Handsome Hearse

However vexatious the times may be for the overwhelming majority of people who have an uncommonly high regard for their lives and have been unwilling to take any least precautions for insuring their continuance, what we are assured on every hand may be the world's last hours are a rich time of harvest and reward for those connoisseurs of human folly who have taken a dim view of what passes for "progress" and have cried in the wilderness that, although he has achieved piffling advances in science, man's intellectual awareness has to date unfitted him for possession of tools more sophisticated than the wheelbarrow.

There seems to be a strong likelihood that man is now about to flush himself down the drain of cosmic time without, in his brief and idiot occupancy of a minor planet, having proved anything or validated his existence.

If it is indeed on the verge of its own taking off on a universal scale and regretful of this circumstance, as it seems to be, the world may in its last moments ponder how it got itself into this fix.

Everyone to his own taste, and the post mortem diagnoses of our own ills will be many and ingenious, but it is the personal conviction of this department that it was the sentimental debauching of the American people who, for a time, held destiny in their hands that did the trick.

The softheads, the humanitarians, the underdog lovers, the pacifists, mush-heads, do-gooders and tolerance advocates, the bleeding hearts from Bangor to San Diego have brought the world to a condition where its total destruction seems necessary to prevent its piecemeal surrender to total beastliness.

Americans have been told by the spiritual beatniks to whom

they have given respectful audience that they should be loved instead of feared, should seek flattery and approval instead of the respect and terror that alone in a murderous world might have assured us of survival.

Faced with the unequivocal facts of life and death in a competitive jungle where fang and claw are the only instruments of self-preservation and the maintenance of order, Americans have prayed earnestly for deliverance in the temples of their several superstitions and turned to baseball as the solution of all ills.

Neither God nor Candlestick Park seems to have been quite the ticket. The folklore of mendacity is replete with the legend of the true believer whose Bible, carried next to his heart, turned the assassin's bullet, but as an expedient of practicality this has never been widely recommended. Prudent men cut their enemies' throats first and did their devotional reading later.

In the end it has been the sentimentalization of the American character that has proved fatal, the childish desire for approval where only terror and respect could be effective. The masters of Imperial Rome who ran the most glittering and successful road show on record and got the most mileage out of it, would have laughed themselves sick if they had been confronted with the concept of "world opinion."

It may be symptomatic of the sick national mentality that, during the most urgent of all recent crises, it has been virtually impossible to obtain the slightest clue to what was happening in the world on mankind's most irresponsibly conducted toy, the radio, without listening in a proportion of fifty to one to emetic singing commercials advocating, presumably as an overture to incineration, an assortment of artifacts such as lipsticks and other cosmetic filth, hairnets and fancy limousines.

The corpse of the nation, with the right shade of face paint and every hair in place, was going to meet eternity in the most expensive make of hearse.

The Myth of 'World Opinion'

Prominent in the Farrago of completely meaningless ideological jargon to which Americans are these days subjected by pollsters, politicans and other merchants of mendacity is the myth of "world opinion," a body of sentiment of which the Caspar Milquetoasts of the United States are instructed to stand in humble awe while the rest of the world gets a horse laugh at our timorous veneration of something that doesn't exist, and if it did would be of no least material consequence.

Pious frauds in public office, scoundrels in Washington and editorial charlatans with a hanker for "significant" thinking pontificate about "world opinion" as though its existence were a demonstrable fact, although the only place it can ever be pinpointed is in news releases by the State Department in this country and Tass in Russia, where "world opinion" curiously enough follows the party line of the moment with amazing exactitude.

"World opinion" is invoked by the Administration every time it wants to rook the taxpayers out of a few billions in some particularly fantastic swindle or as a lever for conning the dolts into going along with underwriting all the current expenses of some tankstop nation whose destinies mean nothing to the United States nor anybody else.

"World opinion" is invoked by political poltroons and hedgers in this country whenever it is suggested that the United States should actively and effectively resent insult and affront to its sovereignty and dignity abroad or protect its investments from confiscation by the revolutionary practice of thuggee in adjacent banana republics.

"World opinion" is the bogey constantly raised to intimidate the United States and prevent it from conduct becoming an independent, powerful and resolute nation with rights and privileges of its own in a world that has largely succumbed to total barbarism.

It doesn't stop anybody else, anywhere, at any time from doing precisely whatever opportunism and self-service may suggest. The Russians have ignored "world opinion." So have the warlords of India when they wanted Goa.

Even among our own friends and presumed allies, the British, the French, Belgians and other civilized nations of Europe, "world opinion" carries little or no weight when policies concerning the national welfare or security are involved. Informed and realistic people everywhere know that "world opinion" is for the birds, the bird in this case being the bedraggled American eagle.

In this pass, and since you know and I know that "world opinion" comes as close to being utterly meaningless and ineffectual as words can approximate, it would be a good thing if it were eliminated from the thinking of the Administration at Washington and from the vocabulary of propaganda everywhere. The emperor's clothes in the medieval fairy story were never more visible. Nor more nonextant.

The Economy of Abundant Trash

Recently they had a learned convocation of doubledomes in Washington in the name of the Center for the Study of Democratic Institutions, an organization whose very style and title might awaken doubts about its validity of purpose. But no matter; the midnight seminars of the savants came up with the thesis—hold onto your hats—that the United States was the first "overdeveloped" nation in history, in a word that Americans had too much of everything: too much food, too much amusement, too much comfort, too much leisure, too many conveniences. "After 1946," deposed Supreme Court Justice William O.

Douglas, "Americans became people living in big white houses on the hill, largely unconcerned with the slums around us."

What the sentiments of the pundits added up to was nothing more or less than an apology for American success, and the whisking sound that is distinctly audible from the cemeteries of the land is made by ten generations of hard-working, ambitious and largely intelligent Americans who made this success possible only to find it rejected and repudiated by its ultimate beneficiaries.

The complaint about American materialism has been a perpetual gripe of do-gooders within and have-nots without as long as the memory of man runneth. It began with the earliest visitors and commentators from abroad who complained bitterly that Americans actually preferred to keep warm in wintertime to dying of cold and the diseases it induced in England and Europe. Dickens concealed the envy that consumed him at sight of American abundance by commenting adversely on American personal habits like tobacco chewing. As recently as the Thirties, Adolf Hitler proclaimed that American decadence derived from eating too much grapefruit, and on his American visit Mr. Khrushchev was pained to find the highways filled with enormous motor cars with, in many cases, but a single occupant. It's just possible that Mr. K. has something there but his comment was based on envious hatred and not any regard for the traffic problem.

Just what is wrong with the house on the hill, Mr. Douglas?

The answer is that there are a great many things wrong with the American house on the hill. Its structure is defective from its cheap wooden sheathing to its roof of tired blotting paper; its plumbing is characterized by calculated obsolescence, and electrical installations are warranted not to run from the day they are put in by union contract labor. Poor foundations or none cause its walls to sag and its sleazy plasterboard to crack, its hardware fittings are pinchbeck and its timbers are unseasoned. It is a fraud and a cheat that is guaranteed to disintegrate well in advance of the date of the last installment to the finance company and it isn't a house on the hill, but a miserable defective shack set down right next to a whole lot more all occupied by verminous neighbors with mannerless issue and the radios going full blast.

If this is the sort of material plenty and superabundance of luxury that awakens the furious envy of Russians and Congolese and Chinese by the million, they damned well should have their heads looked at.

More effective as a deterrent to the war Communism so desperately wants might be some firsthand insight into some of the elements of the American way of life the have-not nations are supposedly so envious of. It is difficult to imagine the most debased peasant living in the most impoverished province of the Chinese hinterland putting up for an instant with the devitalized bread without a trace of nutriment that is commonly accepted by Americans from Bangor to San Diego without complaint. The average electrical installation, washing machine, television set, coffee percolator or vacuum cleaner that is fobbed off on American housewives by the million would be rejected with gestures by the most benighted resident of the Congo. No serf in the lowest echelon of Soviet slavery would be gulled into investing in the trashy appliances that come as costly extras on American motor cars. Any reasonably intelligent resident of Zanzibar would flee from the wasteland of the mind that is indicated by ten seconds' communion with any radio program in the land.

The question may reasonably be asked if the Big Lie isn't the illusion that America is a land of unbounded material opulence rather than a kitchen midden of continental dimensions of complete trash. It isn't worth the war the Chinese and the Russians contemplate in order to steal it, and most of it would disintegrate before they could carry it off. An intelligent appraisal of the American economy would suggest that its components wouldn't be had by any other people as a gift.

Suttee for Vice Presidents

The end result that it didn't take either a Merlin or J. P. Morgan to foresee, namely, that the Asiatic adventure to which the Johnson government has committed the nation was an unmitigated blunder is presently being unfolded.

The whole sorry Vietnam excursion was a major error, not of course from the political and idiot humanitarian viewpoints that dominate the thinking of the bleeding hearts and the beard and sandal set, but from reasons of plain economics. It was and increasingly is a war the United States cannot afford. The potential profit was less than nothing, the advantage ephemeral or altogether chimerical and the cost, to a nation already tottering on the verge of bankruptcy, astronomical.

Notwithstanding the daily reassurances from interested parties to the contrary, your Uncle Sam is up the spout, stone broke and financially in the hands of the Morris Plan. I know, I know there are more motor cars per capita than anywhere else on earth and personal income is at all-time highs. The motor cars are largely defective, most of them aren't paid for, and the personal income is in depreciated paper or shinplasters whose value has been on a steady toboggan since Roosevelt II assured universal bankruptcy by repudiating the national currency.

And yet with a confrontation with the taxpayers (who in the end pay for all military adventures whether justified or as spectacularly reckless as the current one) in the immediate offing, the Johnson administration, which means President Johnson since there is no opposition, still wants to play politics as usual and evade the perfectly obvious fact of life that it can't have its cake and eat it too. It can't have both the war that is its own unappreciated dream child and the Great Society.

President Johnson has got himself out not merely on a limb with his Asiatic adventure, but on the horns of an ugly dilemma of economics which, as is usual in a democracy, he will ask the American taxpayer to resolve for him. He will demand in the name of a variety of holy pretexts that his military imbroglio in Vietnam be financed in its every aspect of waste and costliness and at the same time that the already gasping economy maintain him and Sargent Shriver and all the rest of a mendicant administration in the fullest flower of profligate spending for their own political advantage.

If there is any lesson to be learned from this unsavory imposture it may well be that when an American President dies or is assassinated in office, his Vice President without any evasion and in the national interest should be required to commit suttee.

Let's Have a Rum-Soaked Ballot

One of the most preposterous impositions that has come to be established by entrenched and vindictive bigotry at the expense of milquetoast American taxpayers and voters is the pestilential practice of making it impossible to get a drink in public on election day. Through the agency of this vicious harassment, and since it includes primaries and by-elections, a couple of days out of every year in most States are irrevocably chalked up as triumphs for meddlesome bureaucrats and the insensate snouters of prohibition.

The basic fear behind this pigsty assertion of bigotry is, according to its apologists, that the unwary voter treading a sober and reflective measure toward the polling place might be accosted by solicitous villainy bent on defiling the purity of his

90

franchise and swerving him from emplacing the mark of his choice on the ballot.

In other words, his vote might be purchased for a noggin of squareface.

If votes can be bought for liquor and a price in proof bourbon be set on the ballot, then the ballot is being elevated beyond any status it now owns.

No other limit or hindrance is placed on the influencing and outright purchase of the voter's suffrage with promises of pie in the sky and limitless freedom to pillage his betters through the swindles of social legislation. Political campaigns in the United States are nothing but a universal scheme for the corruption of registered voters with promises which, happily, no politician has the slightest intention of fulfilling.

He can be promised the distribution of cash bonuses from the treasury for his vote, he can be promised the right to tax his neighbor into bankruptcy, to ruin the credit of the Nation, or he can be promised free false teeth and the universal medication of his ailments from paresis to hemorrhoids for his vote, but he may not be solicited with a Martini or shot of bourbon and branch.

Advocates of civic responsibility are loud in powerful exhortations to get out the vote but take no note of the melancholy fact that no man's judgment is as keen or his purpose as pure as when he has taken a belt or two at the nearest bar before getting into a scuffle with the ballot.

This is the heart of the matter. Nothing scares the living daylights out of a politician like the idea of an intelligent appraisal of his candidacy by the electorate. A realistic appraisal induced by alcohol might well reveal him for the fraud and potential thief he is. Hence no booze. Keep the voter sober and stupid at all costs.

As long as American elections were floated on the sea of

hard liquor our sanctimonious snouters now profess to find so shocking, fair winds filled the sails of the Ship of State and all prospects for the future were golden. At an all-time low in the ebb of our national destinies, when the future is no more than a day-to-day gamble, we might well revert to the conduct and institutions of our forefathers, at least for a day. There's nothing in the world to lose.

Kiss of Death for Goldwater

Senator Goldwater has been losing enemies. It is a tactical error which may yet be fatal.

As long as there were allied against him in a solid rank of implacable hostility the sentiments of Governor Rockefeller, Senator Javits, Henry Cabot Lodge, Walter Lippmann, the more irresponsible partisans of what pass for civil rights, Henry Luce, and the internationalist newspaper and magazine press and allied agencies of radio and television that constitutes communications in the United States, the chances of the Arizona Senator were effulgent.

With enemies such as these he couldn't lose. The wild carnival of denunciation, blackguarding and revulsion on the part of persons and agencies held in universal distrust and in some cases detestation by the American people assured his nomination, and if maintained at the pitch of sneering virulence achieved by Washington columnists and radio grunters at the time of the convention had him with one foot already through the door of the White House.

Now there is betrayal on every hand. There has been a decline in the incalculably precious hostility of Walter Lippmann, a once not inconsiderable pundit and political commentator but now no more than the hollow voice of fatigued senescence echoing from the anterooms of eternity. The very tangible asset of Mr. Lippmann's disfavor has somehow been abated to a point where he can mention the Senator's name without the symptoms of towering blood pressure that once brought white-coated attendants running with restoratives against apoplexy.

It is reliably reported, too, that Mr. Goldwater has become discernibly more acceptable among the carpetbaggers of the United Nations. The treacherous rogues in this threadbare road company of the League of Nations have been heard to speak, if not in positively glowing tones, at least in terms of moderated approval of the Senator, a shabby device of the most infamous contriving to discredit him with the electorate.

What must give the Senator's partisans sleepless nights is the possible weakening of the opposition of the foreign-dominated internationalist press of the American East where the opinions of the infected communications structure are the opinions of Moscow, Paris, East Berlin and Warsaw printed under Washington datelines.

Any tolerance for Mr. Goldwater among the kingmakers and in the internationalist press could be the kiss of death. It would be the foulest tactic of betrayal in the long and maculate record of American political treachery.

A Nation Takes Leave of Its Senses

Up until the immediate here and now, the reconstruction years immediately following the Civil War have been the favorite target for national apologists for the American record.

Next to the Reconstruction, however, it is a safe bet that in years to come at greater or less remove, history will point most urgently in embarrassment to the age we are now living in and which may well come to be known as the Years of the Great Fallout Panic.

Posterity will either be convulsed or revolted, according to its lights, by an era in which a great and powerful Nation, and one in the ordinary course of things presumed to be in possession of at least some of its marbles, ran hog wild in self-induced dementia of terror and indulged a panic of obscene dimensions at the behest of cultists and crackpots ranging from Henry Luce and Governor Rockefeller at the top to the self-appointed Minutemen at the thin fringe of sanity.

There never was a clown act the cast of which included such a miscellaneous gaggle of exhibitionists, including statesmen, ward politicians, clergymen of every known denomination and some that crawled out of the woodwork for the occasion, "scientists" who contrived, against all odds of probability, to bring a new dimension of contempt to the word, evangelists, soul-savers, emotional thimbleriggers, knaves, opportunists, irresponsible journalists and salesmen for the most demonstrable sort of trash.

The clergy have horned into the act with holy attitudes and pronouncements of sanctimony to the effect that (a) a true Christian will relinquish to interlopers his space in a fallout shelter of dubious efficacy, and (b) a devout Christian is entitled to shoot anybody who attempts to invade his property. You have mayors of uncontaminated communities who will shoot refugees like dogs and civic supervisors who will welcome them with the municipal band. You have advocates of taking to the hills and advocates of taking to piano crates in the back yard, and there are even so-called radiation suits to don at the approach of doom, much as garlic used to be rubbed about the lintels of the huts of Transylvanian peasants to keep off Count Dracula.

All this whoobab and ruckus, all this screaming for political advantage and commercial profit, all this terror for the justification of the great civil defense fraud, and all this bird fluttering among men of holy orders, in a word, all this evocation of silliness on a positively cosmic scale has as its excuse and warrant an unconfirmed and nebulous potential of peril, a form of contamination that has never been assayed or defined, that many

well-informed people believe to be microscopic and that, in the
end, may not exist at all.

When it's all over and discarded, fallout shelters and anti-
radiation suits litter the desert like empty beer cans, there will
be a time for embarrassed self-appraisal. In the meantime, we
may contemplate with unbelieving revulsion the "peace marchers" converging on City Hall to demand that the municipal
furnace man outlaw atomic fission and make the Communists
behave.

The Threat of the Democrats

There are those who are prone to protest the allegation that
the Democratic party is the party of treason. To evade what
might be construed as a libel on a fairly large group of Americans, let us only say it is a party whose principles would have
appealed strongly to Benedict Arnold. But nobody has ever with
a straight face denied that the Democratic party is a party of
total and overwhelming incompetence economically speaking.

In times of meat and plenty it may be that the national
economy is sufficiently vital to withstand the impact of the
meddlesome quackeries, always compounded by outright pillage
and larceny, which are the inevitable consequences of Democrats in high office.

In times as parlous as those in which we live, when only a
national prosperity sustained at the optimum level can stave off
military disaster, reason totters to think of the debacle that will
ensue if a new nest of Democratic spoilers get their hooks in the
treasury.

The Mandate to Steal

One aspect of the prospect of four more years of Texas in the
White House, if the President's infatuation with mob adulation

doesn't bring him to an abrupt end before that time, is that it will be a happy time for newspapermen.

With Texas in the saddle and in possession of what it will regard as a mandate from the enlightened electorate to continue acting in the Texas manner of grand larceny with breakfast and total embezzlement by noon, it is easy to foresee lively times for the newsmen on the Washington beat. The breath of scandal, it may by confidently expected, will now become a typhoon and the debris swept under the carpet will make the Blue Room floor look like a profile of the Sierra.

The mandate to steal everything in sight has always been implicit in the election of a Democratic administration. That the shortcomings of the Grant and Harding administrations have entered the folklore of the Nation is attributable to the better advertising given the larceny involved by the out-of-office Democrats of the time. The fury of a hungry out-of-office Democrat is that of a woman scorned and his sanctimonious indignation when he discovers somebody else but a Democrat with his hand in the till is fearful to contemplate. When Democrats are detected leaving the dinner table with their pockets full of flat silver it is no more than standard procedure and Republican virtue can't make such a good thing of it.

President Johnson has served explicit notice on the voters, who immediately reseated him in office on the strength of it, that graft and corruption in the highest places enjoy his benevolent regard and that the good offices of the Presidency can be expected in the event of anyone missing their footing on the window ledge while doing a little second story work. These good offices were indeed extended to cover up Bobby Baker who wasn't even a Texan and the country got a fair taste of what can be looked for in the way of extenuation in the matter of Billy Sol Estes who was in fact a Texan and therefore entitled to the fullest possible protective treatment. In covering up these two lapses from the strictest imaginable probity, the President

was just giving a sample of his virtuosity in absolving loyal re-
tainers of blame when taken in economic adultery.

Becomingly he was more embarrassed by *l'affaire* Jenkins
which didn't come within the purview of Presidential tolerance
if only because it didn't involve the economic factor. If the unfortunate Jenkins had only been detected wheeling assets out of
the Treasury in a midnight barrow he would by now have
been accorded a cabinet post.

All of which adds up to a promise of times of teem for
newspapers, the people who get them out and the ultimate consumer who reads them. Stand by for gee whiz accounts under a
Washington dateline of the latest burglary committed by masked
miscreants in hand-stitched boots and Fort Worth accents who
were apprehended loading the Lincoln Memorial into a truck.

Barnyard to Graveyard In One Package

The witless barnyard hanker of the human animal for the
propagation of his own unspeakable species has at last reached
a point where the capacity for the wholesale elimination of life,
now reposing in the arsenals of the world and daily increasing,
is no more than an instrument of what may well turn out to be
a scheme of cosmic order and propriety. If he is going to sur-
vive at all, mankind is going to have to revise his appraisal of the
agencies he has hitherto esteemed benevolent, miracle-drugs for
the preservation and extension of life, human essays in relieving
the lot of backward people who might otherwise accomplish
their own infinitely desirable extinction, and all the massed incentives of state, religion and commercial greed for augmenting
the dreary human parade between the incubator and the incinerator.

It may well be that in the short space of tomorrow Strontium
90 will assume, in philosophical pharmacology at least, the
position now occupied by penicillin or the sulfa drugs, and

where, by a paradox of Gilbert and Sullivan dimensions, the elimination of life is more benevolent than its creation or preservation.

There is nothing cynical in the concept, however unsavory and uncomfortable that factual process may turn out to be. If the human succession is going to continue, and what may be more important in an only imperfectly understood cosmic order, if animal life of any sort is to continue, it's going to be on a diminished scale from what is now practiced without limit or license. It may very well be that *homo* allegedly *sapiens,* having reached the limit of his possibilities, will go the way of other primeval mammals to become part of the fossil deposits of eternity. He hasn't shown much justification for being around, to date anyway, and if mankind cannot resist his own fatal preoccupation with procreation, there is an agency of sanitary purpose at hand to achieve this end. Ironically he will resort to the supreme end product of his disorderly genius to accomplish his own, perhaps overdue, taking-off.

Yet, in the face of this infinite calamity, do you see any marchers for enforced birth control over everybody, everywhere, or any banners with the altogether sensible and sanitary slogan "Ban Babies?" You do in a pig's valise because if such sentiments should be aired with any degree of militancy their sponsors would be had at by church and state with sanctimonious screams that they were advocating violence against the laws of nature and the intent of heaven, it being the manifest intent of heaven and decree of nature that mankind must presently commit suicide by smothering itself.

It makes no difference that the idea of birth control is vaguely seeping into the intelligences of Europeans and North Americans; it has never been heard of, and if heard of violently rejected, in the maggot breeding bins of Asia and Africa where it is most needed.

A really successful famine in China opens illimitable vistas

of potentiality for the eventual betterment of a miserable country whose announced determination is the conquest of the rest
of the world through the agency of unlimited warfare just as
soon as it can get itself organized to this end. Certainly the
Russians who, in some respects, seem to be becoming more
reasonable, won't be persuaded to regard a bang-up famine in
China as anything even resembling a calamity.

A massive famine in India is a more melancholy prospect but
there is completely nothing that more enlightened nations can
do about it so long as the Indians themselves reject any measures which might improve their agricultural economy and continue to breed like the Connecticut river shad. Diversion of the
world's foodstuffs on a purely charity basis, since India can't
pay for them, will be nothing better than a stopgap measure
and encourage the uneducated elements of its population in the
belief that they can go on creating people on a limitless scale
without any form of retribution. The same is true for Latin
America where food production remains static while irresponsible peoples continue to show their unfitness for enjoying life by
creating more of it on a disastrous scale.

The choice is between taking steps to abate the universal
habits of the barnyard, or at least of inhibiting their tangible
consequences, or taking the high road to the universal graveyard. There's no need of the bomb in a world where the pro-
creative couch will accomplish the identical end and in an even
more untidy manner.

CHAPTER FOUR

The Press—Today and Yesterday

After 40 years in journalism, Mr. Beebe thought he knew a thing or two about the press. He loved reminiscing about his raffish journalistic past and he loved cudgeling the cowardly publishers of modern times for their failings.

The Peepul's Friends

The great era of crusading newspaper publishers in the United States, which saw the rise of Joseph Pulitzer, William Randolph Hearst and James Gordon Bennett the Younger, was perhaps also the greatest age of complete hypocrisy on the part of newspaper owners themselves.

Noisy champions of the underdog and vociferous assailants of the well-to-do, these three powerful publishers, Hearst and Pulitzer to a somewhat greater degree than Bennett, were conspicuously bogus in their frenzied espousal of causes to promote what they claimed was social and economic justice. Their piteous bleats for the common man were, for the most part, a fakement of pure rabble-rousing behind which both Hearst and Pulitzer amassed enormous fortunes and practiced all the luxury and extravagance which they condemned in their papers as the vices of the exploiting classes.

Old man Pulitzer, in his palmiest days, when he and Hearst were competing for circulation in the New York that termed their practices "yellow journalism," ran a paper that was practically indistinguishable from *Pravda*. One of his favorite devices was to ascertain the basic cost of some private social bash of the time, such as the celebrated Bradley Martin ball, and break down the total in terms of baby's boots, working men's rent and the annual food bills of needy families.

And where was the owner of the *World* while its columns were roaring in holy anguish over the deprivations of the underprivileged? He was in one of his several palatial homes staffed with English butlers and knee-breeched housefootmen in New York, Bar Harbor or Paris, or aboard the equally well upholstered *Liberty,* one of the largest and most magnificent ocean-going steam yachts then in service.

Butterfield's Bar Harbor Society Grocery (a lovely name)

still, according to Cleveland Amory, recalls filling a single order for foie gras and pheasant for the commissary of *Liberty* which came to $5600.

It was while roughing it in such circumstances of hardship that Old Joe would wire his editors to investigate the life history of each Morgan partner in the hope of finding some remote clue in the distant past to an indiscretion that might tend to discredit the greatest banking house of them all.

James Gordon Bennett the Younger was somewhat less of a phony. Exiled from the United States, at least socially, for a breach of decorum for which his peers could not forgive him, Bennett castigated Saratoga as "a seraglio for the prurient aristocracy" that refused to receive him, but he contrived in Paris to spend a cool million a year on his whims and caprices, which in the hard currency of the nineties took some doing. By and large the moral and social crusaders in the record have had scant use for the classes whose way of life they championed.

The Press and the Code Duello

The last recorded duel fought under the formal terms of the code duello was, it is interesting to note, between a newspaperman and one of his social peers over an imagined slight. James Gordon Bennett (the Younger) and Fred May, the brother of his one-time fiancee, in 1877 at Slaughter's Gap, conveniently located on the Maryland-Delaware border, burned powder at each other, with both the participants chivalrously firing with deliberate intent to miss.

Bennett's second on this historic occasion was Charles Longfellow, son of the good gray poet of Cambridge, Mass. The basic occasion for the quarrel was an episode, now firmly established in American journalistic folklore, in the course of which Bennett, during a New Year's afternoon call on his fiancee's family, couldn't find the bathroom and used the drawing room fireplace instead.

New Year's calls were livelier in those times.

My own predecessor as publisher in Virginia City of *The Territorial Enterprise* in the sixties, Joseph Goodman, participated in a celebrated formal duel with Tom Fitch, editor of the rival *Virginia City Union,* in which Fitch was sorely wounded in the knee and limped ever afterward.

Further to the east a celebrated shooting involved John A. Cockerill, chief editorial writer of the respected *St. Louis Post-Dispatch,* and a fire-eating Colonel Alonzo Slayback, who took exception to the *Post-Dispatch* political sentiments and one fine morning called on the man of type cases with lethal intent. Before, however, the colonel could draw a pepperbox revolver from under the tails of his frock coat, Cockerill had found a Navy Colt under a pile of galley proofs and ventilated the colonel who was carried out in dying condition and leaking bourbon from every seam. Political differences between editors and their constituents at this time in Missouri produced so many duels that a contemporary historian wrote that "it was usually a question of whether a Missouri editor died of whiskey or gunpowder. Largely the gunpowder, being of better quality than the whiskey, was the more effective agent."

The Daily Press as Chicken Little

Only two important professions that I have been able to discover factually and explicitly are dominated by complete malevolence toward the people who keep them in business. One, obviously, is the calling of undertaking which bluntly hopes you may be dead so that they can get your custom; the other is the newspaper profession whose entire being and occupation is predicated on the worst possible news for the readers who buy newspapers and, presumably, patronize the merchants and services they advertise.

It was long ago established as an axiom in the business that good news of any sort never sold a single copy of a newspaper but that the worst possible news of calamity, doom, dissension and disaster boomed street sales and produced gratifying circulation totals. It is a situation where a single rotten apple can corrupt the whole barrel, for, once engaged in the horror sweepstakes, every newspaper is committed to more devastating torrents of terror than have been tapped by the opposition.

But the elements of the press that really cry havoc in ever-mounting spirals of hysteria are the weekly news magazines where doom and gloom unparalleled since the fall of Milton's angels is the standard fare. *Time* and *Newsweek* have devoted their covers to the exploitation of crises until the word has come to be wholly meaningless.

These weekly periodicals with their limited space have room for only the quintessence, extra-distilled, of fear and horror and *Newsweek* and *Time* are primarily Books of the Dead. Their readers, one and all, perished in atomic attacks long ago and their editors are fighting World War XIII with the ghosts of vanished civilizations.

Being moderately realistic fellows, many newspaper owners, publishers, and even the hired help are now and then disturbed by the paradoxical nature of their intentions. If all the customers are eliminated by the end of the world, every day, who is going to buy the Cadillacs and two-pants suits and real estate and foodstuffs they advertise along with the impending end of all things in the next column? To announce with breathless certainty World War III and the end of the human race on the same page with housing lots, special terms to veterans of World War II, on liberal time, doesn't make much sense. Which of these alternatives is the newspaper in question backing?

Fortunately for the economics of journalism, if not for the

vanity of its practitioners, few of the customers except professional humanitarians and hand-wringers in Berkeley, whose ears are attuned to the falling of bombs that nobody else hears, like those noises audible only to dogs, seem to take doom as dispensed in the daily and weekly press of the Nation at face value. If anybody took these portents seriously, the only sales being made anywhere would be sandbags for bomb shelters and survival kits.

As it is, you can't sell Americans on any part of a program of civil defense and the sales of outboard motors, mink stoles, automobiles and sports shirts, none of which are products of the National Casket Co., are at an all-time high.

All this is, as I say, very frustrating to newspaper and magazine editors who have been wishing total disintegration on their readers, lo, these many months without the slightest perceptible impact. Already dead and buried, the American people keep right on buying the merchandise and services which are keeping newspapermen in Martinis and sports cars when they ought to be buying potted beef and decontaminating devices, few of which are brisk movers at Macy's.

Terror All the Way to the Bank

The role of Cassandra in the Greek tragic cycle, whose merchandise was woe unutterable, used to be regarded as vaguely comic. A moderately well-adjusted human outlook on things in general simply felt any such pusher of unmitigated grief to be preposterous, and like Russian novels whose sole burden was the unending gloom of the Ural Mountains, nobody took Cassandra very seriously.

Now Cassandra is not only the loudest voice in the land, her load of perpetual terror is multiplied out of all endurance or probability through the willing agency of the terror press, the terror radio, terror television and the amateurs in terror who hover on the fringes of the professionals and contribute their two cents worth of gloom impenetrable outside the accepted agencies of communications.

Merchants of doom, most of whom never got their names in the papers until the city desk gave them a headline with the word "survival" in it, and university professors, who until now haven't been able to attract attention to their opinions at the faculty cafeteria, suddenly find themselves swept up in a radiant and imaginary holocaust in which their worst mental aberrations, until now a private matter, have been lent conspicuous significance in the public eye. "Scientists" who, until recently, couldn't lay a credible fire in the parlor grate, are now quoted on "firestorms" and "continental disasters" and it's a dull meeting of the PTA that doesn't get itself in on the act of how to avoid incineration in the impending galactic bonfire.

Fear and abject terror invoked by highly expert professionals for purposes of commercial profit have become as commonplace forms of merchandise in America today as breakfast foods or cosmetics.

Terror is confected in wholesale and retail quantities alike by politicians, publicists, vested commercial interests, the newspaper and periodical press, radio, television, the pulpit, practitioners of letters and the movies.

The louder the screeches and the more anguished the hand-wringing of the end-of-everything artists, the greater is their apparent concern for material rewards which they will hardly have time to enjoy in a world doomed to almost instantaneous annihilation. The authors of a horror novel called "Fail Safe," who are among the top ranking marrow freezers of the moment, are currently engaged in copyright disputes on an epic scale over royalties which, in the world cataclysm they foretell, will be completely worthless.

The "Fail Safe" authors are not interested in laying up treasures in heaven. They want their rewards in immediate,

109

tangible form in a world they profess to believe to be on the brink of certain incineration.

Nor is there any record that the author of a *grand guignol* called "On the Beach" ever refused royalties on the best seller or its widely touted film version which was of such grim dimensions that suicides were attributed to it. There are no suicides among those participating in the gate receipts at these assorted previews of hell, who laugh cheerily all the way to the bank after having convincingly demonstrated that, in a fortnight at best, neither they nor the bank will be around at all.

Two of the most assiduous and persistent syndicated entrail watchers who can be relied on to come up with full measures of ghastly forecasts are Drew Pearson and Joe Alsop whose end of the world capers have, over the years and decades, taken on all the aspects of a farewell tour of William Gillette in "Sherlock Holmes." Humanity and civilization have so frequently achieved a bad end in their newspaper articles and magazine pieces as to assume the character of perpetual motion. Yet it is not reported that Mr. Pearson rejects his salary as a mere meaningless down payment on oblivion and it is an established fact that Mr. Alsop lives high on the hog in Georgetown and foretells impenetrable gloom at an extremely favorable rate of remuneration.

As long as the merchants of doom and gloom remain convinced of the validity of property and demand to be paid the going rate for atomizing everything, the rest of us may be excused for taking a dim view of Armageddon, along with the integrity of its prophets.

Madison Ave. Through a Glass Darkly

If the entire flimsy structure of Madison Avenue, with its projection of images, incentives to wastefulness and touting of trash, should one of these fine days disintegrate into irretrievable ruin, a lot of us would cheer our heads off.

110

Not that there is anything inherently wrong with the advertising of services and merchandise when conducted with anything resembling propriety and dignity, but the techniques of promoting the useless, the meretricious and downright worthless have become offensive to perceptive people, and there are signs that maybe the decline of the intelligence dominating big-time advertising has set in.

An institutional campaign currently designed to promote the dairy industry generally, and the consumption of milk in particular, shows a likeness of a glass of Grade A juxtaposed to that of a teddy bear with the pitch: "Which One Haven't You Outgrown?" My instant reaction is in favor of the teddy bear and a determination to have nothing to do with milk. The teddy bear image is fairly deeply embedded in my consciousness; I like bears and I was devoted to the teddy bear of my youth and the suggestion that I should emotionally renounce teddy bears in favor of an insipid temperance beverage conditions me against any possible drinking of milk.

At the other end of the bar, metaphorically speaking, I recoil from the consumption of whisky which is advertised as being "light." The presumption implicit in this approach is that somehow a "light" whisky is better than a "heavy" whisky, but to my perverse thinking it suggests a cheap, ineffective, flavorless and underproof product that all right-minded whisky drinkers should reject.

I want my whisky strong, boozy, potent, full-bodied and of irreproachable proof, the sort that used to be consumed by heavily mustached men in cast-iron derby hats with good solid watch chains across prosperous stomachs. Any abatement of these characteristics simply debases the national drink of all right-minded men and suggests Scotch, which in my book is an active emetic and effeminate, although it never seems so when drunk by Englishmen. Whisky for Americans ought to be the sort that eats holes in the carpet if you spill it.

111

Lament for Toto, the Millionaire Poodle

I often wonder what has become of Toto the millionaire poodle dog. Sometimes he wasn't Toto, but Fifi or Mimi or any other endearing diminutive that somehow suggested capitalist decadence to the Russian mind and he or she existed only so far as anyone was able to discover in *Pravda* and other official Communist publications where he enjoyed a life of superabundant luxury, waited on hand and foot by many menials and living it up grandly on the doggy equivalents of champagne and foie gras and midnight suppers with delectable canine companions at 21 and El Morocco.

Toto (or Fifi or Mimi) made his appearance in the Russian press every so often, notably when a crop failure put a few million serfs on short rations or a government scandal had been uncovered too gigantic in its dimension to be kept from the peasantry. Toto was the beneficiary of the will of a decadent American millionaire who had wrung his ill-gotten wealth from the poor and oppressed of Texas or Oklahoma by driving them to slavery, with cossack-type labor police.

The millionaire, having at last cooled, willed his all to Toto, whose wealth and social position now required a staff which included a personal body servant, a secretary, chauffeur, a resident physician and a dietitian as well as a practically limitless staff of lawyers, investment experts and trust officials charged with the administration of his vast holdings.

The natural corollary to this opium dream of opulence was provided in the Russian dispatches about Toto by the intelligence that while pampered American pets lived high on the hog, millions of the enslaved American proletariat were sleeping under bridges and scrounging in trash cans for the leavings of idle rich dogs and that red revolution was surely at hand any moment to wipe out a scheme of things where capitalist Totos had private physicians while millions rioted for bread.

112

Somebody must have put a flea in the ear of the editor of *Pravda* to the effect that any economic scheme of things where pet poodles live on a scale of luxury unknown to any but party bosses in Russia might, when looked at in the wrong light, make the American economic order seem fairly desirable in a country where nobody at all eats anywhere nearly as well as almost everybody did before 1917.

Toto, the millionaire poodle, disappeared forthwith, presumably a victim of hobnail liver from too much Dom Perignon at the St. Regis.

'Scientist' as a Term of Contempt

A good many years ago, about 1925-26 I'd say, because I was an undergraduate at the time, the end of all things arrived, as it has recurrently arrived before and since that time, with a resounding bang in a Monday morning edition of the old *New York World* of which the then esteemed and now venerated Walter Lippmann was editor.

The end of human life on any appreciable scale, in that remote and unsophisticated age, was about to be accomplished through the seemingly innocent but in fact absolutely lethal agency of the fumes of vaporized gasoline. Wherever the automobile, even then fairly numerous in the land, had been, there death stalked behind, silent, invisible but with irresistible doomsday tread.

A group of noted "scientists" and "medical experts" of unblemished professional probity and the highest possible standing had revealed to the *World's* city editor the horrifying circumstances that survival of life was impossible wherever the air had been impregnated with a polysyllabic byproduct of the internal combustion engine. People who lived in cities knew not the lateness of the hour, unless they lived above the fifteenth story in apartment houses in which case their life span might be extended a few days or hours. Country folk, where the poison was less dense, might linger on for as long as a year or two.

113

But in a short time, as such things are measured, everyone who had ever been near an automobile was for the meat wagon. I forget the precise symptoms, but it seems to me that the bones were going to disintegrate into corn meal or some such, and that only the fortunate Eskimos and happy residents in Upper Assam and the Congo where motor cars were unknown had any chance at all.

Newspaper circulation boomed as readers became interested in what amounted to reading their own obituaries. Many extra papers were sold and, as the story continued and expanded from day to day with gruesome improvements, large numbers of people began to feel their bone structures were dissolving into corn meal and sought medical or spiritual reassurance as their natures dictated.

Curiously no fatalities were reported nor did the authorities in a sweeping fiat abolish automobiles and ban the manufacture of gasoline, although there were many loudly articulate folk who demanded the instant leveling of Detroit, Flint and other guilty communities and the hanging of Henry Ford as the chief agent of universal genocide.

Somehow we survived, even chauffeurs, filling station attendants and others whose occupations exposed them most urgently to the great hazard. The numbers of people whose bones seemed to be dissolving into corn meal were discovered to be consumers of Jamaica ginger, then an occasional substitute for whiskey among the lower classes.

The great gasoline fume terror of 1926 is what makes me today view with something less than alarm the theory prominently advanced in the daily press whenever there is a serious dearth of fires, muggings or droll stories from the local zoo that radioactive fallout is about to accomplish the end of all things and relegate human life to the status of the dinosaur.

It makes me cynical, too, about the incidence of lung cancer among smokers that is daily and horribly attested by "leading scientific and medical authorities." A leading scientific and medical authority is anybody with a Berkeley or Stanford telephone number known to the local city desk as available to doomsday quotation on a dull Sunday afternoon with the Monday paper coming up. Often he turns out to be the janitor of the chemistry building. The phrase "highest medical authority" has come to have about it some of the connotations of "Hollywood starlet," once defined by Gene Fowler as "any female resident of Los Angeles under seventy not actively engaged in prostitution."

Show me any member of a university or college faculty not available to identification as "a leading scientific authority," no matter how preposterous or assinine the mendacity attributed to him, and I'll show you a whole bankroll of three-dollar bills.

The word "professor" was once in the American lexicon a term of respect amounting to adulation until it was usurped by snake oil vendors and patent nostrum salesmen when it finally degenerated into meaning the piano player in a love store. At the rate of its ever-accelerated cheapening, the word "scientist," already degraded by every publicity-minded mountebank and phony until it is little more than a term of humorous contempt, will go the same way. The "cosmic scientist" of the morning editions by afternoon is usually emptying the trash baskets in the physics lab.

Won't Someone Help Me?

Notoriously a cheery and charitable soul with no more malice in my makeup than is contained say, in a chapter meeting of Black Muslims or a convocation of king cobras, I would still like to discover some agency short of assassination of the honest postman through which I can contrive not to receive the West Coast edition of *The New York Times*.

When this journalistic venture was first launched last year, and as a matter of professional curiosity, I did indeed subscribe for the absolute minimum period available in the trial offers.

A nervous and undernourished feuilleton and lacking not only the august magnitude but also the multiplicity of special departments of its black bombazine parent in Forty-fourth street, the West Coast *Times* arrived on my doorstep for the appointed ninety days of my trial subscription, a compendium of the world's crises and miscarriages for the past twenty-four hours, a harbinger of documented gloom, a badly printed and vilely edited capsule of catastrophes.

Its columns teemed with correspondence from the nastier pockets of outrage and violence in Darkest Africa and gloomy forebodings from Moscow. Mostly it recorded the assassinations and scuffles of statesmen in unpronounceable places whose formal attire was a chicken bone through the nasal septum.

I congratulated myself when my ninety days subscription period was up and I could attend the grand guignol of human progress in the more animated columns of my own newspaper and the capers of Minnesota M & M in *The Wall Street Journal*.

But the *Times* continued to arrive. Its flow was undiminished by the circumstance that I had long since ceased to pay for it and hoped to God it would go away. Now and then I received plaintive billetsdoux from the circulation manager saying I wasn't paid up and no longer a member of the club and that he would, perforce, have to terminate our association. Daily I anticipated this bright release, but alas, it was never realized. Unsolicited, unwanted, unloved and certainly unpaid for, the *Times* came daily and ceaselessly to abide with me, like Mr. Poe's raven.

Now I am open to suggestion at any level within the bounds of law how to discourage, abate, divert or otherwise discontinue the arrival of the West Coast *Times*. Legal redress against fellow laborers in the vineyard of journalism, no matter how misguided,

116

is the recourse of a churl and unworthy of professional consideration.

I have discarded as impractical the invocation of the offices of Holy Church because the management of the *Times* and I go to church on different days of the week, mine being strictly rationed to alternate Sundays once in a blue moon.

I am in communication with Miss Rachel Carson in search of a pesticide that will chemically eliminate *The Times* from the mails without killing off the wild life of advertising matter, tradesmen's duns and the screams of anguish from maimed and dying readers of the *Chronicle* which accompany its arrival in the post. But this takes time and patient research while I perish in an undulant sea of plebiscites in Palestine and palace revolutions in Pakistan. Help!

Sad Fate of The Times

Word continues to trickle back from such Manhattan cultural checkpoints as P. J. Moriarity's Saloon and Jack Bleeck's that *Times* men and *New York Times* partisans, between sobs and whilst taking precautions against weeping into their Jack Daniel's and so diluting the True Elixir of Life, are blaming the fiasco of *The Times'* West Coast Edition on the entrenched provincialism of the Trans-Sierra rather than on the shoddy and inept production of a third rate newspaper.

"The West isn't ready for it" is the quavering complaint of the Sulzberger minions, and nothing could be truer. The West isn't ready for the type of professional incompetence the West Coast *Times* represented or for the slightly patronizing attitude of *The Times* management in condescending to sponsor a California dateline as a cultural boon to the gun-toting sourdoughs in the Placerville Diggings.

This is, of course, a predictable gesture of self-vindication on the part of professionals who ought to have known better in the

117

first place but still undertook an invasion that should have required the logistics and determination of the beachhead in Normandy but which was actually attempted on a scale of the Bay of Pigs. *The Times* management made the error of believing that so starved for the Big Time in the field of journalism were the peons working those lazy Spanish ranchos in Monterey—and what's the other place called, Yerba Buena?—that they would put up with a product which in the field of newspapers was the precise equivalent of a second Shubert road company of "The Student Prince."

It was a mistake and it was fatal.

Churls of the Press

In a singularly petulant and churlish outburst the *Nevada State Journal*, Reno's morning newspaper and counterpart of the *Reno Evening Gazette* under the joint ownership of the Reno Newspapers, Inc., recently took Virginia City, that ancient citadel of mining and now the liveliest ghost town in the world, to task for allowing its over-all facade to deteriorate into little better than a carnival midway.

The town's historic C Street where once the frock-coated nabobs of the Bank of California had trod, *The Journal* complained in testy tones, was becoming modernized with neon and chromium trim and had lost almost all of its endearing archaism and continuity with the heroic past.

Nevada journalism, it must be explained, has always had overtones of churlishness about it and its company manners would congeal the marrow of newspaper managements where certain amenities of politeness, if not actual courtliness, are observed in the profession. Hank Greenspun, the free-wheeling publisher of the *Las Vegas Sun* openly refers to the Reno newspapers as "the kept press."

The Reno newspapers themselves have no hesitation about detailing at length the filing of libel suits against other publications in the same field, a breach of professional etiquette that it would be hard to parallel elsewhere in the United States.

The annual meetings of the Nevada Publishers' Association are carnivals of bad feeling and mutual outrage and wherever they are held extra municipal police are assigned to watch them in the interest of abating mayhem and civic tumult. The principal speaker at these shambles of the proprieties need not bother too greatly with the content of his remarks; the trading of insults between the assembled chivalry makes them largely inaudible.

Among the Electric Belts of Finance

In the now almost incalculably distant youth of this writer when, or so it seemed, the returning heroes of The Wilderness and Shiloh were still stacking their swords in the front hall umbrella stand, my literary devotions were paid at the shrine of a series of dime novels that, for no valid reason, were strictly interdicted at the ancestral Beebe manse. All of them were devoted to the acquisition of money. Other paperbacks of the period that circulated among my acquaintances were devoted to Buffalo Bill Cody, Jesse James and the Younger Brothers and they didn't cost a dime but two whole bits. These were dedicated to the theme of gunfire pillage, rapine and violent commotions in or around Missouri but they had scant appeal to the Boy Beebe. His allegiance was claimed by a school of paperback fiction called, if memory serves, "Work and Win" whose starred performers were all Boy Wolves of Wall Street.

I had imagined that this sort of fictional wishing well had long since disappeared from the general ken and that wish fulfillment had become a psychoanalyst's property until in the Palace barber shop, if you must know, I picked up a copy of

119

Barron's National Business & Financial Weekly. In a jiffy I was back in 1910 with copies of "Work & Win" as thick as leaves on Vallombrosa in the bureau under my Boy Scout suits.

I can unreservedly recommend *Barron's* as some of the most delightful reading this side of the "Waverley Novels," transporting the delighted beholder into an ineffable world of increment, wealth and bedazzlements beyond the dreams of Texas avarice, a handbook of pyramiding permutations of potential profit to make the nabobs of the Honorable East India Company shabby panhandlers in retrospect. Here, among the electric belts of investment and the restoratives of lost fiduciary manhood, there open vistas of gain to shame Get-Rich-Quick Wallingford.

It is not to the editorial content of *Barron's* that I refer, but to the advertising columns where the suggestion is explicit that for a paltry fee ranging from a single skin to $80 or $100 anybody can be instantly privy to secrets that will make him independently wealthy for life.

"Four electronic stocks likely to rise on soaring earnings" will be divulged to you as a special introductory offer by "Science and Electronics Investment Letter." The Market Diversions, Inc., offers "Free analysis of salt water conversion stocks." The Value Line advises that "an overloaded industry group has stimulated explosive growth in which we expect stock prices to double and triple."

For a beggarly $5, the Trendline Corporation will let you in on 286 stock charts, "showing daily action" which may well make you the financial peer of William Henry Vanderbilt.

The overall connotation of *Barron's* is that, with such an abundance of avenues to wealth available, the only possible obstacle to becoming a millionaire instanter lies in the matter of choice. So many goodies on the menu paralyze the beholder with indecision akin to that engendered by the list of fine clarets on the wine card at a great restaurant. Poverty, it seems to say, is for boobs.

Only one element seems lacking to the readers of *Barron's* and that is the initial stake with which to launch oneself upon inevitable opulence. But in the dime novels of my youth no mention was ever made of how the Boy Wolf of Wall Street financed his first primeval coup. Margin requirements were different then, anyway.

Journalistic Dandies of Yesteryear

Sartorial elegance is no longer associated with the Fourth Estate, alas, but as recently as a generation ago during my labors in the journalistic vineyards of New York distinctive dress among reporters and editors was as common as the silk hat in Wall Street during the heyday of John Pierpont Morgan the Elder.

All of us reporters on the street were identified by a uniform which included a bowler hat among snobs, but universally a walking stick with a crooked handle to hang over your wrist while taking notes, and a copy of the *American Mercury* folded in the left-hand pocket of our jacket where we also kept the triple-folded sheaf of yellow copy paper all street men carried.

Every reporter I ever knew in 1929 except Red Dolan of *The News,* who was very tough and often spat while interviewing kings, carried a stick. Alva Johnston wore spats as did Edward Dean Sullivan.

Dressiest of all was George Buchanan Fyfe of the *World* who wore a square crowned derby, wing collar and batwing bow tie and was a crackerjack at police headquarters on difficult stories. George fancied a straight stick which he had to carry under his arm when drinking and which often gouged the eyes out of passers-behind-him at bars. If they objected, George beat them to a pulp, for the stick was loaded in the handle end, and then had a waiter throw them out.

Next dressiest was Skipper Williams, senior ship's news man

121

on the *Times,* who always wore a square derby and wing collar with a fold-over tie and gold horseshoe tie pin.

Of course, *The Times* society editor, Fred L. (Free Lunch! Baker, was celebrated for his morning and evening tailcoats, which contained rubber-lined pockets in the tails so that he could take home terrapin Maryland and other desirable chow from the better weddings and debutante parties.

Royal Cortissoz was art reporter when I went to work for the *Herald Tribune* and invariably, in overcoat weather, wore an Inverness cloaked greatcoat and smoked cigars in a holder so long that you knew he was coming around a corner half a minute before he appeared in person.

On the exchange desk was a real veteran named Milton Snyder, a testy old party who had been one of the *Herald's* staff in the incandescent days of Bennett the Younger. Milton used to turn up on war anniversaries and marching days in a Prince Albert frock coat, dented top hat, and a splendid array of tarnished medals.

Ogden Reid, our publisher, never was seen after six out of evening or dinner clothes unless so stiff he couldn't negotiate the pants.

As the evening wore on Ogden tended to become increasingly formal of mien and less stylish of appearance. He would appear at Bleeck's in an opera hat from which the spines had extended themselves through the crown through some dressing room contretemps, and there would be traces of the best claret on his shirt front.

Bleeck would point to them and say "Clos. de Vougeot '99, Mr. Reid?" Reid would think back to dinner and contradict him: "Mouton Rothschild '29, Jack."

Baffling Case of 'The New Yorker'

There are a number of well certified indexes to the approach of senility which your doctor or the undertaker of your choice will be glad to outline to you in some detail. High blood pressure, cheeriness at breakfast, a mellowing political philosophy and an inability to drink more than half a bottle of proof spirits at cocktail time without falling over the fire irons all suggest dark wings hovering overhead and the impending midnight croak of the raven.

Personally and although my locks are hoary I felt until recently that I was fighting a reasonably good rear guard or delaying action against the Grim Reaper and postponing the eventual rendezvous with the dark camel that waits at the city gate at sundown.

Now I don't know. I also wonder if there isn't an absolute if unrecognized medical symptom of senility that has hitherto escaped general attention.

I can no longer read with any degree of understanding the letterpress of *The New Yorker*. Not a damned word of it. Talk of the Town, articles of cosmic scope and dimension, back of the book departments and, most of all the short pieces of fiction about suburban life simply elude my comprehension.

Such has not always been the case. In the long ago Twenties when *The New Yorker* had its beginnings I and my contemporaries couldn't wait for the week's issue to get on the newsstands. Like Henry Mencken's *American Mercury*, *The New Yorker* was an intellectual status symbol.

The folk who wrote and drew for it then didn't do so in double talk or, as we have come to know it, glossolalia. They all seemed to be writing in English and drawing gags that were meant to be comprehended.

Sometimes it took a minute's study to catch the horrid significance of one of Addams's masterpieces of the macabre but that was the pleasure of the thing. Nothing was, as is now the universal intent of *The New Yorker's* editors, deliberately and purposely meaningless.

123

To this generality of rational conduct the book reviews were, and always have been, a dazzling exception. Almost nobody of my personal acquaintance ever heard of any of the books that were reviewed, recognized the names of any of their authors or, often enough, the by-lined book reviewers themselves. They were all novels translated from Icelandic or Hungarian, and Benchley once told me, when in wine, that the entire book department was a contrived gag, an elaborate hoax and that none of the books, authors or reviewers actually existed at all.

Now, in my years of tottering senility, it occurs to me that all the rest of *The New Yorker's* editorial departments have become an extension of the book reviews, trafficking in non-extant ideas and fictitious events and personalities or at least in ideas, events and personalities so far removed from common experience or awareness as to be meaningless.

The delightful paradox of *The New Yorker* is the fact that its advertisers seem to consider cloud-cuckoo-land the most ineffable imaginable framework for their goods and services. Never was complete inscrutability so magnificently upholstered in voluptuary revenue.

The Evolution of an Instant Statesman

The accession to office of a new President has caused a remarkable revision upward of the Washington correspondents' estimate of Mr. Johnson's importance, wisdom, sagacity, farsightedness, benevolence, statesmanship, humanity, rectitude and capacity for progressive leadership. Almost none of these qualities were associated with him when he was Vice President.

A great many people had some difficulty remembering his name as occupant of an office Mr. Dooley characterized as "not exactly a criminal offense but no credit to a man's character." When President Kennedy, yielding to Mr. Johnson's importunities, sent him on a foreign mission to distribute ball point pens among the heathen, the newspapers of the land and the periodical press, too, were surprised that such a person existed.

Today he is the recipient of a Washington press almost as favorable, profuse and emotionally charged as that of his predecessor. Granted, as the journalistic merchants of platitude have been avidly pointing out, the office makes the man, many Americans are surprised that it made Mr. Johnson practically overnight.

He is almost the only example of an instant statesman on record.

Without any least derogation of a man on whose capacity for high office the fate of civilization may well depend, especially if he is re-elected next year, this tumultuous acclaim of Mr. Johnson's importance, wisdom, sagacity, etc., confected on short notice seems ill-considered and scarcely the mature judgment of close observers over a prolonged period of time.

The truth is that Washington correspondents are enthusiastic supporters of whatever administration is in office at the moment, and especially so if the incumbent is a Democrat. Only by investing the principal excuse for their professional existence with almost unearthly qualities of sapience and glamor can they bask in the reflection of the same characteristics.

They made Calvin Coolidge a statesman of the first magnitude, and in the light of that accomplishment arraying Mr. Johnson in the robes of an Augustus should be a pushover.

Bang! You're Dead!

During the missile gap horror of only a few years back, the Alsop brothers, chanting woe like the chorus in "Antigone," had the United States atomized by superior Russian fire power of missiles so often that a ponderable part of the population

125

came to regard itself as permanently dead. It had been killed off by Joe Alsop so frequently that it was beginning to believe in its own obituary.

Scarlet Sisterhood of Newspaper Row

A long-time servant of the caprices and prejudices of my principals, and a loyal hired man available to the mercenary projects of anybody sufficiently well-heeled to support my expensive tastes, I have without reservation subscribed to the ancient aphorism: "Whose bread I eat, his song I sing." I have viewed membership in the crimson sisterhood of Newspaper Row with the cynicism that has characterized all the other inmates of the ink-stained bordello, at least after their apprenticeship and the high ideals they brought to town with them in a cardboard valise along with their extra shirt has evaporated under the pressures of reality.

But it never was brought home to me what an overall bedhouse I inhabited, where the partisanship of great and influential newspaper properties could be purchased lock, stock, and barrel, on a basis of the most meretricious advantage, until the recent national elections of the President and other candidates for office in the autumn of 1964.

Here for all to see and the impression irrevocably engrossed on the memory of generations to come was the spectacle of an overwhelming majority of the American press and communications structure allied in a gigantic cabal of mediocrity endorsed by mendacity, of superficiality sponsored by superciliousness, of sneers from louts and watercloset witticism in support of witlessness, all allied to support a party and man in office of proven corruption because it seemed the safe and prudent course and one totally devoid of honor or integrity.

There is nothing essentially wrong with President Johnson that wasn't wrong with Boss Tweed in New York or Harry Daugherty or Albert Fall of later memory and there is nothing about the Texas gang in Washington that wasn't wrong with the Ohio gang in the Harding years, but the press of the Nation was outraged by Boss Tweed and Teapot Dome. Today it merely indulges in a locker room smirk of boys-will-be-boys tolerance in the face of an Administration whose depth of corruption is only as yet guessed but which has shown traces of what mining prospectors call float, in Billy Sol Estes and Bobby Baker. There will be more and better later.

So when the American Newspaper Publishers Association foregathers in its annual confraternal conclave to determine which course of political policy will in future be supine enough or corrupt enough to bring in the most revenue, they may spare themselves the lofty platitudes about integrity, public obligations, responsibility and all the other sanctimonious jazz that communications moguls admire to hear after the third double Beefeater. It will be just another meeting of the hustlers and they can put their beaded bags on the table while touching up their mascara in pocket mirrors without destroying any illusions about their social status.

When Wellington, interviewing a Napoleonic officer after Waterloo, enquired for the whereabouts of the French general staff, the answer was *"Ca n'existe pas!"* That will do for the integrity of the American press. It doesn't exist.

Lippmann and Lodge at Bleeck's

If, as and when Henry Cabot Lodge is ever elected President of the United States it will be one more tribute to those two greatest of all finishing schools of journalism and diplomacy in the New York Twenties and Thirties, the *New York Herald Tribune* editorial staff and Jack Bleeck's Artists' & Writers' Saloon next door. For Cabot was one of the most brilliant ornaments of the former and an occasional patron of the latter.

Less of a regular than Richard Watts Jr., the *Tribune's* accomplished film reviewer, Cabot was still more familiar at the bar than Walter Lippmann, a frosty Olympian whose office on the tenth floor was reputed to contain a billiard table and grand piano and who almost never mingled with the wayward but jocund serfs on the fifth floor. Lippmann was only remembered as ever being in Bleeck's once although the unique occasion was not without its memorable aspects.

His contract with the Tribune Publishing Company was up for renewal and Ogden Reid, the owner and publisher, would sign contracts no place but at Bleeck's bar so the great tenth floor pundit, not without misgivings, arrived for the signing ceremony in surroundings that were patently not his dish of tea. The misgivings were well founded.

No sooner had Ogden and the great man been served and a fountain pen been produced from amidst the Prince de Galles Cigars in Ogden's pocket than a water connection in Fortieth street burst, cutting Bleeck's off from the outer world and locking the inmates of the moment within as securely as any jail. The great man who may, on occasions of carnival abandon, have taken a glass of sherry before dinner found himself immured with a posse of rumpots who regarded a pint of bourbon before breakfast as the merest precaution against the damp. He emerged palsied and shaken four hours later after the floods had subsided and spent the next two weeks in a nursing home.

Cabot, a fastidious Yankee who would, we always felt, have preferred a vintage Madeira, say a Flying Cloud 1815, made do in democratic fashion with the strong waters at Bleeck's and seemed to enjoy occasional skirmishes with life as it emphatically was not lived in the Somerset Club, Beacon street, Boston. He made up in personal charm what he lacked in any very earthy humor.

On one occasion the late Bill Houghton, then assistant chief editorial writer to Geoffrey Parsons, was telling of a long ago moment of exaltation when, as a city side reporter, he had been introduced to the ineffable and legendary James Huneker.

"Glad to meet you Mr. Houghton," Huneker had reportedly said. "Glad to meet any newspaperman. Once a newspaperman, always a whore."

Cabot was horrified. With outrage in his every accent he looked Houghton sternly in the eye and said: "Why, Uncle Bill, if I believed that, I'd never have joined the profession."

Sigmund Freud Among the Type Cases

As one of the graying and now ever fewer veterans of the *New York Herald Tribune* when it was the greatest newspaperman's newspaper of them all, I am frequently asked whence, please, came the *Tribune's mystique* in that now vanished age of giants? And why did it fade away?

Reason would suggest that with the passing of time interest would diminish in the conduct of the affairs of a newspaper, even in an Augustan age of journalism, if for no other reason than that its survivors are no more than a little band of twitching ancients, like the city fathers who fluttered and piped like birds on the wall of Troy.

Yet its fascination grows instead of diminishing.

One of the veterans now in the Old Soldiers' Home of retired practitioners of daily letters is Stanley Woodward, off-again, on-again, gone-again sports editor of the *Tribune* in its stormiest years and who was at the departmental helm when it became apparent that the hull had been fatally holed.

He was not under the social and moral obligations which obtained with some of us who had eaten salt in the Reid home to keep his opinions of his employers to himself. As a result his sentiments about the decline and fall of the *New York Herald Tribune* from its once Olympian heights are possessed of uncommon validity.

Woodward pulls no punches at all in expressing the sentiment, widely shared but seldom voiced, that the paper's *mystique* stemmed in its entirety from Ogden Reid in his lifetime of authority as publisher and that its decline is flatly attributable to the insistence on the part of Mrs. Ogden Reid, after his death, on directing every detail in the affairs of a great and valuable property to further her own very peculiar ends.

Mrs. Reid, to put it mildly, had a whim of vanadium steel and no least or slightest scruples about using it to interfere with the conduct of every department, business and editorial, of the paper. She was also a rabid feminist and wanted to see as many departments as possible headed by lady editors and executives.

Mrs. Reid surrounded herself with a general staff composed entirely of women, many of them of undoubted ability and executive competence, but all of them hostile to the masculine conduct of an enterprise that was essentially masculine and all of them intent on putting more and more women in key positions. In the end the *Tribune* was an unabashed matriarchy with amazonian females soliciting business from Bernie Gimbel and Jack Strauss and lady hatchetmen spies and informers and agents provocateurs demoralizing the entire structure of the property.

The younger Reids, Whitey and Brownie, dominated by Mamma to a degree that would have aroused interest in Sigmund Freud, encouraged by maternal influence at every imaginable opportunity to depart from the pattern of immaculate good breeding of their father, and their every instinct for catastrophe only tempered by sensational incompetence, couldn't help but wreck the property.

The end came for Stanley Woodward when Mrs. Reid summarily commanded the sports editor to run an eight-column banner head on a women's golf tournament that in the ordinary scheme of things would have rated less than a stick of agate at the bottom of the page. It was symbolic of the end of the great days of the *Tribune* and of a property that was a legend of wonderment overwhelmed in a sea of feminism, momism and a managerial psychosis that would have fascinated Havelock Ellis.

France Strikes Back

The French press at the moment is in the midst of one of its recurrent snits about the debasing influence of the abominable and unclean Americans on the once pure and unstained French national culture.

No doubt the disapproval of all things American in the Paris press has approval in the highest government circles, and the American love of gadgets, cola drinks, television sets, jive argot, fast motor cars, beat whiskers, hankering for publicity and wealthy and dissolute ways generally are the subject of an almost continuous barrage of abuse from the editorial pages.

Anything that is repulsive to good taste and well-bred conduct is instantly identified as of Yankee origin even though it has met with mad acceptance on the part of a large segment of the impressionable younger segment of the populace.

That the identical aspects of life in the America of the moment that vex French editors: transistor radios, Negro slang, maniacally driven sports cars and peculiar attire on the part of juvenile delinquents, are also distasteful to a considerable body of American public opinion makes no difference.

The worse the departure from decorum, the more unhesitatingly it is identified as being American in origin. Somehow the French press has even contrived to invest the obscenities of vulgarity that characterize film festivals at Cannes, a purely French show if ever there were one, with overtones of Americanism.

Connoisseurs of the preposterous are hopefully awaiting the day when the French slang phrase *"C'est d'accord,"* which is very bad French and used to excuse anything, will be branded as essentially American.

When the Ghoul Pool Flourished

I don't know what passes for action in the newspaper city rooms of the land, but I get an idea from occasional conversations with members of the Fourth Estate that somehow things aren't what they used to be. Not that they ever, at least in my recollection, bore any striking resemblance to the urgency of the early Gene Fowler-Damon Runyon era depicted in "The Front Page" or "Five Star Final." Still, there was an atmosphere of hooray not suggested by membership in the Newspaper Guild.

I do recall that on the *Boston Telegram,* before its owner Fred Enright went to the hoosegow for libeling James M. Curley (for God's sake, how?), we had a managing editor named Neal Moynahan who was a real anarchist, and that the only time we missed an edition was when the pressroom foreman, who was also the office bootlegger, slipped while crossing the bridge across a speed press with a case of gin that said Gordon's. Boy, talk about throwing eggs in the electric fan!

The premises of the *New York Herald Tribune* in 1929 had about them a more elevated *ton* if only because we had Henry Cabot Lodge on the staff and Geoffrey Parsons, the chief editorial writer who wore a morning coat, and was also president of the Century Club. An English visitor who was shown through the plant late one evening commented favorably that all the staff wore dinner dress. It happened to be a night when there were 12 openings on Broadway and the drama department, with only Percy Hammond and Arthur Ruhl as accredited reviewers, had called on the city desk for help.

The glory of the city room for a time was the Ghoul Pool, a hat pool from which staff members by lot acquired the name of a likely candidate for an obituary notice. Obituaries of an even 100 elder statesmen, millionaires and names likely to make the death page, were kept standing in type at all times against the contingency of sudden death, and the pool came to an even $100. Names were drawn by members of the pool from a derby hat held by a departmental secretary who stood on the city desk wearing a sash reading "Miss Styx."

Good names such as Henry Ford, President Von Hindenburg, Thomas A. Edison and Mrs. Vanderbilt were regarded as equities and sold at a premium at the bar at Bleeck's. John D. Rockefeller was a blue chip investment and brought $15 when sold by Joe Mitchell to Beverly Smith. A rumor that Grace Vanderbilt was failing drove her up to $25, and Dennis Tilden Lynch, who had purchased her on the strength of a tip from Howard White, our society editor, claimed foul when Mrs. V., hale and hearty, walked to church at St. Thomas next Sunday.

The Ghoul Pool came to an untimely end one day when George F. Baker, a durable Wall Street figure since the Civil War and a Morgan partner to boot, heard that he had been quoted at $15 when Joe Driscoll unloaded him on Lessing Engleking, the night city editor. Mr. Baker, his mutton chop whiskers practically in flames, complained to Mrs. Reid, saying he had heard that William Goadby Lowe, a mere upstart, had brought a higher price, and the Ghoul Pool was suppressed. It had been fun while it lasted, however, and I once made a tidy sum on Calvin Coolidge whom I had bought from Richard Watts Jr. for a paltry $5.

'Community Swoon' of the Press

There is, I think it may be said without reflection on the basic integrity of a calling that has claimed me as a practitioner on a professional basis for nigh onto forty years, a lamentable tendency of American newspapers to think alike and, allowing for minor regional variations, to assume editorial stances that are almost identical.

In particular, the newspapers of California, or what remain of a once noble multiplicity of dailies, are given to what the incomparable John Mason Brown has perceptively called "community swoons."

A classic example of community swoon that Mr. Brown likes to cite, somewhat to be sure before the age of modern journalism, is the case of Charlemagne, King of the Franks, when he learned of the loss of his choicest knight, Roland, in the fated pass at Roncevalles. " 'Christ, God,' muttered Charlemagne, 'in evil case am I,' and tore his beard and wept sore. And with him wept all the horsemen of the Franks. There were twenty thousand in the ranks that fainted on the ground."

This, Mr. Brown notes without fear of contradiction, was perhaps the community swoon of all time. All those twenty thousand knights out cold, with their horses standing by wondering what the hell it was all about, must have set some sort of record.

In much the same manner, although on a less gratifyingly spectacular scale, the presumably responsible press of the nation in general and California in particular is given to a community approach to a wide variety of stimuli. I would like to cite the canonization with which the late President Kennedy has been invested, a holiness and sanctification that would almost certainly have appeared hilarious to Mr. Kennedy himself, who was an expert at self-appraisal.

There is also the great Goldwater smear, a universal campaign of vilification and abuse which must in retrospect be something of an embarrassment to its participants, especially in the light of the candidate they managed to promote in his stead.

The equally sanctified cause of what have widely been touted as civil rights must likewise account for a certain amount of soul searching even among their most ferocious partisans since their achievement now seems to have presupposed a not inconsiderable body of civil wrongs at somebody else's expense.

But the community swoon among the editorial writers of the moment that will, I think, appear most preposterous and certainly the most self-defeating has been the great smear of the membership of the John Birch Society which has been carried to such a degree of ferocity as to elevate it to the estate of authentic martyrdom.

Never very important until singled out by the witch burners of the California newspaper press and certainly at no time in their brief existence any menace to the established disorder of things in the American community, the Birchers have emerged from a prolonged and gratuitous campaign of malignant persecution as a group with a stature which they certainly never before possessed.

As an index of the original Bircher mentality and philosophy of the preposterous, it is only necessary to recall that one of their basic articles of faith embraced the notion that President Eisenhower was in the pay of the Kremlin and the personal agent of the late Premier of the Soviets emplaced in the White House to sell out the Republic to its Russian enemies.

This alone would have relegated the Birch Society to the approximate status of flat earth prophets except for the shrill and insistent flogging of an almost dead horse in the public prints where the unanimity of hostility, public distrust of newspapers being what it is, promptly sowed the seed of suspicion that maybe the Birchers had virtues not apparent to superficial inspection. Continued harassment of these inoffensive and, at one time, inconsequential people not only closed their own ranks against internal dissension, it also gave rise to the suspicion that their cause, however moon-struck in appearance, must have something on the ball.

CHAPTER FIVE
This Wild West

Nevada enchanted Mr. Beebe and California, with the occasional exception of San Francisco, horrified him. He would have been at home in the old West and he deplored the passing of those aspects of it which survived into modern times. His love affair with his latter day home town, Virginia City, was celebrated in columns, books and weekly in the pages of the paper he edited for six years.

Fun Days on the Barbary Coast

Everybody had a good time on the Barbary Coast: the inmates who sniffed nose candy and knocked each other over the head with bung starters as a matter of nightly course; the visiting firemen from the East who couldn't wait to leave their families in suites at the Russ House on the pretext of an important business conference with Sam Brannan; and the reformers who raised mitted hands to heaven to testify to the horror of it all and to invoke celestial aid in its suppression.

Murders on the Coast, be they accomplished by hatchet or derringer, had class and a bravura, something that was missing in homicides elsewhere. The shanghai trade in sailors made use of Rube Goldberg devices like trap doors in the floor and chloral in the already lethal whiskey. Prostitution had a flair about it, a panache of the rowdy-dow when it christened its practitioners Minnie the Pig, the Galloping Cow and Iodoform Kate. Even such comparatively innocuous occasions as picnics to Contra Costa or Marin counties had style, as the merrymakers often took along a cannon and supply of ball ammunition with which to flatten interlopers or, lacking intrusion, their own members.

What picnic in this degenerate age takes along a cannon?

And everywhere, but everywhere, there were orgies past counting and description, lovely rousing orgies of sex, depravity, mayhem, the dancing of clogs and the breaking of glass. "Behind the painted scenes of the melodeon," wrote an enchanted contemporary, "are orgies that may be imagined but not described." The inventory of wickedness was as limitless as a Sears catalogue.

Church folk cheered through the smoke when, on that Day of Doom in 1906, flames finally claimed the Barbary Coast. Me,

140

I would have wept, because the Barbary Coast and I would have gotten along very well. It was a place I could understand. A body could feel at home there.

The Value of Gambling

I'm still all for legalized games in the One Sound State. There is satisfaction in having one's taxes paid by Californians who are themselves residents of a community that frowns on fun and continues with a grim resolution to tax itself into bankruptcy. The thesis that California is rapidly becoming the national nut hatch is amply substantiated by the seemingly limitless population of mudhens, system players and otherwise afflicted of Allah who migrate on weekends to Nevada in the delusion they are going to win. If California ever gets the news and itself legalizes any wide variety of games of chance, Nevada will revert overnight to the witless Diggers and Piutes who originally owned it.

Of all the arguments advanced against gambling, the most preposterous is that the money could, somehow, "be spent better." By this is usually meant the soiled miseries of domesticity and the dreary afflictions of raising a family in a society already suffocating in its own overpopulation. Just what argument can be advanced that a raddled housewife or an assortment of damp and dismal issue is more deserving than Harold Smith or Bill Harrah escapes my understanding. Nevada gamblers of the current generation are shy of personal exploitation to the point of anonymity and of such modest personal habits that the raising of a family, by comparison, appears the ultimate in the conspicuous and wasteful consumption so loudly deplored by Thorstein Veblen.

Getting cleaned at the craps tables is, in actual fact, an economy nobody can afford to pass by.

141

The Curse of No. 4

Nobody knows whence the myth came that Nevadans don't gamble. Residents of Monaco may not be allowed admission to the Casino of the Societe des Bains de Mer at Monte Carlo. In his benevolent overlordship and feudal rule of Florida, no Floridian ever set foot in Colonel Bradley's green and white clubhouse at Palm Beach. But neither statute nor inhibition keeps Nevadans from the craps tables and there's where they pay their own taxes. It gives credence to the entire bootstrap theorem.

All Nevadans except your correspondent, that is. He's not a reformed gambler, or a bankrupted gambler or an ex-compulsive gambler who doesn't dare venture within the sound of shaken dice. He's just a bored gambler. He couldn't care less and it may be doubted if in the past ten years he's won or lost as many dollars even though for a ponderable part of every year he's brought into almost daily contact with every form of opportunity to make himself rich as King Midas.

It wasn't always so. When I first came to these parts to live, the gambling fever coursed through my veins like Jack Daniel's and branch. I couldn't pass a roulette table without seeing if number four wouldn't come up. Dealers in Reno and Virginia City, knowing my fatally flawed character and seeing me enter a saloon, would set up a mendacious clamor, "Four just rolled three times in a row. Four's real lucky tonight. Big action on four." I was convinced that four was magic and that a Druidic spell was woven about it. Friends attributed my addiction more realistically to the fact that on a roulette layout four is at the extreme left of the table where a player is less liable to being jostled and having to reach across other people and where there is room for a drink at the rim of the wheel.

A wicked dealer at Pat Hart's Brass Rail in Virginia City, through some secret mastery over canine intelligence, had my

142

old dog Mr. T-Bone trained, while his master was at the bar, to come over to the roulette table and lay his nose on number four and bark. It was a device that cost me more than Paul Getty spends for Gainsboroughs.

Uncle Len, The Nonpareil

The old master of all Nevada dealers in the days when games were fun was Honest Uncle Len Haffey who ran the wheel in Eddie Colletti and Johnny Zalac's Delta Saloon in Virginia City. Uncle Len looked the part. He was ancient, slightly sinister, with a suggestion of latent hooray under a cockeyed green dealer's eyeshade, and I once persuaded Holiday magazine to run a full page portrait of him in color as the archetypal old-time Nevada gambler in the grand manner of his calling. Which he was.

His wheel was a thing of beauty, nobly fashioned of ornate mahogany some time before The Big Bonanza, not one of the sleazy plastic eyesores turned out nowadays in Detroit, and the green cloth was stained with vintages from the Comstock's youth, perhaps spilled by Jim Fair or the godlike John Mackay himself.

Uncle Len knew how to order wine when the game was lagging at three in the morning or thoughts of home obtruded on the consciousness of the customers, and many's the night we faced each other manfully as the empty Bollinger bottles rose in a bushel basket kept handy for the purpose while the snow mounted equally unheeded outside in C Street where no wheel turned. The cigars were always at hand, Belinda Fancy Tales, and Johnny and Eddie never closed when there was a game going. Night prowlers festooned like snowmen would totter in to proclaim the storm the greatest since the famous ten-foot fall of 1916 and Uncle Len would give the bottle a reflective turn in its cooler.

Now Uncle Len lives a life of affluent ease in retirement, Eddie, the barkeep, took silk and was elevated to the magistracy as Judge Edward Colletti and the long roll and good times at the Delta wheel are no more.

'Restoration,' V.C. Style

Every so often in our ancient citadel of sin and silver in the infrequent lulls between civic outrages, which range from religious warfare to the discovery that the band of juvenile thugs and hoodlums who have been pillaging the community are all sons of first citizens, there is a strange muttering about an elusive something called "restoration."

In Virginia City, the concept of "restoration" is the outright showering down upon the individual residents, property owners and voters of large sums of completely unencumbered spending money by bountiful well-wishers variously spoken of as "the Morgans," "the Rockefellers," "the Fords" and "the Guggenheims."

This uncomplicated philosophy has, in the only recent past, led to contretemps of an embarrassing nature.

Less than a decade ago a smooth practitioner with a fat briefcase and the confident joviality of the professional confidence man arrived in Virginia City and summoned the city fathers and leading saloon keepers in civic conclave with the happy intelligence that he, as an experienced promoter of good works, had unfailing access to the uncounted millions of "the Rockefellers," "the Mellons" and "the Fords" and that these splendid people had authorized him to select Virginia City to be the recipient of their practically limitless benefactions.

To establish his *bona fides* he cited gaudy instances where he had been instrumental in diverting tidal waves of currency to deserving recipients: a magnificent museum of fine arts at Beloit, Wisconsin, a widely acclaimed civic center at Social Circle, Ohio, a vast university of many colleges at Macon, Georgia.

All the Comstock had to do to loose the floodgates of opulence which would make it the wonder and envy of the entire West was to pony up a trifling sum, the merest picayune, say $25,000 to be paid cash in hand to Mr. Bountiful to set the machinery of the mint in motion.

The first citizens of C Street went away wreathed in smiles and counting on their fingers each one his individual take from this abundance of found money.

All except the editors and owners of *The Territorial Enterprise* who had been further afield in the great world than even Reno and had, in addition, read the entire saga of Get-Rich-Quick Wallingford in their youth.

At some expense to themselves in toll charges, they investigated the alleged enrichments, endowments and cultural emplacements at Beloit, Social Circle and Macon, which seemed to have been selected at thoughtful remove from Nevada, only to find them illusory. They did, however, come up with a circular from the Better Business Bureau accurately describing the person and professional attainments of the self-proclaimed keeper of the keys of "the Mellons" and "the Guggenheims" which were of interest to a number of chambers of commerce and police departments in the land.

The proprietors of *The Enterprise* presented their findings to the city fathers of the Comstock whereupon it was found the confidant of the Mellons and Morgans had left the Riverside in Reno without pausing to pay his bill. Did they get any thanks from the community? Come again. They were widely denounced for having deprived Virginia City of benefactions running, with the passage of time, into specific millions.

Happy Days in Virginia City

When my partner Charles Clegg and I removed from New York to Nevada to become residents in what it was even then apparent was the One Sound State in a Union that was becoming a shambles of overpopulation and confiscatory taxation and to undertake the reactivation of the once effulgent destines of *The Territorial Enterprise,* our motivations were several and of a nature both positive and negative.

We wanted out of a New York which had finally and definitely seceded from the United States to become something emetic and "international", and we were enchanted by the discovery of the radiantly individualistic State of Nevada where being a character was a full-time occupation in which the entire population joyously participated.

Virginia City at the time was an unmonumented claim of characters beyond the wildest dreams of the collector and connoisseur of the amiably preposterous.

Unspoiled by the cataracts of tourist trash which have since transformed its once raffish and seedy grandeurs into an outpost of Disneyland, its gorgeous multiplicity of saloons, deadfalls and then-operating bagnios crawled with unreconstructed and largely alcoholic deadbeats, hot water plugs, old-timers of irreproachable pedigree as failures by worldly standards, tall towers of mendacity and battered tilters against the windmills of progress and delusions of responsible conduct in the outer world.

In the year 1948 Virginia City could, I truly believe, boast the greatest density of peerless and unblemished nonconformists in the world. We gladly joined their ranks.

Let us remember in kindness a derelict of fortune who had cooked in the dreadful eating houses of every Nevada mining camp from Hamilton and the Reese river to Rhyolite and Rawhide and was known as Four Day Jack because that was the longest he had ever achieved sobriety on a continuous basis.

Let us, too, stand at attention at the recollection of Zeb Kendall, last of the magnificoes of mining times, who had made and lost half a dozen recorded fortunes in sums of millions and

146

whose name still is engrossed in the pediment of the Kendall Block at Tonopah. Zeb, a rugged and durable grandee and one-time associate in California racing ventures with Wyatt Earp, although well into his latter seventies, was fond of poker and could sit for three days and nights on end in a game at the Delta Saloon consuming an appropriate amount of whiskey.

Apprised that her husband was involved in such a scuffle with the Goddess of Chance, Belle Kendall, fearful for his health, confronted him through a thick haze of the day before yesterday's cigar smoke with the warning: "Zeb Kendall, one of these days you're going to fall dead with a hand of cards and a bottle of whiskey at your elbow!" Zeb's answer was forthright.

"Can you think of any more agreeable way to die, my dear? "

The office of night roundsman in Virginia City changed its occupancy almost with the speed of light at the time of which I write, largely because the representatives of law and order were themselves prone on a universal scale to the nocturnal diversions they were appointed to curb. When one Virginia City Dogberry, summoned to apprehend a gaggle of tough Reno juveniles who had stolen a car and were racing up and down C street tossing bottles through windows, discharged the entire contents of his firelock at the offenders who escaped unscathed he was questioned by the town fathers on his own whereabouts on the night in question. How came it that he had been unable to hit a fair target at close range although contriving to shatter the plate glass window of the Sazarac Saloon, demolish the neon sign of the Tierra Gem and Rock Shop and put three slugs through the windshield of an out of town car innocently parked outside the Old Mr. Comstock Saloon? Had he, in a word, been drinking, while on duty? The roundsman shrugged.

"What else is there to do at night since you closed down the girls? "

Love stores during the early fifties operated on an irregular schedule, flourishing on the edges of town and in well-advertised nests of trailers, well patronized by taxi loads of revellers from Reno for a period of prosperity and then being banished when some special tumult or outrage aroused Virginia City's whimsical sense of civic virtue. One of them for some months promoted its more important traffic in mirth and abandon with a Sunday morning businessman's breakfast of Southern fried chicken reputed to be the best for miles around.

Another similar establishment at prudent remove from the city limits and beyond the reach of public utilities had its own portable lighting plant stolen on opening night by a miscreant promptly hailed as "the meanest thief."

"It was inconvenient," Madame Bertha told a reporter from the *Enterprise,* "but not an essential to our business."

Times on the Comstock have changed now, alas. One by one the old timers have crept to rest, but not silently as in the verses of the Rubaiyat. In winter time they go noisily as all hell, for graves must be blasted from the frozen surface rock of the Lode and loud concussions accompanied by a deal of constructive alcoholism in the town's bars indicate a good man's passing. Most of them deserve twenty-one guns.

California Pot and Texas Kettle

It seems to me from the impregnable vantage point of residence in Nevada, where most of the matters of wordly status and cultural sophistication that are under discussion elsewhere in the West have never been heard of at all, that Californians of all people ought to be most guarded in their denunciations of the melancholy State of Texas.

Blackguarding Texas in general and Dallas in particular has become a parlor sport and major preoccupation and nowhere is it more enthusiastically embraced than in parts of the Union that could well be reminded of the ancient aphorism about residents of glass houses.

No state of the current fifty bonded commonwealths, it seems to me, is less qualified by social, political or any other standards you care to name to hurl the first dornick on the basis of the Biblical qualification of "him that is without sin" than California.

In many aspects of bumptiousness, boorishness, smug self-satisfaction and the insane gratification that comes from bigness in everything from population to bankruptcies and from the supreme viewpoint of complete political ineptitude, California out-Texases the Lone Star State in a dimension of awful magnificence.

Set a blindfolded and impartial observer down in the wasteland of Southern California and remove the blindfold in a spot devoid of instant regional identification through trade names and road markers and it would be impossible for him to tell with certainty if he were in Bakersfield or Waco, Lubbock or Fresno. The same leprosaria of drive-ins, motels and infamies of neon would affront his gaze. The same strangulation of traffic in speedways, the same baboon mentality of "Hey, Mac" familiarity from inferiors, the identical devisings of the Borgias in dens advertising "gourmet" victuals would be the universal norm.

It is probable that he might find himself enmeshed in the cretin ecstasies of a football orgy whose obscene drum majorettes' pouting and pirouetting are indistinguishable in Pasadena from the identical ape-doings in Fort Worth. He would be saluted by his first name by filling station attendants perhaps more offensively in the suburbs of Los Angeles than in the comparatively mannered precincts of Houston.

Nor is the comparison limited to the obvious material aspects of life and casual social contacts. If a piece of litmus paper were to be exposed in Dallas and found to turn blue from ultra-conservatism, it would turn instant red in San Francisco, Palo Alto or Berkeley, the adjacent suburbs of the American

Leningrad. Northern California is nationally celebrated as a cesspool of radical politics, social subversion and academic tolerance of educational beatniks who have been run out of the more studiously guarded portals of Eastern centers of the cultural amenities.

Breastbeaters, bleeding hearts, foes of capital punishment, septic humanitarians and clinical crackpots of every known hue and degree of deviation from sanity abound in the San Franciscan faubourgs the way bogus religious cults and faith healers swarm in the precincts of Azusa and the San Fernando Valley in the Southland. There are more beards concealing more verminous shirtlessness in San Francisco's North Beach than among all the fakirs of India in holy convention assembled.

There is nothing in Texas politics since Ma Ferguson to approximate the infamies tempered only with incompetence of those in Sacramento where the glory of the State's Democrats is a Governor with the mentality of a suet pudding, while the crowning jewel of California Republicanism in 1964 is a one-time hamburger vendor who predicates presidential aspirations on the established fact that his native California now won't have him for dog catcher.

All of which adds up to the fact that whatever meretricious mediocrity or vulgarity Texas has been able to associate with its image finds neck-and-neck competition in the Golden State, which is currently busy patronizing the derelict city of Dallas. The same California that is making childish snootfaces from behind its roadside catastrophes of commercialized cheapness could do worse than to appraise itself as increasingly the dust bin of the West and a social and political disaster area of the first magnitude.

A Notable Death in Denver

The Ship Bar at Denver's Brown Palace hotel is only slightly less cultural than the city's library, having been the scene only twenty years back of a shooting in which the president of a local university was fatally ventilated. In fairness it should be remarked that the Venerable Bede of the bar stools was involved in the gunpowder scuffle only in the capacity of innocent bystander, but Denver cherishes his memory as part of its cultural heritage to this day. No President of Harvard, Denverites like to point out, has ever died in such gratifying style.

The Cult of The City That Was

Congenitally, perhaps, unable to share some of my professional colleagues' unbounded and starry-eyed enthusiasm which causes them to weep tears of impassioned nostalgia whenever the name of San Francisco is mentioned and who stand and uncover at every allusion to the Old Palace, the dollar dinner with a quart of Napa Valley corrosive sublimate thrown in at the Poodle Dog and the halcyon time Before-the-Fire generally, I still find San Francisco the most durable of cities and an emotional tranquilizer without peer save the immemorial metropolis of London.

In London the past is infinitely more durable, valid and immediate than the downgraded present, which is the true mintmark of great civilizations.

Something, on an abated scale, of course, of this self-identification with golden yesterdays explains San Francisco. Many a native reaches for a furtive handkerchief at the evocation of things he never saw. Men born since the Kaiser's war grow lyric at the recollection of Pisco Punches they never drank compounded by the ineffable Duncan Nicol at the Bank Exchange.

Only very old men with the facility of total recall like Uncle Roy Graves, who was driving a narrow-gauge locomotive out of Sausalito when the earthquake came, have any truly clear recollection of The City That Was, but the mind reels at the number of people who will tell you that they themselves often rode the

151

secret elevator that wafted discreet celebrants still seated in their first Pierce-Arrows to the upper floor of private dining rooms at the Poodle Dog.

Only in San Francisco, if I may coin a phrase, are the business meetings of the Historical Society regularly sluiced with champagne, albeit the stuff is of California origin.

I think, however, that the glory of San Francisco's unreconstructed personality is the hatred with which it views the loathesome men of vision who are always wanting to change the city's ways, look to the future and build bigger. Nowhere on earth is the forward looker held in greater revulsion and contempt. The banks that advertise California's industrial expansion, the chamber of commerce wowsers and rancid political jefes at Sacramento who proclaim the largest population in the Union, the architects of vomitous skyscrapers and leprous hotels of Texas dimensions are openly and articulately spat upon as something unclean, and well-bred women draw in their skirts when passing them in the street.

It is a town where housing development promoters enjoy the social status of procurers and San Franciscans look forward to a day when city planning commissioners and State highway engineers won't be able to get life insurance.

I think it is San Francisco's frankly atavistic suspicion of the devisings of modernity and the putrescences of progress that inspires the national jealousy that is a well-established manifestation of the times. In Kansas City or Keokuk big thinkers and forward lookers are treated with slavering adulation. In San Francisco they use the tradesmen's entrance.

In the Best Three-Alarm Tradition

One of its municipal assets that San Francisco has been slow to capitalize on (and it's the only one) is that from earliest times right down to the red hot here and now it has been the most combustible of American cities. It started burning up, as did all

Western diggings, in its shacktown days and was to all purposes wiped out three times in its first decade of organized existence. In varying degrees it has been doing it ever since. Its most sensational effort in 1906 was hailed as the biggest production number since 1871 when Chicago came close to total incineration.

Today San Francisco is the only American city I know of where amusement seekers of an evening have the choice of going to the films or going to a fire. Hotels, rooming houses and so called "housing developments" built on the principle of the open hearth furnace and warranted by the builders to ignite if an occupant runs a slight temperature, burn up with a regularity that provides every morning's newspaper with a fine five column cut showing water towers, extension ladders and people leaping into nets in splendid profusion. Being a fireman in San Francisco is a full-time occupation, honored, envied and photographed, and conflagration is a condition of life.

San Francisco alone maintains continuity with the splendid past, exploding, burning, collapsing on a round-the-clock basis, a pillar of smoke by day and fire by night. Curiously enough the town's municipal boosters don't make a good thing of it the way they attempt to exploit far less exciting assets. In actual fact San Francisco's conflagrations are about the only surviving aspect of its free-wheeling Nineteenth Century youth.

But if the town's official press agents don't know a good thing when it's smoldering right under their collective nose, San Francisco itself knows how to enjoy a good old-fashioned rooming house fire and savors a three-alarm warehouse blaze the way Philadelphians still appreciate old Madeira.

San Franciscans know that a good fire can have about it as much style as a fine dinner. A survivor of one recent major hotel holocaust, according to the public prints, confided to the fireman carrying him down a ladder: "This is the best fire we've had in the place in years."

I like to think that, although it is told of many American cities, San Francisco was in fact the setting for the story of the

153

two immigrants fresh from Ireland and new to city ways who were awakened by the passing engines on their first night in town. One of them went to the window in time to see the Amoskeag steam pumpers racing past, scattering sparks and live coals from their stacks and ash pans, bells clanging and horses galloping. "Quick, Pat, come and look," he shouted. "They're moving hell and two carloads have gone by already."

The Gift of Self-Delusion

Just what fascinates San Francisco with having been the birthplace of that foredoomed vehicle of creaking international futility, the United Nations, defies rational explanation. Somehow, it may be, it equates it with participation in the affairs of the great world on which Americans have so long gazed with the wistful longing of children in a Christmas toy shop. Sagacious in many matters, San Francisco has a gift of self-delusion which identifies it at an exalted spiritual level with events and causes which, in the eventual light of history, turn out to have been the sorriest of street accidents.

The United Nations, already smelling of embalming fluid, was born twenty years ago in San Francisco amidst the pious hosannas of the gullible and deluded. It has staggered down the corridors of time on sleeveless errands of frustration and as an incalculable liability to the United States and finally it came home to San Francisco to die on its twentieth anniversary.

Nobody but a professional politician lost to all shame any longer pretends the U.N. is salvageable, and prudent voices long ago suggested that it be gotten off the premises before, as it has now done, it died in the walls.

The Town That Knows No Hangover

One of the aspects of Virginia City, where this is being written, that your correspondent has long cherished in secret and now

154

reveals only out of compassion for suffering humanity, is one that might not be suspected in the light of the community's fame for having more saloons per capita than any town known to man, including Dublin, Washington and San Francisco.

For some reason as yet unplumbed by medical science but widely recognized by a full hundred years of talented and even dedicated tosspots, the Comstock is hangover-proof. Attribute it to the altitude as being micrometrically adjusted to foil the elsewhere universal katzenjammer. Lay it to the therapeutic qualities of Virginia City water which comes twenty-odd miles by flume, massive conduits and a syphon under Carson Valley from a secret lake in the Sierra high above the mere elevation of Lake Tahoe. Give credit to the long tranquil nights on the slopes of Mt. Davidson where the body refreshes itself in healthful slumber. Whatever may be the cause, and medical science would be well advised to look into the matter, a serious hangover is as rare as jewelry ore in a local antique shop, a truly crashing alcoholic collapse almost unknown.

Conduct among the products that line the back bar that elsewhere would have the happy participant bedded for a week or headed shakily for a drying out home has no worse consequence in C Street than a slight matutinal attack of Irish palsy, a minor affliction quickly allayed by any of a number of talented pharmacists named Mac, Eddie or Pat who practice their benevolent calling at convenient intervals the length of the main drag.

The Big Bonanza is only a memory for historians of the Old West and the deep mines of the Comstock have been in irretrievable borasca, lo these many years, but Virginia City has an imperishable asset passing all other treasure. As the only hangover-proof town in the world it's unique.

Homely Rite of Going for the Mail

Going to the post office for the morning mail in a small village is an experience in decline among an ever-growing number

155

of Americans grown effete and degenerate through dependence on rural free delivery or the motorized post of urban communities. This is a pity because going in person for the mail is a strand with the past, a thread of continuity with a better and simpler world. The true participant in this special form of communion goes for the mail in person. Sending a deputy or surrogate is either a form of aloofness and rejection of what amounts to a civil obligation, or a confession of indisposition. Unlocking the box or forgetting the key and asking the postmaster to please hand the mail through the window is an American rite, as homely as waving at trains or eating peanuts at the ball park.

It is also, for those privileged to participate in this ancestral observance, one of the few agreeable and completely approved contacts one has with the Federal Government. Only the postal service and its personnel enjoy the almost unanimous approval of the entire citizenry. Large numbers of the electorate despise their Congressmen. Many disapprove aspects of the Presidency. The Internal Revenue Service enjoys small affection. But only a churl dislikes the postman. He is almost the only functionary in our national pantheon of occupations, except perhaps barmen, who is held in universal esteem.

In Virginia City, where your correspondent gets his mail in clement season, the morning post office is about the last vestigial trace of community feeling in this ragbag community of ancient glories. Commissioners' meetings are slimly attended unless matters of great moment are at stake. Even the community drunks during which, under the massive pull of a Comstock full moon than which there is none fuller anywhere, all C Street was once accustomed to become as stoned as sailors are now a thing of the past. The shopkeepers and resort proprietors don't know each other any longer. The place is populated with strangers and the old-timers, the professional characters of only yesteryear, have gone away or joined the majority in the town's teeming cemeteries. Gone are the times when what Florence Edwards of the Silver Dollar Hotel called "the rapist's moon" could find the town's first citizens bending chairs and other bar fixtures over each other's heads at the Sazarac or Delta while blood flowed in the gutters and in the morning everybody would ask, "What seems to have happened?" Once, ten years ago, driving up the grade from Reno at five one morning, the writer turned down C Street to find five separate fist fights raging in the sunrise in the middle of the road.

Such community carnivals are now part of the Virginia City legend and walking to the post office for the morning mail is about the only time when the whole town speaks to each other on a predominantly fraternal basis.

Chessman and the Bleeding Hearts

The memory of the late and not specially lamented Caryl Chessman is being kept in a state of moldy green through the self-bailing hearts of newspaper columnists who have contrived to batten off his remains with an economy of waste that would do credit to vultures in the desert. There is also evidence that the case may be flaunted for some time to come as the soiled oriflamme of various groups of political and humanitarian malcontents mounting campaigns against capital punishment.

In such circumstances it may not be amiss briefly to review the issue from the vantage point of comparative tranquillity and to appraise from a small distance the elements involved in the final period of unrestrained hysteria.

The unassailable fact remains that almost none of the characters who contrived to climb aboard the calliope had any least discernible or vestigial concern with Caryl Chessman. The burps of protest against his execution were all from ringers.

The bleeding heart of humanity, for example, was headily represented by a Miss Brigitte Bardot, a foreign film imperson-

157

ator of prostitutes' roles and a non-resident of California, who took time off from waving her mammary glands at the customers to advocate clemency for a criminal eight thousand miles away whose name she had never heard before it was suggested by her press agent.

The all-enfolding teachings of Christ were impersonated by various mangy weirdies in beards who handed pamphlets to responsible citizens and hoped to attract enough attention to themselves at least to become arrested. The disturbed conscience of society found expression in mobs of juvenile delinquents in South American capitals, who smashed windows in loving tribute to a criminal whose crime they didn't know and whose name they couldn't spell. "Students," that somewhat nebulous category of the sexually unemployed, marched and got themselves photographed and in a few gratifying cases got their names right in the papers.

In short the ponderable hysteria and loudest sobbing were on the part of unabashed publicity-seekers, professional breast-beaters and frequenters of the literary pay toilets of the beatniks who had neither stake nor concern in the conduct of its affairs by the State of California.

In the lower echelons of exhibitionism, editorial pages brimmed over with letters from fat housewives couched in the jargon of the soap opera. In the higher brackets of responsibility, Governor Pat Brown kept urging God to attend the press conferences he arranged in Sacramento.

This ragtag of heaving bosoms and monsoons of editorial bathos represented amost everybody except the one group privileged to have some say in the matter: The California taxpayers who foot the bills and for the protection of whose persons and property the law is administered. The letters to the editor were notably lacking the names of responsible folk with some actual stake in the community and the conduct of its affairs.

158

Lacking any evidence to the contrary, it is safe to say that the vast, indeed overwhelming, majority of responsible citizens, voters and taxpayers in California heartily approved Chessman's bad end while lamenting the time and expense, in terms of money and nerves, required for its accomplishment. They might also, if polled, go on record as lamenting that Chessman inspired some of the worst newspaper writing in the long annals of California journalism.

It may be well to bear these facts in mind when opportunists and self-seekers undertake "spontaneous" campaigns for the abolition of capital punishment. The facts may well show that the people of California are in favor of more and faster executions, and for a greater variety of offenses than are now on the statute books, including among them the executions of lawyers involved in the unsuccessful defense of capital cases.

CHAPTER SIX

Bankers and Their Peers

Perhaps because his father was a banker and he himself was a man of some wealth, Mr. Beebe took bankers, banking and money itself quite seriously. While he was fond of quoting Gene Fowler's philosophy to the effect that money was something to be thrown off the back of trains, it is doubtful that he practiced it himself.

Some Sober Notes on Moneymen

If anybody will show me a banker with mutton chop whiskers who makes threatening motions at street urchins with his walking cane while descending from a Pierce-Arrow, he can have my account in a jiffy.

The new and folksy approach to money generally tends to disturb me emotionally. Banks with no teller's grilles or visible police guards, and bank robbers without hats and waistcoats—that sort of thing. I realize that the frock coat and probably even the cutaway morning coat has gone from the American business scene for good, but any banker who is going to have my money in his keeping has got to wear a waistcoat and a hat, and it would help if he carried gloves. Custodianship of money demands a certain nod in the general direction of the proprieties.

In my father's several jugs and those of his father before him there were no female tellers in need of brushing up on their makeup and exuding toothy charm to disguise the fact that there were insufficient funds in the vault to cover unforseen withdrawals.

There was gold currency available to cover every penny deposited by Bostonians who were no fools and would have organized a run on the bank if they had been greeted with any but the barest civility by any member of the management.

In my father's bank in Boston was a particularly menacing looking vice president with a brown beard and old-fashioned tail coat, who sat at a desk commanding the entrance. He always slashed viciously at the mail with what seemed to have been a specially sharp bayonet or disemboweling tool. When a guard apprised him of a caller waiting on him, he would snarl: "What does the rascal want? Turn him out!"

There was a man for my money, although I heard that after hours he was the soul of geniality and, as a hobby, could identify every headstone in the Granary Burying Ground in Tremont Street.

A San Francisco banker who had my unqualified approval was the late I. W. Hellman of Wells Fargo Bank. As he approached a monumental birthday, the employees of the firm were moved to arrange a picnic in his honor. Nothing riotous, just a sort of token of what passes for affection in large repositories of wealth, and possibly a half day's holiday. Mr. Hellman was moved by the news and the attendant invitation. He hadn't imagined anybody downstairs knew he was still around and he was touched. He was enchanted, too, with the idea of a picnic. "But I shall not, of course, be there," he said. Nothing frivolous for I. W. Hellman.

Another banker the current generation of glad handers might emulate was James Stillman, no man to let himself out on a limb or say anything for which he might be sorry. In one of the recurrent crisis of some years back Stillman, according to S. N. Behrman, was closeted for a full hour with Henry C. Frick while the reporters waited for a statement that was to allay the public fears. When it came it read:

The U.S. is a great and growing country.
Signed: James Stillman
Henry C. Frick
This is confidential and not for publication unless names are omitted.

My ideal banker was, of course, the ancient George F. Baker, who wore side wheel whiskers and a square derby hat to the end. He encouraged confidence in depositors just to look at him.

Every traffic officer in Manhattan Island saluted his passing in a vintage Rolls-Royce with two men on the box and a passenger compartment in which it was possible to sit bolt upright. Money was not frivolous to Mr. Baker, who incidentally endowed the Harvard Business School, and he would have taken a dim view of anyone who suggested it was.

Baker deserved the confidence he aroused. On a sick bed at the age of 80 during the 1930 depression, he heard that the stock market had achieved an all-time low. Struggling with the nurses, he commanded a car and headed downtown crying: "I've been in ten depressions and made money in every damned one of them! " He made money in 1930, 20 millions roughly.

The Golden Age of Banking

In my youth, which is popularly supposed to antedate Antietam, traveler's cheques were unknown and when you went abroad you went with a letter of credit, a document of the formidable dimensions of the *Boston Evening Transcript,* drawn by Kidder Peabody and filled with elegant spencerian flourishes which attested that your financial status back home in State Street was good up to a given amount. You presented this to Morgan Harjes in Paris, Baring Brothers or Coutts' in London, received what you required in gold coin, and the amount was inscribed, again with flourishes, in a balance column on the document itself.

But do not, pray, imagine that presenting a letter of credit in that now distant time, say, at Drexel Morgan & Company's London office was something you did by walking off the street and pushing it under the cashier's grille.

You made an appointment, preferably by letter of hand, sufficiently in advance for your *bona fides* to be thoroughly investigated by the Atlantic cable, and when the time came you donned a silk top hat and braided edge morning coat, white wash gloves and umbrella, ordered a per diem carriage with two horses from the hall porter or, if you were a fanatic on progress, a Rolls-Royce with two men on the box, and set out for The City attended by the fluttering handkerchiefs of your hotel staff as though for audience at Buckingham Palace.

Arrived at your banker's, where you were received by a Grand

166

Admiral of the Fleet in dress attire, you were passed through a succession of frock-coated gentlemen in waiting to the inner office of one of the partners where ancestral portraits glared at you disapprovingly as they had at people withdrawing funds since Waterloo. Matters of no least pertinence to finance were discussed while a clerk departed with your letter of credit and tea was served.

After that the partner donned his top hat and took you to lunch at the Junior Conservative Club, explaining that transactions of such moment (it might be all of 50 pounds) required a little time in the counting room, and after a three-hour lunch of Scotch grouse, Stilton and Port you returned to the bank, passed in reverse through the equerries and gentlemen in waiting, received your money in minted gold and went your way.

The Noblest Work of God

Whatever contrary expressions of sentiment he may occasionally be maneuvered into, the basic belief of every American is that the noblest work of God is a rich man. There are runners up for his esteem, baseball players and successful generals, popular philosophers and even scientists. The two dominant and ranking artisans of his most mature satisfactions, chefs and plumbing engineers, get scant attention although their contributions to civilization are immeasurably ahead of those of any statesman or religious leader in the record. Lip service is paid to poets, mathematicians and Episcopal bishops and there has been a wave of religious fervor in favor of the members of the Kennedy family, who come under both holy and fiduciary classifications, and are therefore either doubly sanctified or *hors de concours* depending on your prejudices.

But wealth, its acquisition, retention, increase, display, inheritance and custody generally is the major preoccupation of American intelligence and has been since the first merchant

167

princes of Boston engaged in the China trade in preference to the sermons of Cotton Mather. The American folk hero has variously been John Pierpont Morgan, William Henry Vanderbilt, Henry C. Frick, John Mackay, William Collins Whitney and Huntington Hartford. John D. Rockefeller was suspect for his personal appearance which suggested mean instincts and Andy Carnegie was a blowhard who dissipated the good will he might have evoked with homilies about thrift and other contaminated virtues. Americans like rich men who are also good spenders and there are more biographies devoted to William Randolph Hearst (otherwise a deplorable character), Bet a Million Gates, Diamond Jim Brady, James Gordon Bennett the Younger and Jim Fisk than any statesman you can name except Lincoln and Washington.

Deplorable or not, the fact of the record is that good works and lofty moral character have small appeal to Americans compared to vast wealth if it is handled in the right way; i.e.: arrogantly, ostentatiously and generously. To be acceptable a rich man must be a spender.

Arrogance—Their Endearing Charm

For a good many years now almost the only remembered utterance of Charles Francis Adams Jr., onetime President of the Union Pacific Railroad and later the ranking corporate historian of the railroad scene in general, has been his contemptuous verdict on the rich of the United States who, in his generation, were amassing enormous fortunes in the boom or bust economy of the post-Civil War era, building vast railroad networks between nowhere and nowhere, cornering the commodity markets and generally raising uninhibited hell while their wives engaged in social nip-ups in Newport and Fifth Avenue.

"I have met and known, tolerably well, a good many 'successful' men—'big' financially—men famous during the last half-century, and a less interesting crowd I do not want to encounter. Not one that I have ever known would I care to meet again, either in this world or the next; nor is one of them associated in my mind with the idea of humor, thought or refinement."

The remark coming from a fourth generation Adams, the generation which produced Brooks and Henry Adams, was not without its own aspects of the preposterous. The Adamses from earliest times had been notably the most aristocratic boors on the American scene, to a man, completely devoid of any least discernible sense of humor, without social graces or the amenities of polite living and associations to which their attainment entitled them, and generally curmudgeons.

For Charles Francis Jr., to denounce his financial peers for the very qualities for which the Adamses were celebrated was not without its overtones of hilarity, but he had just been tossed out of office in the Union Pacific by Jay Gould and his distaste may have been heightened by this indignity at the hands of a notorious man of disaster and no social status at all.

The distinguished historian, Allan Nevins, undertakes to refute the ungallant sentiments of Mr. Adams which have been used as a weapon against the "money grubbers" ever since they were uttered and to justify the rough-hewn tycoons of the Nineteenth Century as a cut above Adams' critical estimate of them.

He does so on the ground that, almost to a man, they were philanthropists in the end.

This it seems to me is altogether the wrong approach to an appraisal of the predatory acquisitors. It wasn't their open-handedness, in the face of extinction, with money they notoriously were unable to carry with them that, in proper fact, makes them the arch-heroes of the American legend. It was their magnificent arrogance and disregard for the smirking and emetic aspects of what has since been termed "social consciousness" that made them admired to an incomparable degree by the very people they were plundering, insulting and kicking in the teeth.

It was J. P. Morgan's complete indifference to public suffrage and the grovelling subservience he exacted on every hand and from men of every station that won him the name of "Jupiter" in his own lifetime. Andy Carnegie will be warmly recalled by posterity not for a multiplicity of public libraries but for his instructions to his chief clerk in his Pittsburgh days to physically kick downstairs all and any clergymen soliciting alms or good works, and often as not opened the door of his own office, which was on a lower floor, to add a contributory boot as the man of the cloth went past.

Henry E. Huntington will be remembered for his whim to have Gainsborough's "Blue Boy," which he had just purchased from the Duke of Westminster for $620,000, hung as the merest casual ornament in one of his three private railroad cars and was only deterred by the insurance company.

History will take pleasure in the memory of James J. Hill, not for having almost single-handedly brought the Northwest into the United States, but for having, in retribution for an imagined slight from the townsfolk, erased the town of Wayzata, Minnesota, from the map by ordering his trains no longer to stop there.

Conversely, Jay Gould is remembered with contempt, not for having ruined thousands and nearly wrecked the national economy, but for having hurriedly fled the scene of disaster in a hack with drawn shutters.

Never Mind Your Image

If anything were needed to point up the soupy thinking characteristic of a nation being brainwashed into conformity to the character of Caspar Milquetoast, the amiable little poltroon in the cloth hat, it is the intelligence carried in the press of the

170

land that "Wall Street" is getting worried again about its "image" in the American consciousness.

Wall Street, if there is such an entity, should relax. It never had an image until the mendacious psychopaths of Madison Avenue, a much less attractive thoroughfare in its implications, sold them this bogus bill of goods.

Wall Street, the stock market, big business and money generally have always been at their best when they enjoyed the worst possible press. The captains and the kings of finance Americans have most admired have been the most ruthless, hardest-headed and most arrogant, and the attempts of the image makers to debase them with a sort of wretched humanitarianism has been on a par with the campaign to make bankers folksy.

Ivy Lee, who emplaced a midget on the lap of the Younger John Pierpont Morgan during a Senate investigation, although he was widely hailed at the time as a benefactor of capitalism and a humanizer of big business, in fact did banking and finance generally more harm than Jay Gould ever did, and Gould was a superman of disaster. The midget act cheapened the image of money and worse than that it cheapened the image of the name of Morgan.

Never mind Abe Lincoln or Mr. Washington or even the now godlike Robert E. Lee. The one name at whose mention all Americans, and most of the rest of the world, stood and uncovered in his time was that of the Elder Morgan. That dynastic greatness isn't hereditary was demonstrated when his son permitted a dwarf to be placed in his lap instead of throwing him through the window.

Money, which is pure quintessence of everything that everybody wants most, is above amiability and folksiness. The reason the Texas archmillionaire is held in universal contempt and detestation isn't because, nine times out of ten, he's an illiterate boor, but because he affects the mein and habit of his inferiors.

Rich Texans insist on remaining ranch hands or drill riggers despite ample resources for bettering their estate and persons. Their gestures of philanthropy run to Methodist universities, football teams and drum majorettes, and the polite amenities of wealth as they are observed elsewhere are rejected and suspect. The Texas imagination doesn't extend beyond barbecues and Cadillacs, so that cultivated Houston people who keep English servants, dress for dinner, serve wine at meals and otherwise comport themselves like gentlefolk, do so apologetically or in secret. The great world has yet to come to Texas.

If the oil-rich dolts of Dallas and Houston were worthy of the largesse that chance had showered down on them, they would latch onto the inescapable fact that rich men, to achieve universal respect, should act like their counterparts elsewhere and live up to the estate they have achieved. An oil man with an estimated income of $100,000 a day snapping his galluses and eating at drive-ins is an offense against God and any propriety you care to name.

Show me a man accustomed to the presence and administration of large sums of money who wants it known that he is plain as an old shoe and I'll show you an outsize heel.

Nothing Frivolous About Money

A good many aspects of the current facade of American business leave me cold, but none of them colder than the notion of a warm and friendly bank patronized, presumably exclusively, by warm and friendly people.

Bank depositors, I know damned well because I am one of them, are not warm and friendly people. Where money is concerned they are cold, avaricious and mean, and no billboard depicting an idiot-faced depositor shoving money through a grille with glad helloes to the teller can alter the fact.

Money and its every implication are hard realities and by long odds the most important facts of life a man is apt to encounter between the incubator and the incinerator of the welfare state. Now and then some dolt advances the fancy notion that love is superior in its connotations to currency and the devalued state of the dollar may lend some support to the thesis. On the basis of a forty-cent dollar, love doesn't have to set a very exalted price on itself to be in greater request.

There is nothing, however, essentially frivolous about money and the bank that treats it with jovial familiarity and represents its own function as one of amiable sociability rather than of meticulous trust is simply doing the whole business of banking in the eye.

Most people feel a fundamental distrust for a genial banker. I, who am perhaps more cynical, know flatly and absolutely that a genial banker is a thief and an absconder, at least potentially and probably factually.

Banking is, or used to be, an austere and reputable business that was close to being a profession in its implications of probity and scrupulous conduct. Any attempt to degrade it to the level of a cinema palace or supermarket degrades the merchandise in which it deals. Nowhere is the aphorism that familiarity breeds contempt more applicable than in a bank.

No financial institution should admit, let alone advertise, that it wants business. Its services should be available only on the most stringent terms and on the basis of irreproachable security to suppliants with crooked knee and hat in hand. The attempt to paint a banker as an amiable lout, eager for the affection instead of the terror and admiration of the community cheapens banking and cheapens money. No bank where any officer of importance is visible on its premises or available to casual contact with the customers gets any money of mine. I want one where no employee is permitted in the same elevator with the president and the tellers look like misers by George Cruikshank.

The Boston and New York bankers of my remembered youth looked the part and hired no advertising agencies to say they wanted friends. Everybody wanted to be on good terms with bankers, but the sentiment was in no way reciprocated. I never saw a soft shirt on a banker or a soft hat either until I was out of college, and the sight so unnerved me when I did encounter a vice president of the Old Colony Trust Company in Temple Place without a hat or gloves, even though he wore a three-inch wing collar, that I went directly to the bar in Locke Ober's Winter Place Wine Rooms and got stiff as a plank. The bartender wanted to know if I was in trouble and I told him I'd lost my faith in God.

Where Are The Giants of Yesteryear?

It's been a long time since, as a youth, I sometimes accompanied my father to convocations of the banking mighty and the industrial omnipotent, and I must report that change is abroad in the land, and not especially of a reassuring nature either. When I first began to notice such things railroad presidents could be identified not only by their bold-wing collars, large Havannah Puros and cavalry colonel mustaches, but by a certain assurance with which they commanded what they wanted. An almost godlike magnifico of my Boston youth was Frederick H. Prince, an associate of Frick and Mellon, who carried a riding whip to business meetings and once knocked a groom senseless with a polo mallet for riding him down on his private polo field.

In Pittsburgh recently I found myself surrounded by presidents, executive vice presidents and chairmen of the board of great railroads many of whom, I regret to report, wore no waistcoats, called inferiors by their first names and slapped financial reporters on the back. The principal topic of conversation at this particular rendezvous of the fur trade was, obviously, the impending multi-billion dollar merger of the Central and Pennsyl-

174

vania Railroads. Yet here were men of great substance involved in a massive financial operation, meeting together on the common ground of cold pheasant sandwiches and Martinis in a good will festival that, late in the evening, achieved approximately the exalted level of a college reunion.

It baffled identification or proper evaluation, and I was glad that the greatest financial reporter of his generation, Clarence Barron, wasn't there to see it. Mr. Barron owned and published *The Wall Street Journal.* He wore the glossiest top hat in New York and did his own financial sleuthing when his staff couldn't get a story, and his bifurcated beard was an oriflamme of high finance generally.

Mr. Barron, a big eater, ate himself each year through six progressively larger dinner suits, and when he couldn't get into the largest of them took three months at Battle Creek before starting over again. Pheasant sandwiches and Martinis wouldn't have held him up.

Few of the railroad presidents clustered in the bars of the Duquesne Club like autumn leaves on Vallombrosa looked the part. Almost none acted it. The one spectacular exception to this endless vista of calculated mediocrity was Fred B. Whitman, president of the Western Pacific, who, like Richard Corey in the Robinson poem, glitters when he walks and looks like a casting agency chairman of the board. Mr. Whitman is a Harvard man. On the second day of the bash, he borrowed somebody's business car and left. "I'm going to New York and get stiff," he said. "Perhaps in the Times Square subway station at rush hour where it's more exclusive."

A Disturbing Episode

At a Lake Tahoe resort that shall be nameless, I encountered the president of one of the largest banks in the West. He was seated at a table with two well-known gamblers and a hotel man,

175

attired in a sports shirt of alarming pattern with no necktie. He was drinking highballs which were fetched by a cocktail waitress in an even more alarming absence of much of anything except black silk stockings reaching up to there, secured with crimson garters.

The conversation wasn't exactly depraved but was of an order appropriately low and in keeping with the surroundings, being concerned with Democratic politics.

Since we were all there together, I could see no valid reason for not joining the party for a few belts of Jack Daniel's and branch and attempting to elevate the conversation with Republican politics.

Now it so happens that I have a modest amount on deposit with the bank represented by the presidential sport and that its reputation is a very good one. Further, there is no reason why the banker shouldn't drink whiskey with gamblers who were probably a good deal more important depositors than I. But the episode disturbed me vaguely, in much the same manner that I was disturbed some years ago, late in the evening, in passing the old Fifth Avenue Bank in New York to see several of the tall windows of its counting rooms open somewhat at the top.

Despite the fact that the Fifth Avenue Bank had an open fireplace with a real fire in winter and kept its officers at roll top desks, I withdrew my account the next day and put the money elsewhere, under the dress shirts in my bureau at home to be exact. A bank that leaves its windows open at night isn't a good risk.

CHAPTER SEVEN

The Animal Kingdom

Any species having at least four legs was automatically assured of Mr. Beebe's approval. Conversely, any man or any institution that harmed any animal anywhere invited his wrath. He loved his dogs with a passion only another dog lover could understand.

When The Meek Inherit The Earth

Me, I have always been on the side of Moby Dick. I consider it hilarious when the bull gets his horn into the matador's suit and disembowels him in public. On the lamentably rare occasions when the lion gets the white hunter, I incline to shout, as J. P.Morgan is reported to have done when Theodore Roosevelt announced his impending African safari, health to the lions.

When recently a flight of starlings contrived to down a flying machine in Boston, I was only restrained by the shushing of cooler heads from noisy evidence of my enthusiasm and perhaps some sort of starling award. The starlings were of course branded as antisocial and demands were made for their extermination. This brought the Audubon Societies into conflict with the airlines, a spectacle of rare delight.

If man is indeed, as various moral philosophers and historians incline to believe, approaching the terminal of his existence and about to contrive his own universal taking-off in a wholesale allegory of futility, there are those who will feel it is just about time. He has made it rough from earliest times for the animals who are everywhere his superiors from almost every aspect save his matchless genius for evil and capacity for infecting everything he touches.

No bird, fish or beast of the most debased sort has ever come up with such monuments to his own exalted intellect as Communism, nuclear warfare or jet propulsion and for this negative quality alone the animals would seem worthy of preservation.

Now there seems to be a good chance that just this will happen. Various scientists not actively engaged in facilitating the suicide of the human race see a chance that when man, to the accompaniment of loud screams of his ineffable superiority, has flushed himself down the drain of history, the cycle of animal life will begin all over again.

This could be heartening news for the entire cosmic scheme

of things where man, even on the brink of eternity, is threatening to infect other planets with the incurable diseases of his own devising, were it not for a single fly in this promising ointment. A recommencement of the life cycle on earth might once again produce man. It's all very discouraging.

Day of Infamy in Pearisville, Va.

Now and then there is perpetrated in these United States an offense against human decency in the name of judicial expediency so outrageous and so beyond the bounds of reasonable experience even in the fallible world of courts and law that men and women everywhere on hearing of it may be pardoned for having doubts about the whole structure of justice in the land.

Nobody in his right mind expects the administration of what passes for justice to be unerring if only because it is implemented by common men who, however exalted their momentary advancement in the social fabric, still, as the saying goes, pull on their trousers one leg at a time in the morning. At Judgment Day we are promised flawless justice and that is probably soon enough.

But you can go a far piece down the road of judicial infamy before you will encounter a story of such putrescent administration of callous and brutalized judicial authority as came over the wires a short time back from Pearisville, Virginia.

Virginia's day of degradation was the one in which an elderly gentleman, Jim Laing, was sentenced to four months in jail and a fine of $1000 for not delivering his dog Ricky to the public hangman. Ricky, so they said, had killed a sheep. Whether he did or not is no matter and hardly available to determination at this remove. Dogs do kill sheep and, almost inevitably, the sheep is on the way to be killed by men for reasons no more natural or acceptable than that which prompts dogs to do it.

181

So a Virginia court decreed that Ricky should be, as the phrase delicately has it, destroyed so that the special and holy privilege of killing sheep might remain a monopoly of human beings as God intended. Mr. Laing fought the decision as far as his means permitted, aye even to the Governor's office. The holy and sanctimonious Governor of Virginia, the Honorable A. S. Harrison, Jr., turned the appeal down and arrayed the power and authority of a once-respected commonwealth against an old gentleman and his dog.

So when the time came for Mr. Laing to turn Ricky over to the public hangman he didn't know the whereabouts of Ricky, and the Circuit Court of Giles county in its awful majesty sentenced Mr. Laing to four months in jail for what it was pleased to smirk was "contempt of court."

Contempt of court? What can a court given to such idiot fantasies of arrogance and brutality expect other than the hissing contempt of reasonable men and women everywhere? What can be said of the people of a community who, confronted with the evidence of such septic degeneracy in their servants, do not invade the county seat, burn the courthouse flat and cook the judiciary over the ashes?

Does the Circuit Court of Giles county or His Butchering Excellency, Governor A. S. Harrison, Jr., really imagine that the exercise of the authority of the State to imprison an old gentleman for protecting his pet from the public hangman makes for anything but seething contempt for the executive and judicial hierarchy of Virginia and all its works?

I for one, think opinion everywhere will expectorate on the image of Virginia and that the name of Jim Laing and Ricky will be honored in the land.

So when the time comes to shovel heartless Governor A. S. Harrison, Jr., under the sod and when they come to plant the several hanging judges of the Circuit Court may all the dogs in

Virginia be apprised of the exact whereabouts of these choice locations in the graveyard so that all may use them as canine conveniences.

And may Ricky be the first to avail himself of the opportunity.

On the Side of the Leopards

Not content with killing off what wild life is left to the countryside in the holy name of agricultural profits with the wholesale misuse of pesticides, and as though the record for animal butchery by the American people in other generations were not already shameful enough, American women of fashion it now seems are reaching lethally for another continent to despoil of its animal life.

The National Audubon Society, which conventionally limits its purview to the protection of bird life but occasionally takes a stand on conservation in general, has launched a crusade against leopard coats for women on the grounds that the African leopard as a species will soon be extinct if the style persists in attracting cold-blooded, egocentric and brutal American women.

It takes seven leopards to make a woman's fur coat of their skins and, despite an average price of between $5000 and $10,000 for each garment, more than 1000 were sold by American furriers last year. This figure, according to the conservative Audubon Society, is 80 per cent in excess of the rate of reproduction in the jungles of Africa and the rate of acceleration is increasingly malevolent.

It remained for a Mr. Louis Cohen, president of the American Fur Merchants Association, to state with singular frankness the attitude toward ordinary standards of civilized conduct shared apparently by the pelt mongers of Seventh Avenue.

"I'm sure I don't know what useful purpose leopards serve,"

183

deposed Mr. Cohen in a statement to the press, "but also I don't think there is much threat to them. After all, only the very rich can afford a leopard skin coat."

No useful purpose was served by the plains buffalo in the thinking of the hunters who so narrowly missed making them extinct.

Neither did the herons, bluebirds and orioles that were once fashionable in female millinery, if you take the word of fashion designers and bonnet manufacturers.

Nor did the passenger pigeons serve a useful purpose in the eyes of a generation of American yahoos that eliminated the species from the skies.

It might only be fair in return to inquire patronizingly what useful purpose is served by the existence of Louis Cohen or what validity there is for the mercantile activities of the American Fur Merchants Association? Presumably, the shooting, skinning, tanning and manufacturing into female apparel of this confraternity of commercial murderers would come into conflict with the law. The risk entailed in the procurement of these hides would, therefore, automatically put them in a price bracket only within the reach of the very rich.

The analogy is in every way a legitimate one save for the circumstance that it may be doubted if Mr. Cohen and his Seventh Avenue contemporaries would make very good looking women's coats. There are those, too, who would argue that, being alleged members of the human race, anything deriving from their existence would be inferior to that deriving from other zoological species.

In my personal book, the butchery through the agency of native spears or high powered rifles of the 7000 members of the Fur Merchants Association necessary to make 1000 coats would be no loss to the community.

Purely and simply, the world would be better off without them but the rate of exchange of one fur merchant for one leopard would seem disproportionate. Make it 1000 Cohens per leopard and let's do business.

Happy Hunting Among the Obituaries

Amidst the multiplicity of calamities which throng the columns of the daily press as testimony to man's total incapacity for rational conduct of any sort, there is a recurrent news dispatch, alas, at too infrequent intervals, which brightens my morning for me and makes it a day marked with a star.

These are accounts in which natural forces, or better still the animals of nature, turn on offending or idiot mankind and rend him sorely. An alpinist, perhaps, next to the astronaut the supreme monument to the limitless dimension of human folly, engulfed in an avalanche or bottomless crevasse or hurled to destruction from some hitherto inviolate crag where he had no conceivable reason for being soothes me more effectively than half a dozen capsules of Librium 25.

The intelligence that the test pilot of some improbable hell cart has been incinerated in the stratosphere when his agency of propulsion dissolved around him has the sedative satisfactions of half a bottle of Jack Daniel's consumed in congenial company in an air-conditioned and soundproof grotto.

A fall from even a modest height may well be gratifyingly fatal to a yahoo putting up a television mast, and the pestilential creep who carries a transistor radio in his pocket when walking the street is satisfactory when ground into hamburger by an unheard fire truck.

These are but encounters between *homo sap* and the impersonal forces of natural and contrived physics, and rate comparatively low in the entertainment scale, although there is a compelling grandeur in the delusion of the Federal Government which will flush a number of billions of dollars down the toilet to achieve the moon with the assured prospect that the dolt

185

who gets there will remain emplaced forever as an ultimate and truly cosmic monument to human futility.

Far more gratifying than these agencies for the elimination of man and worthy of greater commemorative rejoicing are the occasions when other and superior animals, harrassed beyond endurance by the beastliness of the human species, turn on aggressive man and shred him to bits.

The shark which engorges a skin diver shrouded in garments of juvenile imbalance and armed with patent weapons for the destruction of marine life that can be of no profit to him I regard as hilarious and a benevolent agent of nature reminding mankind that he cannot, with impunity, invade all the universe. I hear there are squid which can swallow a grown man as one ingests a cocktail canape and they have my unqualified, if removed, approval.

The man-eating tiger which decimates entire Asian villages has my enthusiastic endorsement as an agency for population control.

The trainer who is now and then munched up by a lion as thousands cheer, and the matador who is served to his admirers *en brochette* on the horns of a bemused bull are rich fare for the connoisseur of retribution as part of the natural scheme of things and are only infrequently on the menu, but for the less demanding there is always the hunting season in which hundreds of Americans make sieves of each other while undertaking the elimination of what wild life is left to the countryside. The season for burning powder may even be one of modified rejoicing if one keeps shrewd watch on the obituary columns.

Not all the gunshots that resound in the autumn woodlands signify the death of something wild, and beneath the overtones of rifle fire there runs the cheerful leitmotiv of the ambulance siren hasting the dismantled nimrod to be stuffed and mounted by the taxidermists of the morticians' guild.

186

So, as the firearms manufacturers urge, give your boy a rifle. Don't let anything deter you. The life he takes may be your own.

Looking Backward to the Horse

One of the great and well-established fallacies of the American philosophy, and only removed by the fact of the automobile from being today the universal article of faith it once was, is the belief that the horse is an animal of intelligence, devotion and general good cheer.

The horse is not and never was an animal of very much intelligence, only of great utilitarian availability and sometimes of esthetic satisfaction. Dogs as a race are infinitely more intelligent and a thousand times as devoted. Porpoises, I am given to know when at the dentist's where *Life* magazine is handy, are perhaps more intelligent than even dogs, although I would not remark this in the hearing of any dog of my acquaintance.

My prejudice against the theory of equine sapience had its origins in my boyhood in Wakefield, Massachusetts, where most of the horses of which there were perhaps 15 at a time on my father's farm regarded me with an overt hostility that may have marked them as animals of rare taste and discernment although I never thought so at the time. The big farm horses that worked the hay wagons, tedders and manure spreaders were always stepping on my feet when I was sent into their stalls to fetch them and later, when I was old enough to ride, the saddle horses were always falling under me and, once fallen, rolling on the Boy Beebe with lethal intent.

Later, as a youth on the streets of Boston, I learned that my low estimate of horse intelligence was shared by a majority of the cabmen, draymen, delivery boys, ice men and mounted police who peopled the daily life of a city dweller. The cops' horses were, of course, the pick of their kind and trained to a

187

variety of useful and ornamental attainments, but the cab horses were forever demonstrating that irrational was the name for Dobbin.

"They be stupid beasts, dough-brained like a County Kerry Irishman," was the verdict of Fitz, the public hackman whose stand was adjacent to the apartment in which we lived in winter at the corner of Bay State Road and Deerfield Street. Fitz hailed from County Mayo and taught me to ride a bicycle.

The first street accident I ever witnessed was when Fitz' horse took fright at former-Governor Curtis Guild's new Pierce-Arrow limousine and ran away with his growler careening wildly behind him after it had knocked down and run over its owner. I thought Fitz was killed, but he emerged from the gutter brushing refuse from his person and swearing when he caught up with the beast he'd kill *him*. It wasn't necessary. The animal killed himself running into an ice wagon at the end of the block. Mrs. Guild, of course, as the provocateur of the contretemps, bought Fitz a new horse.

Christmas Is for the Animals, Too

This is the season when a not inconsiderable volume of commercial holiness is evoked by the image prominently displayed in Sunday supplements and department store windows of the well publicized manger in Bethlehem where one of the world's more durable religious ventures had its inception.

There is, however, an aspect of the business of the manger at Bethlehem that seems to me to have been neglected by theologians and partisans of the Christian legend and one which symbolizes in its overall implications the reason I am no communicant of this particular faith or superstition, whichever you prefer to call it.

The source of my reluctance in the matter of revealed religion may be summarized in the midst of the cozy scene of the

Holy Family surrounded by wise men prudently bearing gifts by the question: who's that looking in through the window? It must occur to agnostic intelligences that it is the image of an ox or donkey or other domestic animal who, having done his day's work in the fields, came home to find his accustomed premises pre-empted. The management of the inn had let his space out to another tenant and now the unfortunate beast is out in the cold without his dinner or a place to spend the night.

There have been fanciful artists who have depicted the scene with the aforementioned donkey and/or ox standing by in attitudes of respectful admiration along with the three wise men who started currying divine favor with gifts early in the game, but this I beg to doubt is a faithful rendition of fact. No animal in its right mind is going all out in enthusiasm for somebody who has just taken his bed for the night.

The dispossession of whatever animals may have been involved in the Bethlehem interlude was, it seems to me, a sample and premonition of what was to be the attitude of the Christian establishment on a larger scale and from that time until now.

Animals aren't included in the Christian scheme of things. They aren't included in Christmas either. I don't see the SPCA or any Humane Society listed, along with the Boy Scouts and Red Cross, in the beneficiaries of any community Christmas fund. Christmas charity is only available to those who can exploit their misery pictorially and verbally, a devising not available to puppies, kittens and neglected Shetland ponies.

The animals are as explicitly barred from Christian consideration on its highest and holiest feast day as were the original animals dispossessed from the manger at Bethlehem.

These are some of the reasons why, at Yuletide when the self-constituted and exclusive Christian community is busy perpetuating its own anointed holiness and even ponying up money for a variety of good works to prove to itself something it already explicitly believes, my sympathies are with the animals.

189

There isn't a human frailty or misfortune imaginable to the lexicon of mischance that isn't underwritten today by high-pressure organizations of charity, by billion-dollar foundations with more money than their directors know what to do with, or by the state, eager to purchase the suffrage of mendicancy.

There are no such monolithic and moneyed foundations for the protection of animals. The various Humane Societies, Animal Shelters and the magnificently motivated SPCA have no resources for the high-pressure campaigns mounted in the name of ailments most people never heard of.

There are no homeless dogs or cats or ponies rattling the cup or wearing Santa Claus suits on the corners or rolling their wheelchairs on television. They can't ask for your kindness and if you give it they won't thank you.

That is why my Christmas money goes where I know it is most needed and most deserved. To the animals.

CHAPTER EIGHT

Intelligence from London

His love affair with the city of London lasted throughout Mr. Beebe's life. No other city, not even San Francisco, gave him the all-around satisfaction and the feeling of being at the very heart of civilization and in the very center of all civilized living. All the artifacts of British life, from a bottle of Bass's Ale to the bonnet of his Rolls-Royce, he considered absolutely first-class and the natural requirements of every man of taste.

Where Gout Is A Badge of Honor

To the American visitor to London, accustomed to the depressing spectacle at home of businessmen lunching off a thin sandwich and iced tea, while their absurd womenfolk take Metrecal, the most cheering sight available to daily view at Overton's, Simpson's, Scott's, or any of the multiplicity of West End luxury dining rooms frequented by executives, is that of regiments of striped-trousered representatives of management sitting down to luncheons that may run to better than two hours and include cocktails, foie gras, a thick soup, salmon, lobster or sole with hock or claret, a small steak or partridge, followed by salad, cheese and dessert, all in full-size orders, and a bottle of champagne and port to finish.

The practice of lunching well and at leisure is universal. Englishmen have never taken much stock in the fanatic fads for dieting that recurrently sweep the United States like a pestilence, and they offer in hundreds of thousands a refutation of the widely-held belief in America that weight is a certain inhibition of longevity.

The sight of white-haired, red-faced, monocled Englishmen in the seventies weighing 250 and up, lunching daily year in and year out off five or six substantial courses of unimaginable caloric value with appropriate wines and spirits, and looking forward to an identical way of life for perhaps another 20 years, would give Gayelord Hauser the vapors and drive advocates of the blackstrap molasses diet to madness.

It also gives pause to Americans who imagine that England's widely heralded deficit economy and its consequent "austerity" means a universal diet of skim milk and meatless veal loaf. Gastronomic austerity in England means lunch with fewer than four wines.

Englishmen regard the gout, overweight and liver disorders that can accrue to 70 or 80 years of port and partridge in the light of battle scars won on the field of honor. The other evening at the grill of the Cafe Royal in Regent Street, certainly the most ornate restaurant this side of the Hotel de Paris at Monte Carlo, and one whose rococo mirrors date from the middle Sixties, we watched the arrival of dinner guests in a variety of decrepitude that would amaze Battle Creek.

Valetudinarians, in every stage of decay short of mortification, limped, hobbled, or in a few cases were wheeled by attendants to their regular tables where silver ice buckets bulged with foil-topped bottles and the caviar nestled in beds of strawberry leaves. Each was accorded a reception from the management worthy of the hero of many years of mighty achievement and valiant deeds.

"That's Sir Eric," the maitre d'hotel told us, in the hushed tones reserved elsewhere for the arrival of the Archbishop of Canterbury, as a fine, 80-year-old gentleman was assisted to his place from a bath chair by two reverent lackeys. "Been eating here since the Old Queen's time, regular. Got gout in both feet, terrible, liver like a Rugby football. Our best customer. Great advertisement for the house, Sir Eric."

Not all the captains and the kings have departed, nor the fire sunk on all the dunes and headlands of England.

London Out of Season

Emotionally stabilized by centuries of maturity and national adjustment to the occasional aberrations of the rest of the world, the English cheerfully assume to themselves the blame for such cracks in the national façade of decorum as may be represented by Teddy Boys, Broadway musical importations and extra dry Martinis.

The traveler can go a far piece in London today without encountering any visible or tangible mutations of British character or conduct that can, by the most fevered imagining, be attributed to Yankee influence.

At this season of year and before the great tourist influx that dates from the end of June and the closing of college terms in the United States the percentage of Americans in public restaurants, theaters and hotels is so small as to be microscopic. The impact of American speech, folkways, attire or personal conduct on the London image is so minute as to be, to all intents and purposes, non-existent.

In a few weeks, of course, the air steerage tourist, bandoliered in cameras, hatless, screaming for ice water and accompanied by his native jungle bride and savage young with the accents of Minneapolis and the manners of Fort Worth, will be giving the beadles in Burlington Arcade a bad time by carrying their own purchases and photographing the unresisting guards at St. James' Palace, but for the moment London is as English as it was in the age of Charles II.

The Grouse Get Even

The casualties of the Scotch grouse season, always severe in August and September, are taking fearful toll this year of the flower of English chivalry and, were Parliament in session, it is possible questions would be asked concerning the need for this alarming drain on the national resources of manpower.

Already the prescriptions by Harley Street physicians of Benemid, colchicine and other recognized ameliorants of gout have set a record, and Bath chair rentals to totally disabled epicures laid low as a result of doing battle with the game menus at Rule's, the Connaught and Mirabelle, where the grouse-eating season is in full swing, have set a new and alarming record.

The number of retired colonels and high-ranking civil servants appearing daily in their Pall Mall club windows with a foot swathed in bandages and elevated to a conspicuous level is reaching alarming proportions. The populace often gathers to cheer as a stricken nobleman, one foot encased in a carpet slipper, is eased into his Bentley by solicitous club servants, and nursing homes in Bloomsbury are crowded with gout patients clamoring for release so that they may rejoin their regiments at the Cafe Royal and Simpson's in the Strand.

Even more grave are the tidings reported in the morning papers as this dispatch is being filed concerning the wounding whilst shooting in Scotland on a Deeside grouse moor of Sir Dennis Stuckley, 54, fifth baronet, of Hartley Abbey, Bideford, Devon, and a former High Sheriff of Devon, who is being rushed to London by special overnight train from Aberdeen. A private ward has been reserved for him at King Edward VII Hospital for Officers.

Sir Dennis was injured when he was struck by a number of birdshot discharged by accident whilst shooting the preserve of Sir Malcomb Barclay-Harvey of Dinnet House, Morven Hill. Also slightly injured but remaining with his men at the scene of combat was Brigadier Charles Richard Britten of Kenswick Manor, Worcester, former High Sheriff of Worcester.

The joint accidents partake of insult as well as injury since, traditionally, the English make a practice of shooting up grooms and beaters and even an occasional keeper, but almost never a fifth baronet and former high sheriff. There are almost certain to be grave repercussions in government circles.

One of these may be the creation and award of some special honor for casualties sustained in the ceaseless border warfare with the fiercely individualistic and unreconstructed Scotch grouse. Wounds suffered in the taking of game are regarded by Englishmen as ranking in dignity with those achieved in defense of king and country, and it is possible that Sir Dennis will be awarded another battle ribbon to wear with dinner dress.

The Empire vs. LBJ

Englishmen not only love their dogs, they make their love for them a public article of faith amounting to martyrdom and the impact of the almost pastoral photos taken on the White House lawn of President Johnson holding his beagle by the ears is sure to arouse impassioned protest through the accustomed British channels of formal indignation including "questions in The House" and letters to the editor of *The Times*.

Without waiting for these eventual and foregone demonstrations on behalf of canine rights, your correspondent sought grass roots opinion at its unimpeachable source and fountainhead, a gentleman's saloon bar.

Suitably needled in advance, Mr. Dennis Hawkes, senior barman at the George Tavern, Brown's Hotel, asked loudly and what did we think of President Johnson and his dogs?

The effect was even more cataclysmic than the most depraved *agent provocateur* could have asked. Four hitherto well-mannered dogs of assorted breeds who had been quietly abiding each other's company moored to the hatrack at the door erupted in a dogfight of pre-Sarajevo Balkan dimensions, overturned the hatrack and dragged it snarling and yapping through the elderly West End types accustomed to a quiet eye-opener first thing in Brown's.

When comparative order had been restored, the British major with red mustaches whose bassett hound was suspected of having started the tumult, turned to your correspondent with fire in his eye and Chivas Regal on his breath and demanded to know what would happen to a public servant in God's country, England in this context, who so barbarously used God's unoffending creatures?

"He would be thrashed, sir, thrashed, and I say it with all respect to your nationality, for the bounder he would be."

Here the major looked around for his umbrella as if to demonstrate his sentiments on the person of your reporter, but his Briggs had been thoughtfully removed from reach by Mr. Hawkes much as the trail herders had been deprived of their handguns on entering Abilene or Newton in the seventies.

The reporter, in what proved to be an ill-chosen concept of

198

mild rebuttal, remarked that he was a dog owner himself and would even at the moment be accompanied by his own beloved Towser but for the insane British quarantine regulations governing alien pets.

"You just prove what I was saying," frothed the major. "All American dogs are rabid. I've read it somewhere. You'd loose herds, no packs, of mad dogs on us if given your way. Right here in Albermarle Street. Packs of mad dogs."

A discernible shiver ran through the palsied communicants at the George bar and, having precipitated the gravest international crisis since the seizure of the Confederate emissaries from the *Trent* in 1863, the reporter saw fit to retire, avoiding by a prudent margin the herd, no pack, of hostile dogs at the doorway.

The Decline of Freedom in England

The calculated campaign in England against cigarettes, which can be counted on to extend to cigars if it meets with any success, is an extension of the determination of the current British government to make complete serfs of Britons who are more and more harassed by paternalism while bravely singing that they never, never will be slaves.

Anybody who has ever attempted to get stiff in England knows that it is virtually impossible, the watered spirits, microscopic portions and fantastic prices being what they are, and English drinkers are inhibited by more drastic restrictions in the form of closing hours, Sunday observances and other impediments to personal liberty than would be tolerated by the citizens of Philadelphia. The unsavory truth of the matter is that, from the proud pinnacle of personal liberty, independence and freedom of choice which have been England's principal contribution over the years, to the mores of civilization, Englishmen have been bribed with free false teeth and threatened by arrogant demagogues into a conformity which makes the American intellectual goose step appear a snake dance of dionysiac dimensions.

The pitiful spectacle of a once-haughty race of free men being terrified by the threat of lung cancer evoked by professional quacks for no other reason than the achievement of political tyranny is not a reassuring one. Slavery of a rather repulsive sort is stalking in Temple Bar and the Strand, not as explicitly, but just as degradingly as it does in the concentration camps of Siberia.

We in the United States have learned about the compulsions of professional moralists the hard way. Remember prohibition, when for thirteen long years tens of millions of people had to stay barreled to the hat, some of them against their every taste and inclination, as a means of overthrowing the intolerable tyranny.

It may be too much to hope in the present low estate of personal freedom in the England that was once its source and fountainhead, but a good epidemic of lawlessness and overt contempt for every devising of their pig-brained government may be the only solution.

Cracks in the Moral Façade?

The current Labor government in England has again abolished capital punishment and nothing, on the face of it, could concern me less. England has abolished capital punishment before and come back to sanity and the conventional social sanitary precaution of making it impossible for a murderer to repeat his crime when the novelty of boozy humanitarian thinking wore off.

But there are other, more menacing straws in the wind.

What disturbs me about the tidings from the Tight Little Isle is that, like all too many revealing details of conduct in England in recent years, it indicates a decline in the moral character of Englishmen which once gave them control over most of the

200

known world and established Britain as the most positive civiliz-
ing agency since Roman times. These traces of a decline in national character may perhaps be trivial, but they reveal a
tendency to abandon high standards of thought and conduct
which I, for one and as a student and partisan of things English,
lo these many decades, deplore.

Take, for example, the surrender a few years back of the
hitherto admirably adamant firm of Rolls-Royce to Yankee
meretriciousness when, in what can only be charitably described
as a moment of lapsing sanity, it yielded to swinish importunities
and announced a new Cloud II model with four headlamps
like any production-line heap from Detroit.

Or take the also perhaps inconsequential but revealing matter
of ice in England.

Even in such choice resorts of the international *bon ton* as
the Savoy Grill, the champagne arrived at one's table superbly
presented in a noble silver pail of George III design in the
bottom of which some lightly chilled water sloshed with a handful of melted ice crystals. Churls and bounders who demanded
that their wine be properly chilled with ice mounded up over
the top of the foil as God intended had a hard row to hoe. "It's
not the way we do it, sir," was the most charitable rebuke one
might expect.

Last year, when I revisited those ambrosial premises, all was
changed. To be sure, on its first appearance the wine came to the
table with two cocktail-size lumps of indifferent ice in the bottom of the bucket, but the demand that it be taken back to the
kitchen and actually chilled met with only token resistance.
Where, in other years, wine stewards, waiter captains and
picolos would have ranged themselves in hollow square to resist
the customer to the death and where only the threat of actual
bloodshed could produce a hodful of ice, surrender was the
order of the day and we got our way without violence.

When the moral fiber of national character is so far eroded as to tolerate abject surrender to the whims of inferior outlanders in matters of vital import like icing the wine and the lighting system of The Finest Car in the World, trivial shortcomings like the abolition of hanging can hardly be expected to engage the universal attention.

Outrage in Grosvenor Square

The most shocking outrage against the character and dignity of an older London is, lamentably, the new American embassy in Grosvenor Square, a massive, monolithic, imperial insult to the country to which it is accredited and a tangible advertisement of every quality of aggressive vulgarity and flaunted wealth with which our enemies everywhere are pleased to credit us. Americans forced to do business there do so with batted eyes and, if such is possible, a mantled cheek of shame.

Any of the multiplicity of handsome and ultimately well-bred Georgian mansions available and handy would have been in better taste for a nation in endless search of foreign good will, and if its premises had been insufficient for the vast bureaucracy of uselessness that attaches to our foreign outposts, their offices could have been distributed elsewhere.

When Whitelaw Reid was American Ambassador to the Court of St. James', the Reids were described by Henry James as "incredibly vulgar and palatial people." Their successors and, by implication, all Americans have inherited the Reid mantle in an enlarged dimension of offensiveness.

The Legend of Rolls-Royce

It is a safe bet that, in the 55 years of its existence, Rolls-Royce has been a better hallmark and advertisement for England than all the statesmen of that period, including Sir Winston Churchill, and a greater asset to British prestige than the Battle of Jutland. It has been an oriflamme of breeding and quality, while all other standards have been overwhelmed in the rising tide of universal cheapness. There are other English products and services that have, in a measure, resisted the times; one thinks instinctively of Poole the tailor, Peel the bootmaker, Huntley & Palmer's biscuits, the mutton at Simpson's in the Strand, the Savoy Hotel, Bass's Ale, Lock hats, the hall porters in London hotels and the service on Cunard liners. But none of them measure up to the ineffable legend of Rolls-Royce, the only automobile in history, excepting the Model-T Ford, to create a recognized body of its own folklore.

The Mother of Cities

London, like the Rome of classic times, must be to every perceptive intelligence the mother of cities, the tangible expression of continuity over the centuries which, despite mankind's idiot delusions of progress, is the basic theme of rational life and emotions everywhere.

In London the identification of yesterday with the immediate present is the justification of life itself. In London, style, which is the only excuse for existence and hallmark of civilization, is a perpetual thing, illusive and intangible amidst the mutations of time, but an expression of the validity of life which almost alone the English people have possessed since the fall of Constantinople.

London's Best Bespoke Tailor

Many years ago when, as a very young man, I asked Berry Wall, king of the dudes, to whom I should go for suits, his answer was "Why Henry Poole, naturally! " and the implication was that a man dressed by any other bespoke tailor was little better attired than Happy Hooligan in the funnies.

It was Henry Poole who raised the station of the London bespoke tailor from that of subservient tradesman to arbiter of fashion and an acceptable guest in English country houses where formerly he had used the service entrance. Once, so runs the rune, while the gentlemen, including Henry, were taking wine after the dinner in one of the great houses of the time, a youth unschooled in such matters complained that the evening coat he was then wearing (which had been made by one of the guests present) was a poor fit. Our Henry took a piece of cutter's chalk from his pocket, covered the unhappy boy's coat with cabalistic markings and remarked, "Go see my fitter in the morning; he'll make matters right." The wretched child was marked up in more ways than one, and for life.

The Fat Old Men of London

One of the reassuring things about London is that, contrary to the *mystique* of Gayelord Hauser and the obscene American passion for not eating at all, it is full of fat old men. Amiable old sirs who have to sit at arm's length remove from table continue to dine year in and year out at Simpson's, putting away phenomenal quantities of Black Angus Scotch roast beef, mock turtle soup, roast Aylesbury duckling, boiled silversides of beef, Stilton cheese and gooseberry fool washed down with cataracts of vintage claret, vast pewter horns of bitter, port, and cognac, reclaim their bowlers from the porter and totter off to The City in apparently better shape and obviously more cheerful frame of mind than their Yankee counterparts who have insulted God and their gastric juices with a sandwich and a glass of milk at their desks.

While in London recently, I lunched at Simpson's common table, where single gentlemen are customarily seated together, and watched shrewdly while my most adjacent neighbor, a magnificently rubicund, port-voiced sire in a beautiful pin-striped business suit that must have been fashioned, not by Poole or Hawes & Curtis, but by a sailmaker attacked the menu.

First, with what I estimated to be a double dry sherry, he caused to be placed in front of him a bowl of hard-boiled gull's eggs, the season for plover's eggs being passed, of which he consumed four. Gull's eggs are the same size as conventional hen's eggs with slightly darker yolks and a distinctive flavor which has nothing to do with fish. This was followed by a double order of Lauris asparagus, perhaps the most extravagant of all seasonal whims.

My friend then went into conference with the carver in charge of the rolling table of roast mutton and emerged with a plate heaped high with the world's finest Southdown complemented by roast potato and boiled greens and a full bottle of Mouton Rothschild which was brought by the wine waiter. His simple collation closed with a large wedge of gooseberry tart floating in whipped cream, black coffee and a double vintage port (Crofts '50).

He then courteously apologized for having to leave the table in haste as he had a directors' meeting that would brook no delay. I'd like to be a shareholder in his company which I feel must be as sure, steady, and conservatively managed an investment as were British consols when Soames Forsyte was first becoming a warm man in the pages of John Galsworthy and three per cent was considered appropriate to a prudent gentleman's portfolio.

CHAPTER NINE

Pleasures and Perils
of Travel

Mr. Beebe, in his time, traveled all over the United States and the more civilized parts of Europe when he could find them. He did not, however, travel by air anymore than he would have considered traveling by autobus. If he was going to risk meeting his Maker while en route from here to there, he did not care to do so in the company of people to whom he had not been properly introduced. The one time he was nearly talked aboard a flight to Europe, the unfortunate airline suffered a devastating crash the day before his flight was due to depart. Mr. Beebe's cancellation of his ticket was no surprise to his travel agent who had thought it a clerical mistake in the first place.

No Carriage Trade for the Airlines

I detest and despise airplanes, air travel and everything that has anything to do with getting off the ground. It took the human race a number of hundreds of million years to emerge from the warm tidal meres where life began and it's going to take that much time and longer to make him forsake the earth and be at home in the air.

I don't know a confirmed air traveler who won't readily admit he hates flying, is never completely at ease in a plane and invariably has to get three quarters stiff at the airport bar before he can board one with any degree of assurance. The time he saves in a jet flight to London or Paris he loses by having to go to bed for three days when he gets there.

My distaste for air travel isn't essentially one of physical terror simply because I'm getting to an age and have built-in defects of my own which suggest taking a dim view of immortality. I was flying and loving it before most of the people I now see getting their nerves under control with Jack Daniel's before contemplating an airport were born.

My detestation of flying now derives from the circumstance that on boarding a plane one is, and without any available alternative, locked into a portable pigpen with a lot of people with whom a fastidious person is reluctant to face a trip to New York, let alone an encounter with eternity. I looked forward to the day when private accommodations, my own wash room and reasonable resources of cuisine and space would be available, when I would with glad abandon take passage by air for London, Paris or Ultima Thule.

I now learn that, far from aspiring to this goal, the airlines are seeking to abandon what passes for first-class passage in favor of a universal steerage class. One has openly declared itself in favor of discontinuance of anything even vaguely resembling

210

service, comfort and the usual amenities of polite living in favor of nothing but daycoach flights with all the untidy sweepings of the airports crowded in a common maggot bin of screaming infants and smelly migrants.

This is tantamount to factual admission by the air carriers that they have been unable to attract the carriage trade and that their custom is altogether recruited from the class of persons who would ordinarily travel by bus if the planes didn't offer briefer discomfort and less duration of infamy.

Thus air travel, as a thinkable means of locomotion, has cut its own throat in what amounts to infancy. Rail travel and ocean transport lived long enough to develop polite amenities of living for Pullman passengers and those in first cabin. In the Eighties an overland traveler from Chicago to San Francisco had available to him bathtubs, barber shops, valets, ladies' maids, stock quotations, a wine list with ten choices of vintage champagne and private staterooms with brass beds and ornate toilet facilities. Many people then traveled on the cars, much as tourist cruisers today take the *Lurline* or *Mauretania,* just for the pleasure of being aboard and with no objective of getting anywhere.

Nobody has ever taken an airplane, let alone a jet, solely for the Harvey meals or the extra-length berths and the view from the picture windows. The airlines have now made certain that nobody ever will.

They have rejected all pretensions to service, comfort, agreeable surroundings or acceptable company in transit in favor of the brutal commerce of getting people somewhere in a minimum time and maximum indignity. In a way it's a pity because air travel might have had a future once it ditched the steerage trade.

Super-Snobbism of Staying Home

With the passing of time I feel an ever closer kinship with the

211

Boston young lady from Beacon Street at Dr. Holmes' "Breakfast Table" who remarked "Why should I travel when I'm already there? " Travel is no longer either a distinction or a privilege. It's as commonplace as hamburgers and as populous as a Sunday freeway, so why bother?

I am under the impression that travel reporters and syndicated travel columnists are employed by newspapers to stimulate travel itself and, in a strictly legitimate way, provide reading notices in general terms for the steamship companies and pleasure resorts who advertise so handsomely in the travel sections.

The effect on me is just the opposite and recalls the fiasco that many years ago attended a concerted effort on the part of a group of distinguished art dealers to interest Henry Ford in acquiring a gallery of Old Masters. All the other collectors, Frick, Mellon, Jules Bache, Widener, and Huntington, were oversold and a new market had to be created. Ford as the world's richest man seemed a prospect.

A consortium of dealers got together an extremely costly and handsome catalogue of their available masterpieces. The homeless Vermeers and temporarily unemployed Rembrandts were reproduced on hundred-pound coated stock and Sir Joseph Duveen, later Lord Duveen of Millbank, was chosen to call on Ford and sell him a bill of goods. Ford was delighted with the book and eagerly accepted it as a handsome gift from a group of benevolent well-wishers. When Duveen tried to sell him the originals he replied quite reasonably, why should he spend money on anything that was so handsomely reproduced here in a single handy volume? There was no sale.

The ultimate snobbism nowadays is staying serenely at home while everybody else clamors to be insulted in France and goes to inordinate trouble to be swindled in Rome. Why risk eternity in a jet-propelled cartridge of death with 110 people you've never met socially when the Sunday editions with their travel sections are available and the ice box is filled with Bollinger without the necessity of fighting a supercilious waiter captain for a reservation?

An Augury of Sanity

Through the highly articulate and highly venerated Miss Sylvia Porter, the lady prophetess of the ticker tapes and Sibyl of growth portfolios, the Nation's airlines have come up with a heart-wrenching bleat and dolorous statistics to show that only 14 per cent of the American traveling public has ever used an airplane as an agency of personal transport and that a staggering 86 per cent of Americans when they want to go somewhere steer away from airports as they would from a snakepit.

To this repulsive old reactionary it is an extraordinarily heartening affirmation that Americans have not yet all been brainwashed by the disaster of the Twentieth Century or fallen victim to the contrived mendacities of Madison Avenue in the cause of spurious and demonstrably meaningless "progress."

I think the circumstance that only 14 per cent of all living Americans have ever been close enough to the Wright Brothers' folly to vomit into a plastic container, which has always seemed to me the perfect symbol of air transport, is the most heartening augury for the continued sanity of the Republic since the repeal of prohibition.

The Old Cunard Club Hatband

Nothing it would seem has ever even approached the measure of devotion accorded by partisans of the Cunard Line. Perhaps the P & O of the great days and the Kipling years may have approximated it, but a truly indoctrinated Cunard passenger is never really at home aboard anything else.

It is an affectionate contagion that neither ships' companies nor passengers are immune to. Old-time smoking room stewards with battle ribbons obscuring half their mess jackets look wistful when they mention serving in "the old *Saxonia*" or "the old *Mauretania*" just as the memory of long-vanished but endearing wonderments are evoked in graying passengers by mention of the *Aquitania* or *Samaria*.

Perhaps the most dramatic demonstration of the regard in which Cunard has been held by Americans over the years was that evoked by the sinking of the *Lusitania* which aroused the American public to a pitch of incandescent fury and led ultimately to the end of the German Empire. A much-loved ship whose speed and beauty were household legends, it was the barbarous destruction of the vessel itself fully as much as the loss of life entailed that branded the Kaiser's military hierarchy as huns and monsters. American public opinion was far more incensed by the *Lusitania* than by the invasion of Belgium.

If there were such a thing as old ships' ties or hatbands, the Cunard Club colors would be worn by men who would consider wearing a Harvard Club band or that of the Racquet Club on their boaters a naive ostentation.

They are a little band of brothers who may very well, when the time comes for the final crossing, dig in their heels and refuse to go until Charon hoists the reassuring house flag with the golden orb and lion. Folk who wouldn't dream of an Atlantic crossing by any other agency than going Cunard are unlikely to settle for less when they come to embark for the Styx.

The Deep Water Sailor in Me

One of the peculiarities of ocean travel that has unquestionably made itself apparent to other voyagers as well, but that has impressed me since I first crossed the Atlantic aboard the *Aquitania* more years ago than I like to think, is the reluctance

214

of naval architects to allow seafarers to know they are aboard ship.

Aboard any Atlantic liner of my acquaintance, from the old *Devonian* in the Boston-Liverpool service down to the *United States* where these vagrant sentiments are being typed, it has been necessary to go topside and fight one's way through innumerable fakements of dry land architecture to get so much as a glimpse of Old Debbil Sea or a whiff of salt air.

All known schools of architecture and decor are invoked to convince the voyager that he is emplaced on terra firma: Georgian grand stairways, Federalist lounges, Palladian smoking rooms, and private suites ranging from Louis XIV to Third Empire and from Spanish mission to New England colonial. The men's bar, no longer as God intended populated by men only, but by women in stretch pants and screaming issue without manners, might as well be the King Cole bar of the St. Regis or its counterpart, the Pied Piper at The Palace. The main restaurant on any first-class ocean greyhound out of New York or San Francisco is indistinguishable from the Ritz, the Colony or the Pump Room.

Circular life preservers honestly engrossed with the ship's name and home port are collector's items and you can't find a ship's Waterbury clock outside the Nantucket Whaling Museum or the New York Yacht Club. Patent stabilizers preclude any suggestion of roll even in hurricanes, and staterooms are air-conditioned to eliminate any trace of salt.

At risk of being toasted as crisply as a passenger on the *Morro Castle,* I'd like to see teakwood where heaven intended teakwood to be. The restaurant wouldn't be harmed by portholes against which the rise and fall of summer horizons would be visible. Air conditioning, a boon in St. Louis and a necessity in Houston, doesn't seem to me necessary for a stateroom on the North Atlantic.

Don't mistake me; I have no hanker for the rowing benches

of Phoenician galleys or the open decks of Eric the Red. I hear the salt pork in Fall River whalers didn't compare with the *crepes suzette* of the *United States,* but I have no objection to knowing I'm on the ocean blue. Perhaps a brass porthole instead of French windows would do it.

Rancor Vincit Omnia

The dubious aspects, it seems to me, of air travel are more sinister and deeply imbedded than appear in the mere statistics of probability of being barbecued on a peak in Darien while your luggage goes merrily on to Spitzbergen. These are the casual inconveniences and risks every man must resolve for himself daily and are probably no more than those involved in Russian roulette or drinking Manhattan cocktails.

The black camel waits at the city gate at sundown for everyone and if a man chooses to die nastily in the public gaze and the company of a lot of people he doesn't know socially, that's his business and no matter for general concern. The world is full of dry divers, ledge sitters, bridge leapers and addicts of self-defenestration, and if a man wants to play games with eternity, it's his own affair. There is, let's face it, a certain macabre fascination in seeing whether one puts a period to it all via the ptomaine that sets in from eating airline dinners or splattered on a mountainside in the Sierra.

The grimmer aspect of promiscuous and miscellaneous air travel, however, is that its ready availability makes a great deal of trouble for entirely innocent bystanders who may well regard an airport as a sort of leprosarium and wouldn't be caught dead in a flying hellcart.

The world is full of unrest these days. Hatred, distrust and malevolence are on every hand. Don't rely on my say-so; just read the morning paper which is a long, hysterical *grand guignol,* all of it based on the fundamental circumstance that

216

people hate people and that nobody, in the end, can abide anybody else.

That this distaste may be well-founded is neither here nor there. A profound and abiding dislike of his fellow apes is probably the one and certainly the only thing that identifies man as a rational animal. But, wholesale and on a world scale, human animosities have to date inevitably led to wars, revolutions and other inconveniences that excite the disapproval of posterity and their rejection by everybody who doesn't immediately profit by them.

Every contretemps in the contemporary world can be attributed to the fact that somebody has gotten a good, candid look at somebody else. You can cultivate a deep and abiding hatred for the guts of somebody you meet face to face, and travel can be relied on to see to it that you do indeed encounter him face to face.

The season is now at hand when a number of million Americans with more time and money at their disposal than they know intelligently what to do with, will take quick, cheap and uncomfortable air passage to foreign places where they will sow hatred and distrust for everything American on a scale otherwise to be achieved only by declared warfare. Ignorant mono-lingual, camera-bearing apes certified by the State Department for export as bona fide Americans will go to unimaginable extremes of ingenuity to make themselves and the United States detested wherever they get a chance to take photographs of holy places to the outrage of other peoples' religions and demand cola drinks in wine-growing countries. They will clamor for admission to formal London restaurants in business suits and demand to know why their own idiot brand of decaffeinated coffee isn't served them in Brazil.

In France the native Yankee tourist will cultivate hatred on a national scale by his disparagement of French cuisine. In Italy he will outrage religious sentiment by permitting his wife to

217

enter holy places with her head uncovered. In Spain he will cultivate universal enmity by making rude remarks about the Spanish chief of state.

Wherever he goes his cameras, hatlessness and loud flannel-mouthed conduct will assure him of being a bad taste in the mouths of all classes and kinds of people. His wife will guarantee hostility and his children may bring about a shooting war.

So have no fear for the burdensome responsibilities entailed by American assumption of any position of "world leadership." It won't happen in our time or as long as planes fly laden with potential disaster in the form of American manners for export. They will take care of everything the most dedicated isolationist could ask.

A Bas La France

I wouldn't visit Paris or any part of France, even the Bon Auberge outside Cannes, on a bet and any small change I may be able to spend in Simpson's in the Strand or Brown's in Dover Street, the recipients are welcome to. Nobody has ever gotten anything but a square shake for anything he bought in England, but the tales of survivors and refugees from French rapacity as they disembark from planes and steamers clad in the traditional barrel are heartrending.

Anything you can buy in France you can buy right here at home often cheaper and always from somebody who at least makes a pretense at ordinary manners and decencies. No Frenchman ever expects to see a customer return to his premises no matter how wonderful the cuisine or the acreage of the wine card. The help have seen to that. The French don't like anybody including the French and there is a widespread suspicion that they use mirrors, not to shave in the morning like other people, but to make threatening faces at themselves.

The Great Excuse for Flying

The whole premise of air transport in the United States that important business executives must get somewhere else from where they are with practically the speed of light is simply fraudulent. There is no business deal in history, including the launching of United States Steel by J. P. Morgan and Charles M. Schwab, that couldn't have been done with $100 worth of telephone calls, and 99 per cent of the "big deals" which see tycoons slamming off across the continent with briefcases bulging with comic books could be done by first-class mail.

The importance of flying in the business façade was explained to me recently by a ranking executive as we stood in the bar of the St. Regis in New York spending his stockholders' money on the world's best Martinis. "I almost never am at my office any more," confided this six-figure salary in an Italian natural silk suit. "I am much too important to have anything to do with the home office, so I am conspicuously and all the time away on important business trips.

"People trying to get in touch with me are told by a secretary consulting a carefully detailed itinerary that, I'm at this very minute on United Flight Eight out of New York for Dallas, that I leave next morning for Tampa for a two-hour meeting, and next morning after that I'm due in Chicago for a two-day conference. This gives me a chance to see three or four shows in New York, do some shopping for my wife at Neiman-Marcus, and two straight days in the Pump Room is about all I can take nowadays.

"Of course I fly. If it weren't for flying I'd have to spend at least part of the time at my desk seeing people who know much more than I do and my entire importance to the firm, which is based on always being somewhere else, would evaporate. A

219

businessman at his own desk isn't half so impressive to the jerks who own our stock as he is kiting around from here to there on imaginary missions of the greatest urgency.

"One of the new economic laws is that an executive is important in inverse proportion to his availability at his office. Our stockholders demand that we waste time and money flying on errands that could as easily, and in some cases better, be done by mail simply because being in the air has been made part of the image of the important businessman.

"Me, I'm all for it. I'm important as hell in my organization for the simple reason that nobody has been able to reach me at my desk for two years now. Let's have another quick one before I go to a really vital staff organization meeting. It's at the Four Seasons."

The Jet Set and the Hell Cart

One of the most hilarious items of recurrent newspaper reading concerns the multi-billion-dollar international project in bankruptcy embarked on a while back by England, France and the United States to produce a supersonic, superexpensive, supernoisy and supermeaningless flying machine.

The justification advanced for pouring an unbelievable amount of taxes sweated out of the people of these three countries down the drain of total futility was that it would cut the flying time between Paris and Tokyo by two hours, certainly the greatest milestone in human progress since the invention of the wheel and a daily necessity in the lives of millions.

This fantastic hell cart, evolved on the drawing boards of the mad scientists of three nations in imbecile congress assembled, was going to be the veritable capstone of Twentieth Century progress, and the most impressive monument to the transcendent genius of *homo sapiens* since the beginnings of recorded time. When it was perfected and in full flight future generations would be smitten with amazement at the truly fantastic boon of being able to get from Paris to Tokyo in ten hours instead of twelve. The wonder was how the human race had contrived thus long to get by without this patently basic necessity for its continued existence.

The Paris-Tokyo implications of this grandfather of all swindles was, for some inscrutable reason, the one which most rejoiced the hearts of its proponents. That you might also be able to get from the Pied Piper Bar at the Sheraton Palace to Jack & Charlie's at 21 West Fifty-second street in an hour, a not inconsiderable and valid achievement, was never audibly mentioned.

And only scoffers unworthy of public audience, and perhaps in the pay of Moscow, somewhat timidly pointed out that the sonic boom unavoidable to the progress of this doomsday wagon would destroy property in a 50-mile swath across the American continent and make the major population centers of the United States located within 30 or 40 miles of an airport totally uninhabitable. This was, when hesitantly advanced, denounced as a consideration so childish and puerile as to be unworthy of adult intelligence in the face of the ineffable achievement of being able to get half way across the world without having to go to the men's room.

The glory of the project on a civilian basis was infectious and spread practically instanter to the military whose fly boys in Washington announced ecstatically that it would enable the movement of a full division of troops with all its equipment to the Congo in a matter of minutes and thus facilitate practically instant war. This estimate was later reframed in less specific geographic terms to spare the feelings of what are known in some circles as "the emergent nations."

Now, at the latest report, the bloom is off the supersonic cartridge of cremation, at least in its international aspects. When the English taxpayers got the news of what it was going to cost to get a gaggle of dolts from Paris to Tokyo in two hours less time they let out a screech of anguish.

To compound this unspeakable treachery, aircraft experts in the United States have set their sights on an even less plausible folly and gone helling off towards newer realms of fantasy more involved with the transport of masses of dolts than with the speed of their arrival.

Only the French, as alone in their glory as Sir John Moore in his grave at Corunna, persevere in the hell cart dream, exhorted to frenzies of rage at their delinquent partners by Le Grand Charlie for their reluctance in cutting the time between Paris and Tokyo by two hours. It is conceivable that there are persons of comparative sanity in France who may wish that the General himself would take one-way passage to Tokyo, in which case a few billion francs more or less would be well spent, but they have prudently kept silence.

The news that American aircraft planners are now evoking opium dreams of planes designed to take simply more people at a crack from Paris to Tokyo will not improve their image of sanity, but at least it will have the effect of dampening enthusiasm still further for the international cartel of total folly involved in the supersonic project.

Not only is it preposterous to imagine that such numbers of people have any legitimate business that will take them from one place to another at any such speeds, but the effect on international relations of exposing the people of one country to such copious sweepings from the maggot bins of their neighbors can do little to further the cause of international amity and, eventually, peace.

CHAPTER TEN

The Good Life

Two of life's pleasures, eating and drinking, were of absorbing interest to Mr. Beebe throughout his life. As a child, he delighted in enormous banana splits at the Wakefield town square drugstore in his native New England. As an adult, besides a well-stocked larder, he maintained a cellar composed of equal parts of Jack Daniel's sour mash whiskey, Bollinger's champagne, Booth's House of Lords gin, and the finest of French dinner wines. It was, therefore, one of Mr. Beebe's pleasures to write about restaurants and hotels and food and drink, good or bad.

A Hollow Mockery, A Shabby Swindle

A week or so ago the perpetrator of this column threw caution to the winds, became lost to all prudence and blew the works on a case of Dom Perignon champagne. In the event you don't know about Dom Perignon it is a specially reserved bottling of the best wine manufactured by the old established firm of Moet & Chandon. First produced in the now legendary 1921 vintage, allegedly as a salute to the memory of Dom Perignon, traditionally the inventor of champagne but, in fact, a mere pleasant myth, the Perignon Cuvee was an enormous success in restaurant circles from the beginning. For one thing it was put up in a squat, heavy and uncharacteristic hand-blown bottle, hand-corked with the product of contented cork trees in Portugal and the conventional wire to secure it reinforced by knotted cords, the whole handsomely and impressively sealed with great gobs of dark green wax.

It was an impressive presentation and the wine was as good as its billing, which is to say excellent. It was also very costly and remains the most expensive item on the champagne card today in such restaurants as can afford it on their inventories.

For the service of this treasured nonesuch, I selected an auspicious evening when there was company of an exalted social status and when the cook had outdone herself. The champagne arrived, chilled as the Antarctic in a silver bucket that had belonged to the last of the Czars.

Mindful of the solemnity of the occasion, I undertook to open the bottle myself and reached for it with a knowing ceremonial flick of the rare Irish linen napkin that would have done credit to Oscar of the Waldorf, when suddenly I recoiled as from the presence of a swamp adder in the centerpiece. Beyond all question it was the familiar green bottle; undeniably I had paid a king's ransom for the stuff. But all was now a hollow mockery,

226

a shabby swindle, a treacherous and deceitful fakement, for where once had been the noble and useful green sealing wax was twined around the cork in its stead a nasty blob of miserable plastic.

As God is my judge, there was a plastic foil on the cork of a bottle of Moet & Chandon's Dom Perignon Cuvee Champagne, the noblest and most exalted handiwork of nature contaminated by the nastiest devising of man's infinite genius for trash.

At that precise moment a cock crowed and I heard the echo of the horn of Roland, betrayed by Ganelon; Brutus and Benedict Arnold walked across the lawn and peered in the window. No treachery more damnable, no chicane more debased had been contrived since the betrayal of the Great Inca.

It was as though the radiator ornament on a Rolls-Royce had turned out to be pinchbeck or the trade name of F. W. Woolworth were to be discovered on the hem of the Veronica. No greater imposture would be involved if the Declaration of Independence were found to be a forgery or John Kennedy exposed as having worn a wig.

Golden Caviar of the Czars

The Christmas season is upon us and with it the coated paper catalogues of nationally known specialty shops dealing in a variety of costly merchandise ranging from such absolute essentials of human existence as "kocktail krutches for disabled drinkers" to gold-plated paddles for assisting the circulation of water in the bath tub. How civilization arrived at even its present state without the existence of these artifacts must give pause to the more profound thinkers in our midst.

Such is not the case with an item advertised as "Romanoff's Imperial Golden Russian Caviar As Reserved for the Czars" and selling at the rate of $130 for fourteen ounces with a glass caviar serving dish thrown in as lagniappe. This basic necessity for the maintenance of subsistence living is only harvested at the rate of fifty pounds a year, explains the vendor, hence the price.

The last time your reporter encountered at first hand "The Golden Caviar of the Czars" was in the Pump Room of the Ambassador East Hotel in the late thirties. Ernie Byfield, the restaurant's creator, was very much alive at the time and was widely recognized as an advocate of caviar to still the hunger pangs of the carriage trade.

Byfield, when your reporter arrived in the Pump Room fresh from the amenities of The Twentieth Century Limited, was in conversation with Ben Hecht and also in a state of demonstrable outrage. The source of his grief was a tin of otherwise blameless-looking caviar that had inexplicably emerged a yellow-brown that might, in moments of extreme optimism, be described as "golden." All Russian caviar in those days came from Amtorg, the Russian Trading Company, and the tin bore their stamp.

"The stuff's been imperfectly processed by the lousy Russians," snarled Byfield, "and all the copper lining has come off the inside of the tins. They won't take it back and it's not fit for human consumption. What in hell am I going to do with it? " Everyone had one of the Pump Room's celebrated six-ounce Martinis and your reporter was forced to depart on his professional occasions aboard The Chief for Hollywood. As he was leaving, a look of what might have been inspiration was beginning to suffuse the features of the swarthy Mr. Hecht. "One more of these hell-burners and I'm going to have an idea," he was saying.

A fortnight later found your reporter, this time eastbound, pausing for refreshment in the identical premises and it was apparent that something new had been added to the already elaborate Pump Room menu.

A clip-on flyer of the sort usually advertising the daily special or chef's suggestion had been run up on heavy gold printer's stock with a massive black representation of the double-headed

Imperial eagle of Czarist Russia. Wading through a thicket of whiskered cutups in fur hats drinking vodka out of bottles, the reader was informed that the Pump Room was specially privileged to offer, and on a strictly limited basis, a rare gastronomic taste thrill, "The Legendary Golden Caviar of the Romanoffs, The Prized Treasure of Generations of Czars" of which only a miserable fifty pounds was caught annually. The price was $10 a spoonful.

"The customers have gone wild about the Golden Caviar of the Czars," deposed Frenchy, the maitre d'hotel. "They are wolfing it like hot dogs with circus mustard. The original twenty litres that so vexed Mr. Byfield is almost gone. We are scraping the bottom of the last tin!

"Even now the chef is experimenting with fifty pounds of ordinary black caviar and a sort of gold paint he has borrowed from the pastry department where they use it on wedding cakes. Yesterday Mr. Byfield bought himself a new Jaguar and Mr. Hecht came by for lunch. He and the boss drank four bottles of Krug's Private Cuvee and they laughed and laughed all afternoon. Mr. Byfield gave Mr. Hecht a gold wristwatch."

Farewell to Romanoff's

The demise in Hollywood of Mike Romanoff's restaurant has been attributed to the conventional decline in public taste and manners, excuses we have heard whenever a restaurant has folded, lo, these many years. "People just don't care about eating well any more," Mike has been quoted as lamenting, "and they won't dress decorously enough to warrant the maintenance of a first-class establishment."

Either or both of these dolorous complaints would have been valid in any other community than the Los Angeles tenderloin given over to films and the people who are associated with them. There never was a film actor, if you except a handful of truly civilized sophisticates like Adolph Menjou and Madeleine Carroll, who knew a truffle from an escargot and the large majority of film stars, who have to spell out the menus with their lips and point out the dishes they think they'd like to the waiter with their forefingers, couldn't care less.

Running a first-class restaurant with an advertised clientele of film stars is a contradiction in terms. The basic customers were mentally afflicted weight-watchers, and the rubberneck trade that came to look at them were congenital hamburger munchers.

Mike came up against the facts of life at the great gala soirees for Oscar Awards where the flower and chivalry of old Bel-Air and the proud nobility of Laurel Canyon turned up to lose their imitation tiaras in the tomato aspic and spill Thousand Island dressing down their evening shirt fronts.

These occasions of noble ceremony which were advertised to achieve at least the level of regal stateliness of the Field of the Cloth of Gold and the elevated gastronomic estate of Talleyrand dining the ranking ministers at the Congress of Vienna, often turned out to be low shambles in which the delicate fare confected by the *chef de cuisine* was thrown in the faces of rivals by reigning screen favorites for causes real or imagined and ending with a climactic production number in the lobby where one of the gentleman guests knocked Romanoff cold as a Volga sturgeon while the departing *hochgeboren* stampeded across his prostrate body in an effort to escape before the cops arrived.

Punching Romanoff was part of the heritage of low comedy that characterized his restaurant from the time he was financed to go into business by the late Robert Benchley in a moment of positively supernal whimsy. Benchley wanted the superphony premises of all time, managed by the country's most outstanding social fraud and patronized by the creme de la creme of Hollywood's bogus grandees and neon-lit courtesans. It appealed to him as a concatenation of fraudulences that was the essence of everything Hollywood, the films and the people connected with them stood for. Romanoff's restaurant was a monstrous parody of the grand manner, populated strictly by ringers, fakes, touts, studio pretenders and adventurous and posturing nobodies. Benchley, the author of this wicked jape, regarded a night at Romanoff's as the equivalent of an evening at the *Grand Guignol* in Paris, a synthesis of horror and washroom humor.

Long after Benchley's death, when Romanoff's was still the leading buffalo wallow of Hollywood's bad-check magnificoes and professional confidence men, Mike got delusions of grandeur which prompted him to open two branches elsewhere. The manner in which the grand closings of these establishments followed their grand openings with approximately the speed of light suggested that Hollywood's low comedy, like Vouvray and some of the lesser known vintages of the Moselle, is a property that doesn't travel. Romanoff's was never taken seriously by anybody above the status of a third-rate studio press agent as a restaurant. It will have to be Mike's unhappy epitaph that as a restaurateur, he was just as authentic as he was a scion of the old Russian nobility of a pre-1917 St. Petersburg. As an impostor, he was a prince.

The Great Days at Bleeck's

Nobody in his right mind could have characterized the late Jack Bleeck's saloon in 40th street next door to the printing house of the *New York Herald Tribune,* either in its palmiest flowering as a speakeasy or later raffish respectability as the Artists' & Writers' Restaurant, as a poor man's club.

Steinie's Type & Print, a couple of doors removed, where the pressmen and compositors drank might have been a poor man's club, or the Greek's joint across the way, but you couldn't describe as a resort of underprivilege a bar at which on a single evening the patrons included Ogden Mills, Secretary of the Treas-

231

ury of the United States; his cousin, Ogden Reid, publisher of the *Herald Tribune*; Edward H. Manville, the asbestos roofing magnate, and his son-in-law, Count Folke-Bernadotte of Sweden; Miss Tallulah Bankhead, a play actress; Beatrice Lillie, Lady Peel, ditto; Richard Maney, the highest paid theatrical press agent on Broadway and the treasurer of the Shubert Theaters, Inc.

Bleeck was pleased with his uptown connections and the occasional patronage of the mink and monocle set, and he waged a perpetual sort of jungle warfare against the garment center tradesmen who attempted to get service from him. He once impaled to the bar with a long-tined chef's fork the hand of one who was reaching covertly for the modest free lunch. "That will teach the s.o.b. to be so grabby," he growled.

But most of all Bleeck admired the members of the working press.

It was an admiration that was wholeheartedly reciprocated by the working press so that in time Bleeck's became not only the most celebrated newspaperman's saloon in the world but the very prototype of that universal institution.

The tone of Bleeck's from the very beginning and lasting until comparatively recent times was set by the editorial staff of the *Tribune* and the city desk took it for granted that a reporter not at his desk or known to be on assignment was available at the bar there.

There was of course the conventional fringe of political hangers-on, municipal judges, police inspectors, some very tough and competent members of the plain clothes hierarchy, and other court favorites at Bleeck's own table in the front room.

There was the inevitable Jeweler Joe, a reputed dealer in hot ice, who could turn up anything from a wristwatch to a diamond tiara on half an hour's notice; a boozy parish priest known amiably as Father Daffy, and the horse players who monopolized the beat-up phone booth placing bets for the judges and other sporting members of the clientele.

James J. Walker, in the years after he was mayor and was now czar of the garment industry, was an occasional patron, dapper, charming and thoughtful of friends as ever, certainly the most beloved if slightly disreputable mayor the city ever had.

By the time I had arrived in Bleeck's in 1929, Gene Fowler had long since shaken the dust of the *New York American* from his well-shod feet and was making $1000 a day, payable in cash at the end of each day at the studio in Hollywood because he didn't think the industry was going to last till Saturday.

His occasional descents on Bleeck's, already a living legend and often accompanied by Spencer Tracy, denuded the *Tribune* city room of its staff who stood around beaming in the reflected and alcoholic luster of the most chaotic character in the record of New York newspaperdom. James Gordon Bennett not excepted.

One of the little-known conveniences at Bleeck's was a fire escape hatch, as required by law, which led through a stout steel-shuttered window in the men's room. It communicated directly with a narrow alleyway in which was the stage door of the National Theater which fronted on 41st street. Players in dramatic nonesuches at the National, if they were careful not to soil their fine raiment on the dusty sill, could get to the bar in Bleeck's and back to their dressing rooms in a fraction of the time it took to go around the block.

It chanced that, long ago, playwright Owen Davis, a fecund man of exits and loquiturs, confected a shambles called "De Luxe" into which he wrote a minor part for his son, Owen Jr. Ownie's lines and businesses were few but essential to the meaningful continuity of the play. On opening night with the chivalry of New York in the audience, Ownie became bogged down at

233

Bleeck's and was apprehended, just as his cue was coming up, by a wrathful stage manager who snaked him through the emergency hatch and on stage in the nick of time.

The handsome juvenile, bemused with brandy and blinded by the sudden transition from gloom to calcium, stalked woodenly stage front, glared menacingly at the audience and then stumbled over the stage apron and footlights into the fiddle section of the orchestra.

Fights were relatively infrequent at Bleeck's despite the high voltage content of authors, playwrights, drama critics and actors who formed much of its clientele. The only one that made the wire services was the night a now-forgotten playwright named Jack Kirkland took umbrage at a review of one of his products by drama critic Richard Watts, Jr., and floored the bespectacled and diffident Watts with a haymaker from behind his back. Bleeck, enraged beyond speech by an assault upon a regular customer by a comparative stranger, came out from behind the bar and flattened Kirkland with a blackjack which was providentially at hand. With fully 50 accredited reporters witness to this stirring encounter, it could scarcely fail to make the public prints.

It was upon this epic occasion that Bleeck laid down his celebrated dictum of proper conduct: "We don't allow overly intoxicated customers in this joint."

Other Times, Other Moriaritys

Because he is evidently and amply aware of the uses of publicity and sees to it that no accredited reporter ever gets a check even if he's been bathing in Bollinger, an amiable saloonkeeper in New York named P. J. Moriarity is by way of becoming a national character.

But to an older generation of serious drinkers, Moriarity's doesn't mean P. J.'s no doubt agreeable sluicing premises.

234

It meant the address at 216 East Fifty-eighth street where Dan Moriarity and his brother Mort ran New York's most celebrated and certainly most respectable masculine speakeasy throughout most of the Twenties and until repeal of the infamy that made them rich, respected and, by many loyal customers, beloved.

Dan and Mort were old time East-Side New York Irish. They spoke with a brogue, had important connections in the right police and political circles and drank their own whiskey. Their customers were the elite of New York's masculine saloon set, professional advertising and newspapermen, well-mannered cutups and the less impulsive and more solvent undergraduates of New Haven and Princeton who lived within commuting distance and spent the evening there as educationally as in the university library.

Dan tolerated neither breaches of the peace nor of gentlemanly rectitude. You held your liquor or you didn't come back. At 216 there was the conventional steel-sheathed door under a brownstone stoop with Judas hole, chains and throw bolts and the customers could be cased in the light of a glaring arc lamp which providentially was in just the right location in the all-brownstone block. Or maybe Dan had it put there.

A daily regular at four every afternoon was Charlie McCrae who came up from Wall Street on the East Side subway and refused to speak to anyone, even his own brother at the bar, until Mort or Dan had served him a triple Martini which he inhaled at a single swallow. After he had had three of these benevolent arrangements he went home to have cocktails with his family.

There were two prices at Dan's: two bits for the O'Gradys, Currans and other neighborhood Irish, and six bits for Vanderbilts, Mellons and Whitneys of whom there were many and thirsty, too. Martin Curran, the doorman at a nearby apartment house, was the only non-Catholic Irishman Dan admitted and

235

on one occasion Martin, slightly in wine, shattered the usually well-bred tranquility of the place by booming: "Dan, could a Protestant bastard buy one for the house?"

Another doorman regular was Joe O'Grady, who called carriages at Bendel's and whose uniform was so magnificent that he was once introduced by Sherman Hoyt to some visiting British yachtsmen as "Admiral O'Grady of the U.S. Navy" without arousing suspicion.

Sunday mornings Dan's was Manhattan's leading temple of the hangover, the sufferers crouching motionless and noiseless at the bar, many of them with silk top hats resting on the hatrack by the door preparatory to passing the plate at St. Thomas's or St. Patrick's, trying to get up courage to take the first sip of brandy milk punch that would make or destroy them. It was forbidden to drop a pin lest the noise shatter the therapeutic silence.

When closing hour came at night, usually about three o'clock, Dan or Mort or whoever was on varied the honored British call of "Time, gentlemen" with the query, "Have you no homes? " Many of us had no homes but Dan's and I wish I could hear him say it again.

The Hamburger Came in Heroic Couplets

Everybody by now is aware of the poetic menu, the bill of fare that plays "Hearts and Flowers" among the entrees and invokes the dulcet accents of Swinburne in setting forth the *ragout a la Deutsch*. It summons pure poetry to the counter in truck stops and reaches a lyric pitch comparable to a philharmonic orchestra encountering Brahms in restaurants of more exalted *ton*.

The adjectival menu is, of course, aimed at the flowery detailment of dishes whose more classic French names would have no meaning for the peasants now dining out in ever increasing numbers. It saves the waiter captain from tedious explanations that Florentine means with spinach and Perigordine with truffles.

It was the invention, as far as such things can be accurately ascribed, of the late Ernie Byfield of the Ambassador Hotel in Chicago whose Pump Room established itself in the '30s as a midcontinental restaurant of effulgent dimensions. Much of the Pump Room's reputation derived from its patronage by film celebrities commuting between New York and Hollywood and by the generality for whom a menu might as well have been printed in Etruscan as the French of conventional culinary usage. To con these glamorous dolts into splashing around in the best of everything, Byfield dreamed up a menu which, without insulting the customer to his expensive face with a bald or literal translation of the items into English, let him get the news about the chef's suggestion and the plat du jour. *Caneton a l'orange* emerged as "Tender Breast of Choicely Selected Long Island Duckling Lovingly Sauteed and Flavored With a Delicate Essence of Juicy Oranges From California's Most Favored Citrus Groves."

Once launched on this raging sea of verbiage, Byfield himself became so bemused by the possibility of elevating sauerbraten to the godlike estate of ambrosia that he was lost to all restraint or reason. Menus at the Pump Room came to rival the collected works of Keats and Byron, anthologies of noble fancy which only escaped the intimate second person with thee and thou by a slender margin. Deerfoot sausages were presented to the alarmed customers as "Selected Morsels of Happily Endowed Piglets of Irreproachable Pedigree From the Verdant Massachusetts Countryside Near Olde Southboro Enhanced With Sapient Infusions of Rare and Costly Spices Culled From the Forgotten Lore of New England Cookery."

The imagery of the Lake School of Poets was invoked to advertise roast beef hash, and sole and flounder arrived bedded in classic similes and romantic allusions. The chef at the Ambassador sent out in a hurry for the collected works of Racine, Catullus and Henry Wadsworth Longfellow, and Roget's *Thesaurus* took its place on the shelf along side of Brillat Savarin and Fanny Farmer.

Executives anticipating a simple luncheon while sewing up a deal in women's wear found themselves scuffling with pure Wordsworth. Unthinkable became the service of vegetables that were not succulent, fish other than those choicely selected or desserts not devised in inspired trances by esthetes who combined the expertise of Blum with the vocabulary of Milton.

It is impossible today, of course, to encounter a menu, outside of such impregnable citadels of haute cuisine as "21" and Le Pavillon whose patrons are reasonably sure of their French, where ground round isn't garlanded in wreaths of classical mythology and the nobler strophes of Ronsard. The memory of Ernie Byfield is imperishably secure in culinary folklore as the originator of the service of everything in flames and everything on wheels, but he will be immortal as the first restaurateur to get Lake Superior Whitefish on the menu in iambic pentameter.

Have You Dined With Lucretia Borgia?

Lest any reader of these vagrant paragraphs should suspect from previous exclamations of delight over London restaurants that I am in the pay of Her Majesty's government, and gorging myself nightly on grouse and foie gras on the cuff in the town's most lordly pavilions of transcendental gastronomy, let me here and now depose for all time that I have discovered in London's aristocratic precincts what is certainly the most overtouted luxury restaurant in England, and perhaps one of the worst conducted in the entire world.

Any prolonged research into its ancestry must lead inevitably to the kitchens of Caesar Borgia and his inventive sister who gave a new dimension to Italian gastronomy. It flourishes on the sucker trade of American tourists who will eat anything as long as it doesn't attack them at the table itself with all the symptoms of cholera morbus. ————— gets the dying off the premises and has strict house rules against patrons having convulsions in the men's room, but aside from that it is indistinguishable as a chamber of horrors from any of Mme. Tussaud's waxworks.

To begin with, ————— has not yet heard about refrigeration. Ice is as foreign to the conduct of its affairs as manners in the Kremlin.

Mounds of oysters repose on the backbar of its oyster counter with no vestigial trace of chilling, the salads are served ready to ignite at the touch of a match like so much wood shavings, and the Chablis is poured so warm as, quite literally and in my view, to crack a glass in half. In repairing this contretemps, the waiter took the precaution of placing a silver spoon in the next glass to prevent similar damage.

And if you have ears for further horrors, let me tell you about the broiled fresh lobster at ————— which arrived at table nicely browned to the eye with underneath a farrago of shredded fish meat of the approximate consistency of pureed spinach instead of lobster intact in its shell and undefiled as God intended. The waiter was happy to explain the cause. All lobsters in the kitchen, he said, were first boiled and then the meat extracted and put aside in quantity so that it might be mixed with the appropriate ingredients for Thermidor, Newburg, Mornay, or whatever when it was replaced in the shell, and this applied to broiled "live" lobsters as well.

The service at —————, too, is a little bit of the old European tradition in which posses of moustached garçons foregather in little groups of six or eight in corners of the room scratching their bottoms and discussing Balkan politics at the top of their voices, while the champagne boils in the ice buckets and the salad smolders on the plates of patrons.

If this column may take the liberty of giving advice to

it readers, its unqualified recommendation is that American tourists to London stay away from ————. The life you save will be your own.

Never a Dull Moment at Brown's

Like all too many English institutions dating from the well-to-do days of the Nineteenth Century, when personal privacy was esteemed as the breath of privilege by mannered Britons, the private hotel is rapidly disappearing from the London scene. The phrase itself is an ambiguous one, but it generally means a premises with regular, long-established clientele which has no need of patrons with whom it is not already familiar. It is filled from year to year and knows who everybody is on its guest list.

Most celebrated of all private hotels until the passing of its owner during the last war, was Rosa Lewis's Cavendish, a premises of low moral tone and the most elevated imaginable social rating since it attracted nothing but ex-kings, grand dukes, American millionaires, Greek shipping princes and Arabian oil men, and was so grand in the conduct of its affairs that it stocked champagne only in magnums.

It figured largely in Evelyn Waugh's "Vile Bodies" and until its end enjoyed a reputation for Edwardian style perfumed by associations of Rolls-Royces and romance at the *Debrett* and *Burke's Peerage* level, Rosa, the reputed ex-favorite of Lord Ribblesdale, a sporting peer, drank drink for drink with all the guests and was the delight of Sunday editors on two continents. Long before he was American Ambassador, Jock Whitney used to stay there upon occasion and recalls that it was expensive, even for a Whitney who is also a Vanderbilt.

Well, lacking the Cavendish, Brown's Hotel in Dover Street, where these strophes are being penned, will do in the conservative eccentricity sweepstakes tempered with good breeding and a sense of performance and propriety that has endeared it to generations of English "county families" and Americans with a taste for authenticity.

For Brown's is the McCoy. Nothing in London is more so.

As evidence, I would like to suggest the circumstance that all the doors in every private apartment have door stops to hold them open because, over the decades, the building has settled in such a multiplicity of places that nothing in it hangs true.

The eldest permanent guest is a beldame who occupies a single bed-sitting room, but begins her day with an even dozen champagne highballs made with Bollinger and Hennessy's twenty year, which she knocks back before descending to the main hotel parlor where she starts the serious drinking of the day, always in vintage bubbly. A virginal old party, she will allow no strange waiter to enter her rooms, although she recognizes Dennis Hawkes, the head barman, and Stubbs, the senior waiter. But if a new man attempts to come in with her morning drinks, she pelts him with a barrage of rolled toilet paper kept racked and handy for security purposes. Of late, she has made a practice of holding the end when launching a rocket cluster, and guests, finding the fourth floor corridor festooned in bathroom tissue know that a new waiter has been routed.

The lifts at Brown's, a comparatively recent innovation in Dover Street chronology, lifts that, in any other scheme of things, would be on view at the Smithsonian, are approximately the size of a child's coffin and require the pressing of four separate manual controls for their proper activation. A few years back, a guest of note and value, "a duke, no less," as Dennis the barman will tell you, became trapped between floors in one of these contrivances, which contain no trap or escape hatch, and was there several hours. "His condition was pitiable," recalls Dennis, "but we kept him alive with pitchers of Martinis lowered from the fourth floor through the grated ceiling."

More recently a similar contretemps overtook one of Brown's ascenceurs, this time incredibly peopled with eight descending patrons where three constitute a dangerous crowd. They were there for 40 minutes because the incident took place while the house electrician was at his tea and could not, naturally, be recalled to duty. When finally released, the guests, being Brown's regulars, were damp with perspiration but unruffled, all but one housefootman whose shame was great because his stiff paper wing collar and shirt dickey had dissolved entirely and he was forced to appear briefly, with an expanse of hairy bosom showing beneath a neatly knotted black bow tie riding with no collar to sustain it.

It is this sort of atmosphere of latent gala that attracts a host of native characters in tweeds, monocles, Edwardian whiskers and bishop's gaiters who manage to look like the cast for a production of "Disraeli."

"You see all those retired cavalry colonels, foxhunting squires and elderly ladies with Ann of Austria curls in front of their ears who start taking tea in the lobby at 9 and have to be swept out at closing hour?" Mr. Hawkes asks. "Absolutely genuine, every one of them. Not a ringer amongst them. Your Mr. S. J. Perelman only last year ventured to doubt the authenticity of our choicest retired admiral, he's the sort of lavender-faced one in the corner, who claimed to have been present whn Lily Langtry dropped the ice cube down King Edward VII's collar.

"Mr. Perelman was challenged right there but we got him out the side entry before the admiral could get his foot out of the umbrella stand."

Battle of the Regency Bar

What may turn out to be a substantial contribution to a new lease on the good way of life whose decline in the Nation's largest and most cosmopolitan city is the subject of almost continuous lamentations came into being in New York when the Regency Hotel, the first new hotel of formal dimensions and of a strictly luxury order to have been opened in nearly 30 years, was inaugurated with a resounding social bang.

There was a brief reception followed by a modest but nutritious collation of Beluga caviar *au blinis,* boula-boula soup, *delices de sole Regence* with a Pouilly Fuisse 1961, *noisettes d'agneau Lavalliere* complemented by Chateau Margaux '57, salad, *peches Melba,* petit fours and enough of Mme. Taittinger's champagne to float a medium size battle cruiser.

The guests were largely recruited from the ranks of the ambassadors, ministers and secretariat of the United Nations, a pool of casting agency freeloaders listed in tabulated form by all advertising and publicity agencies in Madison Avenue according to constant availability when gratuitous chow is in prospect and with suitable marks on the indexed cards of those known for their taking ways with hotel silver.

The presence of the U. N. has accounted for the sharpest rise on record in the disappearance of tableware, table linen and portable items of hotel decor. In compensation it has eliminated all necessity for small-time conversation in New York since no two members of the U. N. personnel speak the same language and none at all speaks English.

A microscopic minority enclave or English Speaking Union rallied in hollow square formation at the pre-prandial bar and included Geoffrey Hellman of *The New Yorker,* Charlie Van Rensselaer of the Hearst papers and, according to reliable report, successor to the ill-fated Igor Cassini, Julia McCarthy of the *Daily News,* two very hungry unemployed staff members of *The Times,* a *Herald Tribune* refugee, Chuck Clegg, the Virginia City nabob and magnifico, and your correspondent.

Clegg was of special use as intelligence operative because he speaks several languages and could mingle unsuspected with the enemy milling around the oysters Rockefeller, and it was because of his reports that Hellman, who emerged in the hour of crisis as a tactical leader of the first chop, was able to make the

243

most strategic disposal of the force at his command.

Amidst scenes of fearful carnage we repelled suicide charges by wave after wave of prominent Peruvians, massed Mesopotamians, fanatic French and assorted shock troops of Egyptian under-secretaries, Iranian mercenaries, Arab dervishes and Congolese tribal chieftains, all inflamed to battle madness by double Martinis.

Bloody Maryed but unbowed, our little band of brothers stood together near the shrimp in aspic on a spot which shall be forever England until the last cavalry charge of monocles and economic advisers was repulsed, as at Waterloo, by a sunken ditch down by the hot canapes.

"This is hallowed ground," proclaimed Hellman as luncheon was announced and the tide of battle swept past us toward the boula-boula. "An imperishable shaft of bronze should rise here to commemorate the immortal spot where a valorous band of patriots were to the last able to obtain bourbon and branch without asking for it in French. Gentlemen, we have made history."

The Legend of Crepes Suzette

A short time back an old gentleman who ran a restaurant in Florida and had in recent years enjoyed a reputation somewhat in excess of his true capacities as a chef, but no more than he deserved as a dedicated and venerable gastronome, went to his reward and it was announced at length and in detail that Henri Charpentier had been the inventor of the Crepes Suzette.

The dispatches covering the death of Mr. Charpentier went into detail, all of it familiar to experienced reporters—only with other names, dates and places—of how Mr. Charpentier had inadvertently set aflame a serving of ordinary sweet French pancakes he was preparing for the then Prince of Wales in Monte

244

Carlo and royalty, enchanted, as was its then custom with having its food burned, said: "Henri, what have you done to these pancakes? They are indeed superb."

From there on the legend is familiar to that universal character, every schoolboy, for fat Edward, when the chef said he proposed to name them in his honor, insisted they be named instead for the pretty girl with whom he was lunching and whose name it turned out was Suzette.

There you have a legend in one of its almost numberless variations that is fully as worthy of learned research and a doctoral thesis as the origin of "The Chanson de Roland" or the story of Burnt Nyal in the Icelandic sagas. The origins of Crepes Suzettes are a good deal more various than the versions of the death of King Arthur.

Almost all the versions of Crepes Suzette folklore agree that it was first created in the presence of fat Eddie, the Prince of Wales who later became Edward VII. He is appropriate as a participant in the epic because he was indeed a getter-around in the lobster palaces of his time and finally ate himself to death in a stylish manner no monarch has since been able to afford.

The setting is also almost invariably either Monte Carlo, Nice or Paris, which were then in their heyday as resorts teeming with grand dukes and big-eating kings and Balkan munitions salesmen.

Now and then a variation on the Edwardian theme turns up when it is discovered that the dessert was first served to Manuel, King of Portugal, also a big eater.

The true glory of the folklore of Crepes Suzette lies, however, not in the variety of its places of origin or the identity of the exalted first customer who is seldom of less status than an archduke, but in the vast multiplicity of claimants for the honor of being its inventor. In the early 30s when I was on the staff of the *New York Herald Tribune,* I was sent to get a Sunday feature

245

interview with the inventor of Crepes Suzette who, at the moment, was a worthy fellow named, if memory serves, Malnatti, head of the banqueting department at the Biltmore Hotel.

Mr. Malnatti was in the very best tradition of the inventors of Crepes Suzette, and opened with the classic or Tchaikovsky gambit which begins: "I was just an assistant waiter captain in the Savoy Grill at the time, but I remember it as if it were yesterday.

"His Royal Highness had lunched extremely well: smoked Scotch salmon—it cost six shillings a slice in those days—clear turtle soup with sherry, a trifle of my own invention of plover's eggs served with hot mustard mayonnaise, roast grouse, for it was in September, done just 12 minutes, and an endive salad with flecks of truffle in the French dressing.

"His Royal Highness then turned to me while wiping the French dressing out of his whiskers and said: "Well, Malnatti, so far so good, but what shall we have for the dessert? Something to please this pretty lady from the Gaiety chorus whose name is Suzette! And I said, "If Your Royal Highness will permit me . . . ?" You know it from there.

I didn't ask Mr. Malnatti what Edward was doing in London in September or lunching in public with a Gaiety girl. That is a serious infraction of the rules of the Crepes Suzette game. Mr. Malnatti at this point called for a chafing dish and the appropriate allied matters, and ran me up a fine dish of Crepes a l'Orange awash with approximately a pint of Hennessy Three Star although the hour was 11 in the morning, and I went back to my desk radiant with the wonder of it all and only having fallen down once getting into the taxi.

That was my first interview with the inventor of Crepes Suzette, although I have encountered them since by the score, Henris and Phillipes and Raymonds and Oliviers and Raouls beyond tally. The time, the place and the recipient of the primal crepes differ wildly.

246

I even found one certified originator who had first devised them for the Khedive of Egypt. Leopold of Belgium, Victor Emmanuel of Italy and the Grand Duke Cyril were often mentioned.

One thing is absolutely necessary to a proper classic rendering of any version, however. It is the magic phrase: "If Your Royal Highness will permit me . . ." The press muffed that one in its account of Henri Charpentier.

CHAPTER ELEVEN

Heroes and Rogues

Mr. Beebe observed the mighty of his time from John Pierpont Morgan the Elder to Lyndon B. Johnson of Texas and made sapient comments on all of them. Those who enchanted him most were those who did things in style and he reserved his deepest contempt for the man who could not live up to the demands that life made upon him.

Bennett and the Mutton Chop

James Gordon Bennett the Younger, a heller in his private life which was virtually indistinguishable from his public escapades, had a private and wonderfully simplified standard of gastronomic excellence. He lived well and high in all regards and was a not inconsiderable patron of the great culinary traditions of France as witness the time when he purchased, lock, stock and brandy barrel, a place that pleased him on the Riviera and turned it over to his favorite waiter to run. The waiter's name was Ciro and the name Ciro entered into the lexicon of fine food as legitimately as Maxim or Sherry, if less effulgently than Delmonico.

Bennett's gastronomic yardstick and a standard by which he measured the standing of any eating establishment in any country was its preparation of broiled English mutton chops. The management might boast the presence in its kitchen of a saucier with as many blue ribbons and awards as My Own Brucie. The plover's eggs might be hastened by private courier from a secret wagon road in a remote part of the Scotch Highlands. (Plovers like to lay their eggs in wagon tracks, a circumstance that adds materially to their scarcity.) The Lauris asparagus could be as thick as a pickhandle and the Channel sole still flopping as it became Meuniere. These were not lost upon the tyrannical and impetuous publisher and owner of the *New York Herald* and its Paris counterpart. He appreciated the good things of the world and paid amazing sums to have them served at his variety of villas, town houses, country estates and seagoing yachts.

But the grilled Southdown mutton chop remained for Bennett the benchmark from which to pass judgment on everything else from soup to souffle, or as the late George Jean Nathan had it, from cocktail to Bromo Seltzer.

252

The classic and crowning testimony to the tempestuous millionaire's devotion to the world's most ineffable and one of its least commonly available items of table fare is cited by Richard O'Connor, Bennett's biographer, when the publisher was summoned back to New York for the dedication of the new Herald building in what is today Herald Square. The project had engaged the architectural genius of Stanford White. Several million dollars in an era of hard gold money were involved, and the event was in every way a momentous one in the annals of a great metropolitan paper.

Bennett's steamer docked early on the appointed morning and the great man sought his favorite New York club, the Union, for alcoholic and gastronomic solace before the dedicatory ceremonies. To the horror of spectators in the dining room, the mutton chop arrived overcooked. History draws a veil over the scene of outrage that ensued, but it is in the record that Bennett threw the offending entree together with its heavy silver platter at the club steward, smashed his proffered silk hat over the ears of the cloakroom attendant and booked passage on the first outgoing liner which was sailing that afternoon.

The Senator and the Dixie Cup

I have before me as I pen this melancholy chronicle the reportorial evidence of the depths of demagogic degradation and personal cheapness, often suspected but infrequently so cheerlessly advertised, to which the estate of United States Senator has fallen in this evil hour of the Republic.

It concerns a moment of revelation, a brief instant of shabby truth culled from the pages of *Harper's*, detailing the sidelights of a recent international yacht race at Newport.

"Senator Pell," so states the account referring to United States Senator Claiborne Pell (Dem-Rhode Island), "was asked to officiate at the prize ceremonies, to award the stakes and be the first to utilize the (prize) cup. He declined, presumably on the grounds that his constituents might disapprove of photographs of him standing on a yacht club lawn quaffing champagne from a silver tankard. When photographs were taken, Pell kept shrubbery between himself and the photographers. As for the champagne, he had that out of a Dixie cup."

It is a revealing vignette of quivering political poltroonery, an exquisite example of the mucker pose among the highest placed recipients of public trust, a United States Senator hiding out behind the petunias for fear a news photographer might apprehend him in the reprehensible society of gentlefolk and quaffing an innocuous beverage with which generations of more distinguished Senators then he will ever be were accustomed, and in the full public gaze, to brush their teeth or use as a chaser to stronger waters.

Does the gentleman from Rhode Island actually imagine that, in a society where journeyman electricians working a 25-hour week drive to work in Cadillac limousines and even the lower echelons of labor leaders customarily spend the winter in hundred-dollar-a-day suites in Miami luxury hotels, a glass of sparkling wine taken on a country club lawn is the sort of thing that toppled the Romanoffs from their throne? That a Dixie cup furtively drained at a safe remove from the photographers is prudent to avert mob violence against the arrogant and bloated monopolists of decadent capitalism?

For the reverse of this emetic hypocrisy, Senator Pell might take a backward look at the record of the peerless Senator William Andrews Clark of Montana, a magnifico who invariably traveled with two private Pullman Palace Cars, one for his whiskey and one for his guests. Or refer to the late and equally revered Senator Boies Penrose of Pennsylvania, who invented the elixir of life that is today sold commercially as Southern

Comfort and kept half the Upper House stiff as sailors for a week celebrating his achievement.

Or Nevada's Senator John Percival Jones, who found it prudent to own a Turkish bath establishment in San Francisco as an accessory to his sojourns in the Palace bar. Or the splendid Senator Edward O. Wolcott of Colorado who, when charged by the political opposition with having dropped $350,000 in Ed Chase's gaming rooms in Denver, roared: "It's nobody's goddamned business what I do with my own money. Besides, I'd won it the day before at the race track!"

In the person of Senator Claiborne Pell (Dem-R.I.), the estate of the toga would seem to have come a long way since those times. All of it downward.

The Other Mr. Johnson

In his autobiography, written in the closing years of an incredibly long and adventurous life, Nevada's peerless Senator William Morris Stewart describes an interlude at once sordid and hilarious in Washington immediately following the shooting of President Lincoln.

During the long and terrifying night after the assassination in Ford's Theater when it was apparent that a widely contrived plot against the entire Federal Government had been partially successful and when it was obvious that Mr. Lincoln could not live, some difficulty was experienced in locating Vice President Andrew Johnson who, in a certain matter of hours, would be called upon to assume the responsibilities of the Presidency.

The task of seeking out the Vice President and bringing him, but instanter, to the White House, was delegated to Senator Stewart, possessor of the most patriarchal beard in all Washington, who called a hack and started a search through Washington's more notorious dives, deadfalls, bagnios and stews. Fol-

255

lowing a trail of broken glass and smashed plug hats, Nevada's silver solon had little difficulty in catching up with the Vice President of the United States, but his troubles had only begun.

Discovered in a mean lodging house, Mr. Johnson was patently in no condition for a rendezvous with Destiny. He was stiff as a plank and inclined to be quarrelsome about the whole absurd business. He attempted to take liberties with Stewart's whiskers and urged him to share what was left of a bottle of Old Reprehensible. He had also been actively ill and his frock coat was sadly in need of a laundering or, better, burning in its entirety. His stock was soiled beyond repair and he had lost one Congress gaiter.

Getting the President-designate of the United States sober enough to take the oath of office and in reasonably presentable case presented a major crisis but one to which William M. Stewart, with a lifetime of mining town crises behind him, was entirely equal.

Recruiting cab drivers, city detectives, waiters from all-night restaurants, a barber and valet from Willard's and other co-workers, Stewart turned Johnson into a coffee urn, got him shaved, sent for fresh linen and formal attire, walked him up and down the block and, in less than three hours, had him at least presentable. It was a notable example of the legislative branch of the Government forcing the executive branch to face up to its obligations.

Some Thoughts on John Kennedy

To many Americans the memory of President Kennedy means many things. Beyond all cavil or partisanship, he was a first class person who brought to the White House a style and cachet of superiority, literacy and intelligence it had not known in the Twentieth Century. To clinically minded observers he was, too, in the terminal stages of the occupational disease of politicians and actors, a morbid hanker for reassurance by mob contact and for mob favor that was in his case immediately and factually fatal.

One View of Bobby

A year or two back before the assassination of President Kennedy had established the Kennedy cult of adulation which has, for the time being anyway, eliminated all touches of humor from the image of a man who in his own person had an uncommonly fetching sense of it, the story was widely being told of the occasion when the three Kennedy brothers were in a plane together and the other passengers were speculating on the possibility of eliminating all Kennedys forever by tossing them from the window.

"We could throw out John Fitzgerald," proposed the first conspirator, "and make the Republicans happy."

"Or we could throw out Ted," proposed another, "and make the other Kennedys very happy indeed."

"Better than that," suggested a third. "Let's toss out Bobby Kennedy and make everybody happy."

Sam Insull Moneyed Churl

A short time back the author of these paragraphs had occasion to be in the East on business.

Incidental to the ingestion of astounding quantities of caviar and the best bourbon at the Duquesne Club in Pittsburgh and the Chicago Club by Lake Michigan I became aware of a curious socio-literary phenomenon which seems worth reporting.

This was a concerted and patently well-financed and organized campaign at a variety of levels to whitewash the memory of the late Samuel Insull, a Chicago pseudo-tycoon of the Twenties and Thirties, whose paper empire, when it inevitably collapsed,

257

carried thousands of small investors to ruin and saw Insull firmly established in the rogues' gallery of his age.

Never actually convicted of any criminal offense, Insull soon died broken, aged and widely detested. His manners which were those of a boor and his ignominious flight which forced United States officials to chase him half way around the world before they laid him by the heels did nothing to endear him in the public eye although he had been liberal in public works and gave Chicago a magnificent opera and many other cultural benevolences.

Now forces are apparently in operation to restore the image of Sam Insull to some of the luster it enjoyed before his giant Insull Utilities Investments, Inc., and Corporation Securities Company went up the spout with such resulting chaos and bad feeling that Insull himself had to ride in a bullet-proof limousine with inch-thick windows and heavily armed private police.

Insull biographies, perhaps family-inspired, are beginning to appear suggesting that perhaps the old man wasn't such a scoundrel after all, just the victim of a bad press. His motives were misunderstood. Economics professors in Eastern universities are writing to reprove me for unkind remarks about old Sam in a recent book, suggesting that he was on the receiving end of a conspiracy headed by the rascally J. P. Morgan and that his services in the formation of General Electric back in 1891 entitle him to a place in the ranks of the benefactors rather than the wreckers. The current generation of Insulls in Chicago are blameless folk, highly esteemed in the community and not without influence.

My suspicion is that they are trying to make heroic bricks without the essential straw. Insull had more strikes against him than were represented by mere Federal indictments. He was a testy fellow in his high-riding days, arrogant to inferiors and generally regarded as a moneyed churl. He fled the country when the bailiffs were at the door which, like taking the Fifth Amendment, is widely regarded as an explicit admission of guilt. And he didn't get away with any loot. In the end he died broke.

In other words, he was the type that gave embezzlement a bad name.

Americans want their robber barons in the heroic dimensions of the elder Morgan, James J. Hill, Henry C. Frick or William Collins Whitney, on the theory that grand larceny demands the grand manner. Even that supreme man of disaster, Jay Gould, commands reluctant admiration because he died loaded with loot. Andrew Carnegie, on the contrary, although he contrived to unload his steel holdings for $492,000,000 cash on the barrelhead in a single transaction, is remembered with contempt for his sniveling parsimony and sanctimonious platitudes about virtue and morality. Americans don't want their malefactors of great wealth to get caught picking up the small change on the bar when paying for the drinks.

Soss for the Gander

When subjected to occasional if infrequent fits of melancholia, usually induced by a falling off of abusive mail to myself or my employers with the consequent suggestion that I am getting mellow (the first appreciable symptom of senility), I turn, as some people do to Sherlock Holmes, inventing new kinds of omelet or kicking small children on the city sidewalks, to a contemplation of the shifting but ever-fascinating image of Mrs. Wilma Soss, the lady wolf of Wall Street.

Mrs. Soss is the militant, perpetual and untamable baiter of board chairmen, heckler of corporate dignitaries who have aroused her ire, and resolver of chaos out of order at annual meetings of corporations in which she owns microscopic shares or holds the proxies of dissident investors less available to personal scufflings in the board rooms.

For some years now Mrs. Soss has thrown an ever longer and

259

more menacing shadow over what, except for her presence, should be decorous foregatherings of shareholders in General Electric and U. S. Steel. It is safe to say that the very name of Mrs. Wilma Soss can freeze the marrow of Roger Blough.

Mrs. Soss dresses for the occasion when organizing a cavalry charge against, say, the President of Consolidated Edison. Once she appeared at a stockholders' meeting attired in deepest mourning to suggest that the corporation was practically moribund; on another occasion she lent a touch of fantasy to a similar convocation of risk capitalists in a Gay Nineties outfit with a muff, chatelaine watch and feather boa to imply that management hadn't improved its technique since Dewey took Manila.

Of late she has taken up an electric megaphone capable of throwing the human voice two or three miles with which she refutes the logic of corporate officers when they attempt to explain passing the last quarter's dividend. The mere whisper that Mrs. Soss is in the elevator is enough to make ordinarily self-possessed chairmen of the board start looking around for exits and calling for reserve platoons of company police.

To the best of my knowledge and belief, Mrs. Soss is the first woman to lend anything even vaguely resembling color and commotion to Wall Street since the incomparable Hetty Green, who was also a nightmare to frighten the daylights out of the robust and piratical tycoons of her time.

The annals of American wealth are peopled with the names of women, but they have all been on the spending end. Few of these well-upholstered ladies went near the marts of trade in person. Mrs. Soss, an oddball of the first chop in an age of dismal conformity, deserves well at the hands of her fellow citizens even outside the drab world of commerce.

Roger Blough may be a tireless toiler in the resistance forces of sound money, but I rejoice to think of Mrs. Soss in full charade attire, routing the regiments of vested darkness and blowing a conch horn amidst the templed money changers. Perhaps there is room for a statue of her, larger than life and imperishable in bronze, along with George Washington on the steps of the subtreasury.

Uncle Otto—The Ideal Millionaire

My most vivid recollection of Palm Beach in the golden winter of 1926, next to the fantastic sums in play at Colonel Bradley's casino, was the little drama that was enacted every morning at noon on the Breakers Hotel bathing beach. Although they may well have been there since after breakfast, attired in the black cotton stockings then required of women and the half-sleeved uppers requisite in gentlemen's bathing suits, none of the assembled Stotesburys, Cosdens, Biddles and Wideners had been near the water.

Promptly on the stroke of noon a plump, amiable little man with upturned white moustaches and semi-oriental complexion put in an appearance and made his way, smiling and bowing right and left, resolutely to deep water and began swimming up and down blowing like a porpoise and obviously enjoying himself immensely.

Instantly the water was peopled with swimmers and the word circulated in the adjacent cabanas and under prodigious parasols: "Uncle Otto has come. We can swim now."

All his life the appearance of Otto Kahn was a signal that "Uncle Otto has come; things can begin to happen." Bathing at Palm Beach was only a dramatization of an extraordinarily vital force of American public, banking and artistic life.

A few years later, as a ship's news reporter in New York, I was able to appreciate even better the impact of anything Otto Kahn might have to say or think on the great world of finance he represented. Other moneyed moguls were entrusted without question to the regular duties of ship's news reporting. Montagu Norman, Thomas Lamont, even J. P. Morgan the Younger were

261

regularly entrusted to our interviews when arriving aboard the *Berengaria* or *Olympic.*

But when Otto Kahn arrived from Paris or London the *Herald Tribune's* financial editor Norman Stabler himself stirred his stumps and went down the Bay on the early revenue cutter. The least misinterpreting of a flick of the financial eyebrow of Uncle Otto, the most trifling misquotation could have consequences that transcended ordinary disaster.

As the banker who handled the affairs of Baltimore & Ohio, Chesapeake & Ohio, Great Northern, Illinois Central, Missouri Pacific, Southern Pacific and others of the imperial carriers of the age, Kahn in a period of very few years became an immensely wealthy man and achieved such standing in the financial community that the eccentricity—as any concern was then regarded for the arts—of becoming a patron of music and the theater was conveniently overlooked.

As a culture lover to his fingertips, Kahn set joyously about the congenial task of financing artists, singers, musicians, poets, ballet dancers, playwrights, composers, producers and publishers on a scale never before undertaken in the United States until the coming of the overpowering family foundations which are a manifestation of our own time.

Inevitably as the legend of his truly princely generosity spread, he was surrounded by solicitous moochers, frauds, mountebanks and third-raters, but despite his availability to the most patently spurious touch artists, he came up with a surprising number of winners, esthetically if not financially.

His first and most celebrated beneficiary was, of course, New York's Metropolitan Opera whose destinies he guided through the incredible tantrums, intrigues and perfidies of a veritable zoo that included Gatti-Casazza, Chaliapin and Lawrence Tibbett and, in a penultimate chaos of temperament and contractual infidelity, Diaghilev, Nijinsky and the Ballet Russe.

A more successful economic gesture was his financing of

Morris Gest's fantastic production "The Miracle" with Lady Diana Cooper which required an outlay of $600,000 in a day when many Broadway productions were staged for less than a tenth this sum. The spectacle was a resounding success and closed a national tour in San Francisco with the only public appearance by Gest, a notorious cry-artist, at which he had not wept. Wags remarked that this in itslef was "The Miracle."

Much loved and, for a rich man, much admired, Uncle Otto was the focal point of New York's brilliant artistic and literary life.

No American was ever more truly a Medici in the spaciousness, imagination, variety and magnitude of his interests and benefactions, none more an authentic magnifico in his person and the style with which he invested all he touched.

"Kahn was the ideal millionaire," wrote Beverly Nichols. "He used his money with taste, kindliness and understanding . . . He was a patron of the arts in a sense that has been little understood since the Renaissance. In short, he was a very considerable dear."

Adlai, the Society Burglar

There is more than meets the eye in the widespread and wistful hankering to have Adlai Stevenson in public office. Professional Democrats and irresponsible longhairs seem to feel that Stevenson is an "intellectual force." But there is even a fugitive feeling among Republicans, and responsible people generally, that it would have been a good thing for everybody if Stevenson had won the Presidency.

The truth of the matter is, whatever clowns, flunkies and farmers Americans will tolerate in other offices, they have consistently shown that they prefer to have a gentleman, or reasonable facsimile thereof, in the White House. He might be a loud, brassy gentleman like Roosevelt I or a class renegade like

Roosevelt II or a gentleman ex officio like Harding, but over the years the White House has been the address of more gentlemen than it has jerks.

Americans realize that their elected President is the nominal head of a hostile government dedicated to the pillage of their country generally. Obviously, therefore, they would still sleep better at nights if they felt they had been allowed to vote a gentleman thief into office, a sort of Raffles or Jimmy Valentine who at least wouldn't spit on the carpet while looting the sideboard.

This, it may reasonably be assumed, was the source of the latent hankering at all levels for Stevenson. Stevenson was obviously born in the house on the hill and is accustomed to being seated above the salt at table. He can converse with the great of the world without getting into fisticuffs. His urbanity is unquestioned and his forebears were in American politics at least without attracting impeachment proceedings.

In the socially impeccable precincts of Stockbridge, Massachusetts, legend tells of a series of burglaries among the summer homes of the well-to-do that were accomplished with such dexterity and finesse that the word got around they were the work of a "society burglar." One night, however, the hitherto blameless second story man was moved to open a bottle of champagne in the pantry of one of his victims and in so doing managed to pop the cork, thus destroying the illusion of the "gentleman burglar." Could he have been elected to the highest office, many folk feel, Stevenson would of necessity have been a burglar, but not one to pop the cork of a champagne bottle.

A Wreath for Gene Fowler

Death, when finally he called on Gene Fowler, was not exactly a stranger to 12323 Helena Drive, an address in Los Angeles that its owner was fond of saying was the combination of one of W. C. Fields' safe deposit boxes. The last of the great newspaper names of the New York twenties had long been on bowing familiarity with the old fellow with the scythe and had come to terms with him as any sensible man will with the inevitable.

"I come from a family with a long tradition of deathbed scenes," he said of the Fowler forebears, who lived and died with great energy and character in the Shining Mountains of Colorado, and it may be presumed that when he walked out among the roses in his garden and flagged down a barge for the trip across the river, he did it with style and in the manner of a king. Fowler had an air about everything.

It is perhaps significant that, despite the fame deriving from Fowler's long years on the staff and as managing editor of the *New York American,* the times of teem and theme of wonder in his life had their setting in the West. It is possible that he will be most substantially remembered for "Timberline," his joyous and impious tale of Fred Bonfils and Harry Tammen and the *Denver Post,* and for Captain Trolley, the raffish mining editor of "Salute to Yesterday," rather than for the mighty and the witty with whom he walked in the more urgent newspaper world of Manhattan.

Certainly as he grew older he lived again more lovingly in the Denver of his boyhood and revisited with more eager anticipation of mind his grandfather's mining camp shack where the old gentleman thawed sticks of dynamite in the same oven in which he baked sourdough biscuits. His home was in the Shining Mountains of the heart.

The last years of his life, the carpet slipper years in the California sun, were a time of mellow, if declining, fortunes. He had made, he estimated, better than a million dollars in the films and all of it had gone to deadbeats and on imprudent loans, a fact which never for a moment saddened him. I have before me in his handwriting a letter with the immortal sentiment that epitomized his economic philosophy: "Money is something to be thrown off the back of trains."

Much gusto and much remembered greatness have gone with him from a world Fowler loved but regarded as not strictly here to stay. Perhaps his most fitting final salutation he had already written for Captain Trolley, who raised his eyes to the mountain summits where the last light of a long day lingered and said:

"So they were when I came. So they are now. So they will be tomorrow and tomorrow and forever. Now the strange journey is done. I need not wonder where I shall sleep tonight."

Jack Hines, Gentleman Adventurer

Every so often when some venerable figure in the community, preferably a bartender, pugilist, newspaper reporter or member of some similarly exalted profession dies, his passing is hailed as the "end of an era." Jack Hines' death might have been a conspicuous occasion for such sentimental evocation of the glorious past, for he was that now-vanished phenomenon, a barroom Galahad and gentleman adventurer. His mantle of gentility never slipped from his shoulders even when he was engaged in some of the saloon brawls in Yukon City still remembered with awe and wonder as epics of the Jack London-Tex Rickard-Wilson Mizner era.

My first recollection of him was when he was singing for his supper in the Garden Court of the Palace Hotel, attired in a braided-edge morning coat and the single eyeglass with which he stared down some of the toughest ruffians from the Barbary Coast to Nome and from Nome to Tonopah.

The Garden Court crystal chandeliers and electroliers vibrated with such intensity when he sang "The Road to Mandalay" in a gashouse baritone that the management was apprehensive for their safety. Jack was not averse to a glass of Jack Daniel's after the tiffin hour entertainment was over—glass, hell, half a bottle, and we became warm friends despite a disparity in our ages.

Born in San Francisco in the gaslit early Eighties, Jack lived his life amidst the marginal hooray of the last great mining excitements. Arriving on the scene too late for the Comstock, although he was well known to many of the heroic figures of those bonanzas, he early eschewed the well-upholstered San Francisco drawing rooms to which he had entree in favor of the less reticent pleasures of Market Street and the cocktail route, and as a youth enjoyed considerable local fame as an amateur boxfighter and ballad singer in the clip joints of the Barbary Coast. "I always told my mother I was a piano player in a bagnio," he used to say, "because it was the truth."

The Alaska gold rush was made to measure for Hines, where he arrived, monocle in place and ready to make doll rags of anyone who resented it, in the legendary company of frontier chivalry that included Soapy Smith, Rex Beach, Mattie Silks, queen of the Denver madams, Wyatt Earp, late of Dodge City, who made a fortune running a saloon in Nome, and the aforementioned London, the Brothers Mizner, Rickard, and the cream of the sporting fraternity of the American continent.

In a moment of youthful exuberance Hines married, apparently not too wisely, since his wife shortly tired of the northern lights and decamped on an outbound steamer with the Polish Count Constantin Podorski. Hines followed them when he heard they had set up light housekeeping in then-booming Goldfield in the Nevada desert. "I guess I was impetuous," Hines told me 40 years later, "but I had to follow the fellow into a number of places where the liquor was very bad. I was seasick all the way from Alaska, too."

Provoked by such a catalogue of affronts, Hines walked into Goldfield's fashionable Palm Grill one evening while Julius Goldsmith's band was playing dinner music and shot the pusillanimous Count Podorski four times in the head. Once in my hearing at Palm Beach, Mrs. E. T. Stotesbury asked Jack if it was true he had killed a man. "My gentle lady," said the Sweet Singer of the Yukon, "I blew the fellow's waxed moustaches all the hell and gone over that dreary pothouse. I doubt they have the place cleaned up yet."

No penalty, of course, attached in those times to avenging the honor of a gentleman and Hines lived out his declining years in the clement climate of a new and happier marriage in La Jolla.

Aunt Alice at the Opera

Although all Bostonians of her generation were familiar with Mrs. Jack Gardner by sight as, indeed they were with another lady magnifico who was her contemporary, Miss Amy Lowell, my contact with the city's great patroness of the arts was accomplished on a single unique occasion, but one so blindingly splendid as perhaps to merit a place in the record.

At the time of which I write the effulgent Boston opera company annually performed for a season in the farthest reaches of Huntington Avenue where the Boston Opera House lurched against the municipal skyline. My elderly and much loved Aunt Alice Carpenter, a grande dame of formidable mien and overwhelming presence, and by every standard Isabella Gardner's peer save in the realms of fine arts, had asked me to squire her to an evening performance of "Aida," or perhaps it was "Carmen." The billed performance was so inferior to my Aunt Alice's that it is lost to memory.

My aunt in the prophetic mood of elderly ladies who had long outlived their husbands felt that this might well be her last appearance in the Boston society of which she was so handsome an ornament, and to lend style to the occasion, instead of soliciting one of my father's cars and chauffeur, I arranged for what was certainly the last public horse cab in Boston to attend our going.

We dined grandly at the Touraine Hotel and there was a

great deal of wine. Alice was arrayed in a pearl choker dogcollar a good six inches deep which elevated her chin to a haughty degree but in no way prevented her absorption of a large quantity of Mumm's '14.

It was a good dinner and we rolled grandly through the socially dubious purlieus of Huntington Avenue to the brillantly lit porte cochere. I had apprised Mr. Mudget, the courtly and equally elderly manager of the Opera House, of Alice's impending arrival and, full fit and glossy hatted, a white-satin-lined cloak over one shoulder, he was on the sidewalk to receive us.

It was a good entry, but nothing to what was to follow.

Alice's box was in the second tier. The maid on duty relieved her of her wrap and, on my arm, Alice stepped down from the dressing room level to that of the box itself which in turn was divided by still another step. Her progress was not unnoticed and opera glasses were turned our way from all over the house.

That progress, however, was inhibited by the dog collar and the haughty angle of the Carpenter profile, so that to my horror and that of half a thousand spectators Alice kept right on going, firmly lifting a leg over the enclosing red plush rail and stepping grandly out into space.

I was able to apprehend her in mid-air just before gravity began to assert itself and retrieved her to a well-bred patter of applause from the adjacent boxes and here and there a subdued "Well played, sir." From the box immediately below, however, into which she would inevitably have plunged, came the patrician and carrying voice of Mrs. Jack Gardner.

"Not tonight, Alice Carpenter," it said. "You know very well that this is your box only on Tuesdays and Thursdays. Stay in your own box on Mondays and Wednesdays."

Crazy Cliff, The Merry Mortician

The current pother in the public prints over the exalted cost of dying in California could not but bring to mind the life and good times, far away and long ago, of Crazy Cliff, the Merry Mortician of Newport, Rhode Island. Cliff's name was formally Robert Clifford, but to an entire generation of New York newspapermen he was Crazy Cliff and he would have resented any more decorous approach as an affront to his well-defined character.

"Le style est l'homme meme," was one of Cliff's favorite aphorisms.

Cliff claimed that an undertaker with any sense of the proprieties should look like a ghoul and was at pains to create the illusion in himself. He had sad, bloodhound features of graveyard hue and a red nose of J. P. Morgan dimensions on which W. O. McGeehan claimed he was able to light a cigar. He wore the funeral apparel of his calling, a black morning coat and heavily weeded top hat on days when on professional call, and seemed to many of the more literate patrons at Bleeck's to have stepped right out of a drawing by George Cruikshank.

"Death, it's hilarious" was his favorite cry when in wine, which was anytime after 10 in the morning when the bar opened, and several of Bleeck's more sensitive customers who were advanced in years took their patronage down the street to Steinie's Type & Print Club when Cliff was in town.

Cliff was in the habit of sneaking up behind drinkers at the bar with a pocket tape measure and taking their dimensions. "I see something with silver handles and tufted white satin," he would mutter as the palsied prospect turned around. Harry Staton, the *Tribune* syndicate manager, said he gave the place a bad name. Many patrons, on the other hand, drank more when Cliff was in their midst. Bleeck regarded him in much the light he regarded the oversalted Saratoga chips in the free lunch, as a thirst promoter.

Cliff, as the leading mortician of Newport, had inside information on the probable mortality amongst the socially elect who had named him in advance as the recipient of their terminal patronage and a warm understanding existed between Cliff and Stanley Walker, the *Tribune's* ambitious city editor. If a Bonsal or Gerry or Goelet was skirmishing with the Grim Reaper, Cliff let the library know in time to have a full dress obituary in type and so beat the *Times*. "The black camel is stalking in the driveway" was the way he announced an impending demise of upper-case dimensions. In return the paper always noted that Robert Clifford was in charge of arrangements at St. Thomas or wherever.

John D. Rockefeller fooled everybody by dying in Florida and this treachery was denounced by Cliff as "conduct unbecoming a scoundrel."

Crazy Cliff's greatest triumph over the competition and a strategem in which he rose to dizzying heights was the case of a truly notable Vanderbilt for whose obsequies he panted with a great longing. "To plant this character would be the capstone of my career," he told Henry, the barkeeper at Bleeck's. "It would be a mandate loud and clear to the Four Hundred to die with Clifford. None of the other bastards in the business would get a smell of a classy corpse after that."

The Vanderbilt in question had a Newport villa from whose master bedroom window a long chute descended at a gentle angle of incline to the waters of Buzzard's Bay. Down this the owner was accustomed to slide in bathing attire each morning before breakfast for a dip. Afterward his valet reeled him back with a long rope and winch. Mr. V. read his mail on the way down, throwing invitations to be accepted to one side, bills and other inconsequential matter to the other. Cliff stationed a boy with a spyglass in a tree on a promontory commanding a view of this scene of privilege. One morning the boy arrived breathless at the saloon patronized by Cliff when in Newport. "He's carrying part of his mail into the water with him," he announced.

"I knew he was failing and that it wouldn't be long now," de-

271

posed Cliff, "so I went to the family with a rock bottom proposition including a private train to New York. All Vanderbilts had private trains then, dead or alive. And you know what? I got the business; now I'm the Ward MacAllister of embalmers."

Bill McGeehan was by now getting on in years and had promised his business to Cliff at what was reported in Bleeck's to be a cut rate in return for various favorable mentions in Bill's column. McGeehan spent his last spring with a ball team in Florida and every evening filed his copy to the telegraph desk with the signature "No black camel." One night no wire came. Cliff got the business.

Skipper Williams, Heroic Liar

In 1929 when ship's news was an important assignment and expert reporters were sent to meet the arriving *Berengaria* and speed the departing *De Grasse,* none of them was more vivid in recollection than the ineffable Skipper Williams of the *New York Times.*

The Skipper was a completely unreconstructed English Cockney, born within sound of Bow Bells and a character who would have been more believable in a Broadway comedy like "You Can't Take It With You" or "Twentieth Century" than aboard the 6:30 cutter out of Quarantine.

He wore a high-crowned, square, derby hat of the style affected by the peerless mutton-chopped banker, George F. Baker, a wide aperture wing collar, a horseshoe stickpin in a folded cravat and elastic-side congress gaiters.

In addition to the charm of this rich garb and an accent right out of Bernard Shaw, the Skipper was a tall tower of mendacity, a liar of majestic dimensions to ensmall Baron Munchausen, and he was a deadly professional competitor.

Every so often *The Times'* Sunday editor, Charlie Lincoln, a man of such noble mein as he raised a foot to the bar in

Bleeck's Saloon that in another incarnation he had surely been a Roman senator, would allow the Skipper space in which to lie officially in the Sunday paper. On such occasions he would produce a laborious three or four thousand words about a fictional Marmaduke Mizzle, the Mincing Lane Caraway Seed Merchant. The Skipper considered them hilarious, the greatest thing since Pope and Addison, and solemnly warned friends against their impending appearance in the Sunday paper.

But the Skipper's value to his principals was in laying false trails to outwit the other ship's news reporters. He had no compunction about telling younger and more gullible staff men from the *Herald Tribune* or *Sun* that tomorrow's incoming ships were so unimportant that he wasn't even going down the bay.

He would then slyly board the 6:30 cutter at the Battery and come back with an exclusive interview with Thomas Lamont or some comparable eminento and the rest of us would get dark looks from the city desk and be threatened with assignment to West Side District Court if we didn't mend our pipelines.

Finally it got so that nobody trusted him and the other reporters on cutter assignment formed an informal detective pool to shadow the old man's movements. When he headed for the Cunard office or the Barge office at Pier 9 radiating innocence, all concerned would be alerted and the pack would arrive baying at his heels in triumph just as he was uncovering some stupendous exclusive on the *Empress of Britain or Ile de France*.

Aside from his heroic mendacities, the Skipper was the most massive mooch in the record and would pillage incoming liners the way the Goths sacked Rome. He would eat sparingly for a day or two before the arrival of a particularly well victualed boat where he was on close terms with purser and chief steward. He would then board the early cutter to Quarantine and take two hours going through a Cunard breakfast menu from Southdown mutton chops to Yarmouth bloaters and from lamb's kidneys Turbigo to eggs Vienna with nine kinds of hot bread and strong tea in proportion.

As the ship cleared the Narrows going up the harbor he would refresh himself with a free shave, haircut, shine and suit pressing in the barber shop at the expense of Sir Ashley Sparks, resident manager for Cunard, round up an interview or two and, at the last moment as the ship was tying up, sit down again to the full luncheon treatment. He would then go ashore waving with dignity to customs with all the whiskey he could hide about his person, which was capacious.

I never saw him stiff or yet completely sober and the vision of him swarming up a rope ladder over the highsides of the *Olympic* in the dark of a sub-zero morning with loud encouragement from the cutter crew shouting "They got kippers for the Skipper" was something to remember. Sometimes he would go down harbor with outgoing ships and spend the night on the pilot ship where the destruction of steaks and whiskey was legendary. Everybody welcomed the Skipper. He told such wonderful lies. And as a steward on the *Franconia* once remarked of him in malapropian admiration: "The gentleman from *The Times* is a real gastropod."

The Bastard Who Made Good

Almost alone within the memory of living students of the world's great and powerful in the category romanticized as "merchants of death" was the charming if remote figure of Sir Basil Zaharoff who, before World War II, was generally credited with being the most powerful and active of all commission merchants dealing in such commodities as machine guns and slightly used battle cruisers.

Sir Basil lived up to his billing. A man of profound mystery and elusiveness, bearded and inevitably attired in an Inverness cloak and slouch hat, he flitted ghostlike between the capitals of

Europe on The Blue Trains and Simplon-Orient Expresses of the period, picking up coded telegrams as he went and holding converse with conspiratorial emissaries of the great powers in the private gaming rooms at Monte Carlo.

Sir Basil, alas, was about the only merchant of death you would like to encounter in the corridor or a wagon-lit threading the snowy passes of the Carpathians on a winter night, the urbane incarnation of mystery, intrigue and wicked wealth. The Krupps, like the du Ponts, appear to have the hearts of stock jobbers and the personalities of greengrocers.

When Zaharoff died he got a bad press. Ordinary reason might suggest that a cause of his lack of universal esteem was that in every European and Asiatic war from the latter 19th century down to the 1939 conflagration, he had been a motivating power, supplying one side or the other but most usually both, with the advanced weaponry with which to turn peasants into fertilizer. Deaths explicitly attributable to him ran into the millions, but few of his obituaries held this against the old gentleman.

What outraged editorialists in London, Manchester and Paris, although less in the United States where the saga of rags to riches is part of our national epic, was that Zaharoff, for all the titles, honors, crosses, ribbons and orders to which he was entitled, was of dubious birth, a climber, self made and obviously an *arriviste* on a truly magnificent scale. In a word, Sir Basil was no gentleman.

It didn't matter that wars erupted and thrones tottered at Zaharoff's whim, that prime ministers were his lackeys, general staffs on his payroll and that he manipulated for his own advantage the largest staff of spies, saboteurs and provocateurs in the world. All these were incidental to the fact that he may have been born on the wrong side of the blanket and that at one time it was definitely established that he had been a runner for a love store in Constantinople.

275